Key Account Plans

The practitioners' guide to profitable planning

Lynette Ryals
MA (Oxon), MBA, PhD, FSIP

Malcolm McDonald
MA (Oxon), MSc, PhD, DLitt, FCIM, FRSA

ELSEVIER

AMSTERDAM • BOSTON • HEIDELBERG • LONDON • NEW YORK • OXFORD
PARIS • SAN DIEGO • SAN FRANCISCO • SINGAPORE • SYDNEY • TOKYO
Butterworth-Heinemann is an imprint of Elsevier

Butterworth-Heinemann is an imprint of Elsevier
Linacre House, Jordan Hill, Oxford OX2 8DP, UK
30 Corporate Drive, Suite 400, Burlington, MA 01803, USA

First edition 2008

British Library Cataloguing in Publication Data
A catalogue record for this book is available from the British Library

Library of Congress Cataloging in Publication Data
A catalog record for this book is available from the Library of Congress

ISBN: 978-0-7506-8367-8

For information on all Butterworth-Heinemann publications
visit our web site at books.elsevier.com

Typeset by Charon Tec Ltd (A Macmillan Company), Chennai, India
www.charontec.com

Printed and bound in Slovenia

08 09 10 11   10 9 8 7 6 5 4 3 2 1

Working together to grow
libraries in developing countries

www.elsevier.com | www.bookaid.org | www.sabre.org

ELSEVIER   BOOK AID
International   Sabre Foundation

Contents

Acknowledgements

This book is based on our experience in researching and teaching key account planning for a number of years. We owe a debt of gratitude to all the key account managers and leading companies that have shown an interest in our work and invited us to help them plan. In particular, our thanks go to the companies who are members of the Cranfield Key Account Management Best Practice Research Club and who have sponsored much of the research on which this book is based. We are also grateful to the enthusiasm and determination of the hundreds of key account managers who have attended our courses in key account planning at Cranfield and elsewhere.

Many people have been kind enough to contribute directly to this book. First, there are the companies that have provided case examples that we refer to. Some of them have asked not to be named for reasons of commercial sensitivity, but our thanks to them all. We would also like to mention the colleagues at Cranfield School of Management who have commented directly on portions of the manuscript; in particular, Dr Ruth Bender and Keith Parker, who assisted with the chapter relating to customer profitability analysis. We would also like to mention the support provided by Lindsay Bruce, Dr Iain Davies, Dr Sue Holt, Lynne Hudston, Peter Mouncey, Beth Rogers (now of Portsmouth Business School), and Diana Woodburn. All of them have contributed to our research into KAM.

On a personal note, we would like to thank Tim Goodfellow of Elsevier for the energy and enthusiasm to get this book under way, and for the effective and persistent chivvying that encouraged us to complete it. Our families, Joy, Roy, and Vincent Ryals, and Margaret McDonald, have been a great source of support. We are grateful to Anna McDonald for typing half the chapters and co-ordinating the first complete draft of the manuscript.

Professor Lynette Ryals
Professor Malcolm McDonald
September 2007

Introduction

Key accounts are business-to-business customers that are of strategic importance to the supplier, and key account management (KAM) is an integrated process for managing these relationships profitably. Fuelled by the globalization of world markets and the unprecedented level of merger and acquisition activity that stock markets worldwide have witnessed in recent years, KAM has become a topic of major importance for suppliers in their dealings with these larger and larger customers.

Sadly, all too many KAM programmes come unstuck, leaving customers disappointed and suppliers out of pocket. Years of research and teaching in KAM have indicated to us that the main reason why KAM programmes fail is because there are no key account plans.

The key account plan is an essential part of world-class KAM. It is a strategic plan for an individual relationship with a specific key account. The plan sets out how the supplier intends to manage the relationship and is supported by a wealth of detail about the customer's markets, business, competitive position, and end markets. The plan also contains details of the strategies and approach that the supplier will use, as well as the team of people that will be involved in managing the relationship. Although this is a strategic plan, it should be accompanied by a detailed action plan showing how the key account plan will be implemented over the coming months.

Our aim with this book is to promote good practice in key account management. KAM is recognized as one of the most important developments in business-to-business markets to emerge in the past decade. Yet, too many organizations are paying lip service to KAM and too many key account managers are unsure how to develop the key account plans that are essential if they are to implement KAM successfully.

■ About this book and who it is for

This book is for practising key account managers, for senior sales people, and for key account directors and commercial directors who manage KAM teams. The information it contains is also hugely relevant to major account managers who manage major (although not key) accounts, and to sales people who are involved in complex selling and relationship management.

The book is in two main sections. The first section (Chapters 1–8) is about how to develop world-class key account plans that will support and develop your company's most important relationship. This section provides detailed guidelines and a wealth of tools and techniques for analysing the customer and for developing powerful and effective customer management strategies. It is intended for practising key account managers but will also be of use to major account managers and to sales people who manage customer relationships.

The second section of the book (Chapters 9–13) deals with all the other issues that suppliers need to address to deliver world-class KAM. This includes information about organizing for KAM, KAM performance measurement, the key customer perspective, and the role and skills of a KAM manager and KAM team. This section is for experienced key account managers who want to further develop their understanding of the process; it is also for key account directors, sales directors, and commercial directors who are looking to implement KAM within their organizations or who want to improve an existing KAM programme.

The final chapter in this book (Chapter 14) sets out a step-by-step system for preparing a strategic plan for a key account. Effectively, this chapter provides all of the main frameworks and templates that a key account manager needs for the development of a key account plan. Checklists and reference notes are also provided, together with some worked examples. In addition, there is detailed hands-on information about how to prepare a 1-year action plan. This chapter draws together the most important tools and techniques described throughout the book into one convenient chapter.

■ How to use this book

Key Account Plans is intended as a guide for practitioners, for the people at the sharp end of customer management. It contains many tools and techniques plus a wealth of pro-formas and worksheets to show how the tools should be implemented. This is not a book to be kept in mint condition on your shelves. We hope that you will keep it on your desk and write on it as you go. Please feel free to adapt the tools and to annotate; we would love to hear from you about how you use the planning tools we have set out here, in your own company.

Good luck with your key account plans!

SECTION 1

The Plan

CHAPTER 1

Why you will lose your best key accounts if you don't prepare a strategic plan for them

Summary

Chapter 1 explains the need for preparing strategic plans for key accounts and positions it firmly within the broader domain of corporate planning and marketing planning. We strongly recommend that those who have bought this book read this chapter carefully.

■ The need for strategic plans for key accounts

Managing powerful customers profitably is perhaps the biggest issue facing suppliers today as markets, particularly in Western Europe and America, mature and as inexpensive versions of goods which were hitherto only supplied by the West flood into their markets from lower cost countries such as China. One major response from most organizations is to put pressure on their suppliers because, as can be seen from Figure 1.1, the easiest and quickest way to increase margins which are under pressure is to cut the price paid for external goods and services.

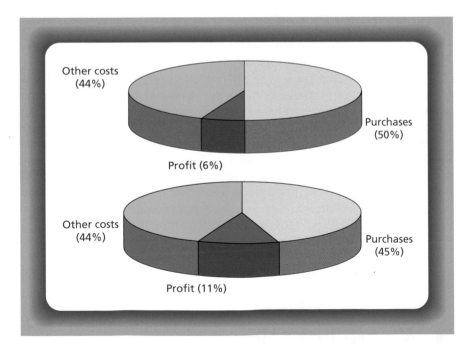

Figure 1.1
Double your money: cut spending on purchases (Purchasing: adding value to your purchasing through effective supply management' Institute of Directors, September 2003).

The problem with this approach, however, is that price cutting is finite (how many pence can be cut from a pound, cents from a euro or a dollar, etc.), whereas value creation is infinite and is limited only by our creativity and imagination.

So increasingly, purchasing directors are beginning to take account of the potential benefits of fostering a small number of truly strategic relationships with a privileged group of suppliers. Such relationships, however, are few and far between, because no organization has the time or the resources to align their R & D, purchasing, manufacturing, logistics, information technology (IT), finance, service, and other functions with the equivalent functions in their customers' businesses in anything other than a few, special cases.

When it happens, however, our research at Cranfield has shown that such relationships are the wellspring of profitability for both parties and totally justify the effort.

Key account management (KAM), then, is without doubt the major challenge facing business today and is fraught with difficulties in conceiving, planning, and implementing it, involving, as it does, organizational change.

With over 10 years experience of researching buyer/seller global best practice at Cranfield, we know what are the requirements for successful KAM. Without doubt, one of the biggest barriers is the type of people who are asked to implement KAM programmes, for KAM is as different from selling and sales management as chalk is from cheese. Our experience over the years has shown us that key account managers must be experienced senior executives, fully trained in analytical techniques, financial analysis, strategic planning, political and interpersonal skills, and indeed, the very skills required by a successful general manager or chief executive officer.

The point we are making is that it is most definitely not a *sales* role and people who are trained to sell and who are rewarded accordingly rarely make good key account managers.

The purpose of this book is to set out in a no-nonsense way what a top-notch key account manager needs to know and do in order to build profitable relationships with powerful customers. This inevitably means spending time on analysing the customers' businesses and DNA prior to producing a strategic plan guaranteed to build profitable relationships for both parties. It will focus on putting together *strategic* plans for key accounts prior to implementing the first year's plan, for, as John Perton of Boston College said "The good thing about not having a strategy is that failure comes as a complete surprise and is not preceded by a long period of worry and depression". It is amazing to us how many major accounts are lost because the supplying company has little more than sales forecasts and budgets for 1 year only and how surprised they are when they are dropped in favour of another supplier who has taken the trouble to work out a longer term strategy for working together.

■ We are not talking about forecasts and budgets

Don't be fooled into thinking those words from John Perton about lack of strategy and failure represents just an academic trying to score points by

Table 1.1 Britain's top companies (Management Today)

Year	Company[1]	Market Value[2] (£m)	ROI[3]	Subsequent performance
1979	MFI	57	50	Collapsed
1980	Lasmo	134	97	Still profitable
1981	Bejam	79	34	Acquired
1982	Racal	940	36	Still profitable
1983	Polly Peck	128	79	Collapsed
1984	Atlantic Computers	151	36	Collapsed
1985	BSR	197	32	Still profitable
1986	Jaguar	819	60	Acquired
1987	Amstrad	987	89	Still profitable
1988	Body Shop	225	89	Still profitable
1989	Blue Arrow	653	135	Collapsed

1. Where a company has been top for more than 1 year, the next best company has been chosen in the subsequent year, e.g. Polly Peck was rated top in 1983, 1984, and 1985
2. Market values as of 31 December of each year
3. Pre-tax profits as a percent of investment capital
Source: From Professor Peter Doyle, Warwick University

being clever, as hundreds of companies all over the world have found out to their cost. Indeed, up to 1990, every UK company with the highest return on investment either went bankrupt or got into serious trouble. Neither did the best performing companies in sectors up to 2000 fare much better, with the likes of Marks & Spencer, ICI, GEC, and others either going out of business or systematically destroying shareholder funds (for evidence, see Tables 1.1 and 1.2). Some of these companies have since recovered, such as M&S, BT, and BA. Some have been acquired and are now profitable, but the lessons to be learned in the historical context of those decades are still highly relevant for companies enjoying high growth in the 21st century.

Before going into further detail about the paramount importance of having a strategic plan for key accounts covering a period of up to 3 years, however, let us dismiss once and for all the mind-bogglingly puerile belief that all the directors and senior managers need to do is to write down some numbers that these become targets and eventually, budgets.

Apart from the fact that Mickey Mouse or Donald Duck could do this without any training, it only ever works in growth markets with little competition. For example, research into the banking sector in the UK threw up the following interesting observation:

In Company X, value creation was merely a matter of protecting market share and managing costs.

Table 1.2 Britain's top companies

Year	Company[1]	Market Value[2] (£bn)	ROI[3]	Subsequent performance
1990	Maxwell Communications Plc	1.0	5	Collapsed
1991	Imperial Chemical Industries Plc	8.6	13	Collapsed
1992	Wellcome Plc	8.3	40	Acquired
1993	ASDA Group	1.6	7	Acquired
1994	TSB Group Plc	3.7	20	Acquired
1995	British Telecommunications Plc	22.2	17	Not Profitable
1996	British Steel Plc	3.3	19	Collapsed
1997	British Airways Plc	6.1	7	Not Profitable
1998	National Westminster Bank Plc	19.6	14	Acquired
1999	Marconi Plc	29.8	22	Acquired
2000	Marks & Spencer Plc	5.3	7	Not Profitable

1. Each company was a FTSE 100 when selected
2. Market Values as of 31 December of each year
3. Pre-tax profit as a percent of Equity & Long Term Debt
Source: From Professor Malcolm McDonald

> The data show that the company X business model is in effect a "money printing" machine, therefore the challenge for strategists lies in how they can act as responsible stewards of a resilient business model.
>
> Cranfield Doctoral Thesis (2005)

There are, however, always consequences of such behaviour. It is interesting to note that, of Tom Peters' original 43 so-called excellent companies in 1982, very few survived because of a fixation with excellent tactics at the expense of strategy (Pascale, R.T. (1990). *Managing on the Edge*, Simon and Schuster).

Take, for example, the hypothetical example of InterTech given in Figures 1.2 and 1.3. (Based on a real example, but disguised for reasons of confidentiality). Figure 1.2 shows the kind of information typically discussed at board meetings, most of which are based on forecasts and budgets.

A glance at Figure 1.3, however, shows that on every market-based dimension, the company is losing ground dramatically and is likely to suffer serious consequences the moment the market stops growing.

Here are some recent quotes from well-known sources:

> Improvements in a short-term financial measure such as economic profit can be achieved through postponing capital investments, reducing marketing and training expenditures, or by divesting assets, each of which may have a positive effect on near-term performance but could adversely affect long-term value creation performance. Nevertheless, when incentivized with bonuses to 'manage for the measure' this is exactly what many managers will do irrespective of the consequences on shareholder value.
>
> (Simon Court (2002) "Why Value Based Management Goes Wrong", *Market Leader*).

Performance (£ million)	Base year	1	2	3	4	5
Sales revenue	£254	£293	£318	£387	£431	£454
– Cost of goods sold	135	152	167	201	224	236
Gross contribution	£119	£141	£151	£186	£207	£218
– Manufacturing overhead	48	58	63	82	90	95
– Marketing and Sales	18	23	24	26	27	28
– Research and Development	22	23	23	25	24	24
Net profit	£16	£22	£26	£37	£50	£55
Return on sales (%)	6.3%	7.5%	8.2%	9.6%	11.6%	12.1%
Assets	£141	£162	£167	£194	£205	£206
Assets (% of sales)	56%	55%	53%	50%	48%	45%
Return on assets (%)	11.3%	13.5%	15.6%	19.1%	24.4%	26.7%

Figure 1.2
InterTech's 5 year performance.

Performance (£ million)	Base year (%)	1 (%)	2 (%)	3 (%)	4 (%)	5 (%)
Market growth	18.3	23.4	17.6	34.4	24.0	17.9
InterTech sales growth (%)	12.8	17.4	11.2	27.1	16.5	10.9
Market share (%)	20.3	19.1	18.4	17.1	16.3	14.9
Customer retention (%)	88.2	87.1	85.0	82.2	80.9	80.0
New customers (%)	11.7	12.9	14.9	24.1	22.5	29.2
% Dissatisfied customers	13.6	14.3	16.1	17.3	18.9	19.6
Relative product quality	+10	+8	+5	+3	+1	0
Relative service quality	+0	+0	−20	−3	−5	−8
Relative new product sales	+8	+8	+7	+5	+1	−4

Figure 1.3
InterTech's 5 year market-based performance.

- Ninety per cent of US and European firms think that budgets are cumbersome and unreliable, providing neither predictability nor control.
- They are backward-looking and inflexible. Instead of focussing managers' time on the customers, the real source of income, they focus their attention on satisfying the boss, that is, the budget becomes the purpose.

- Cheating is endemic in all budget regimes. The result is fear, inefficiency, sub-optimization, and waste.
- In companies like Enron, the pressure to make the numbers was so great that managers didn't just doctor a few numbers, they *broke the law*.
- People with targets and jobs dependent on meeting them will probably meet the targets, even if they have to destroy the enterprise to do it (Simon Caulkin (January, 2005). "Escape from the Budget Straightjacket", *Management Today*, pp. 47–49).

Finally, on budgets, a major bank has been criticized for its contribution to personal debt of £1 trillion in the UK.

Employees are set tough targets for selling loans and double their low salaries, which encourages customer abuse and leaves many borrowers facing ruin.

Banks are no longer there to help customers find the most suitable solution.

"We have a target-driven culture that staff must hit targets"
(A major bank, 10 May 2005).

Consider also the often puerile and backward-looking process by which quantitative objectives are set.

Take the following hypothetical example, shown in Figure 1.4.

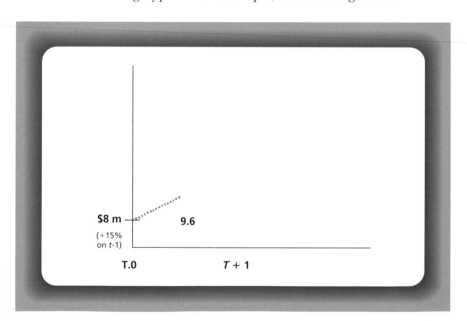

Figure 1.4
How not to set targets

From Figure 1.4, it can be seen that in the current year, this company achieved a 15% increase in sales revenue over the previous year. But, being optimistic, the chief marketing officer set a so-called stretch target of plus 20% for next year, giving a target of 9.6 million which, if achieved, would satisfy the budget holder.

However, consider for a moment a different and more professional way of setting an objective for next year. If the market addressed was a growing market, a strategic objective might be "to be market leader in three years time". In order to achieve such an objective, the chief marketing officer would need an assessment of market size in 3 years time – say 100 million. Market leadership in this particular market would be, say, 25%. So, representing this in Figure 1.5 and extrapolating *backwards* from this target would give a target of 15 million next year, not the backward-looking historical target of 20% (9.6 million).

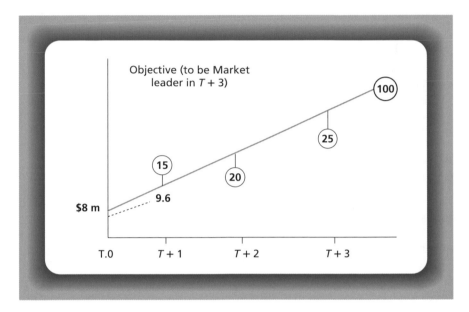

Figure 1.5
Using corporate objectives to set sales targets

Every single element of this company's resources including R&D, HR, IT, etc. would be totally different if the current budget had been 15 million as opposed to the backward-looking 9.6 million. Consider also where, in a typical tactically orientated company, the 8 million on which the original forecast was based came from. The answer, of course, is the company's own database.

Yet it has been consistently shown over the past 50 years that sales people sell the products they find easiest to sell, often at the maximum discount, to the customers who treat them nicest. Such sales go into the database, of course.

Consider also the kind of knee-jerk, macho management-by-objective targets that are often set by senior managers without considering the unintended consequences. A classic example of this is the desire to cut costs by reducing working capital, such as inventory. If the logistics manager is paid a bonus to make such reductions, then these reductions will be made. So the poor unfortunate customer asking for 100 widgets and 200 didgets, on being told they can only have 50 of each, decides to go to a more accommodating supplier. The consequence of the lost sale is lost in the system, because the logistics manager has achieved the objectives set and so has the finance director. But the database on which the next year's forecast is made is impervious to all these and in most cases is merely a reflection of the organization's own stupidity!

Even the great Unilever, when losing market share to Proctor and Gamble, realized that their forecasting and budgeting system was holding them back and, in a presentation in 2006 to a research club at Cranfield, a senior financial manager said:

> "We used to spend £ ½ billion out of a £50 billion turnover just on budgeting.

All it led to was setting the *lowest* sales/profit target (and under no circumstances exceed it) and the *highest* marketing budget (and under no circumstances underspend it).

The consequence was appallingly bad behaviour on the part of everybody.

We were

- boxed in by too many targets;
- defined "success" in the wrong way;
- too inward- and backward-looking;
- set the wrong performance targets.

Our previous negotiation of budgets was a bit like allocating planes, tanks, etc. across the army by giving each division one aeroplane and one tank each, rather than putting the resources where they could be the most effective. Unilever's planning system was worse than communist Russia's old system – i.e. so many bricks, etc. But *never* have any left over. That's why you would frequently find buried bricks, buried bulldozers, and the like! Unilever's new system is more about helping people win than holding them to account. Now, when you meet people, you can't tell what function they're from, because they are just talking about the business".

Readers will doubtlessly be clear by now that the authors of this book have little patience with managers who believe that forecasts, budgets, and tactics are all they need to do.

Even so, we still need to clarify even further the importance of strategy and why it must always precede tactics rather than being an extension of them.

Figure 1.6 shows a matrix in which the horizontal axis represents strategy as a continuum from ineffective to effective. The vertical axis represents tactics on a continuum from inefficient to efficient. Those firms with an effective strategy and efficient tactics thrive continuously (Box 1). Those with an effective strategy but inefficient tactics (Box 2) merely survive. Those firms to the left of the matrix are destined to die, as too much emphasis is placed on tactics, thus avoiding the underlying strategic issues surrounding changing market needs. Any organisation doing the wrong things more efficiently (Box 3) is destined to die more quickly than its less-efficient counterparts. It is a bit like making a stupid manager work harder, thus doubling the chaos and probably offending twice as many customers!

Already, companies led by chief executives with a proactive orientation that stretches beyond the end of the current fiscal year have begun to

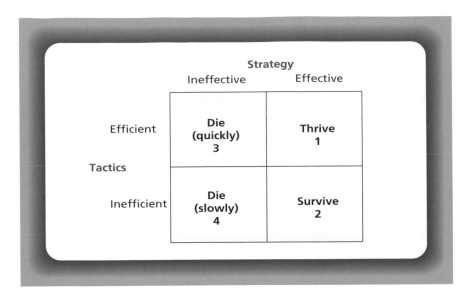

Figure 1.6
Strategy, tactics and business success

show results visibly better than the old reactive companies with only short-term vision.

Figure 1.7 shows the old style of company in which very little attention is paid to strategy by any level of management. It will be seen that lower levels of management do not get involved at all, while the directors spend most of their time on operational/tactical issues.

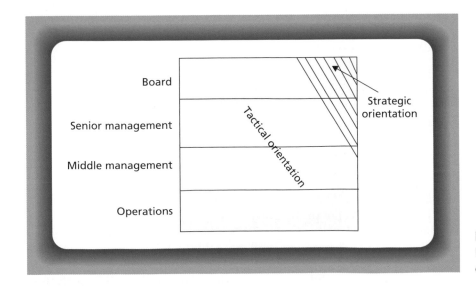

Figure 1.7
Low strategic orientation

Figure 1.8 is a representation of those companies that recognise the importance of strategy and who manage to involve all levels of management in strategy formulation.

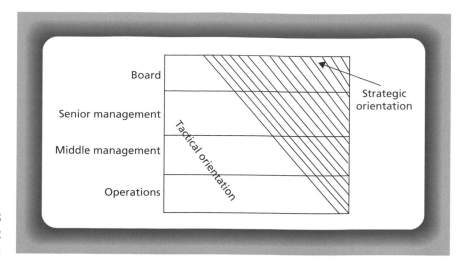

Figure 1.8
High strategic
orientation

The rule, then, is simple:

● Develop the *strategic* plan first. This entails greater emphasis on scanning the external environment, the early identification of forces emanating from it, and developing appropriate strategic responses, involving all levels of management in the process.
● A strategic plan should cover a period of between 3 and 5 years, and only when this has been developed and agreed, should the 1-year operational marketing plan be developed. Never write a 1-year plan first and extrapolate it.

The emphasis throughout this book is on the preparation of a *strategic* plan for key accounts. The format for an operational or tactical plan is exactly the same, except for the amount of detail.

■ The strategic planning process – a brief introduction

Strategic planning in the very best companies starts with the setting of corporate objectives.

Corporate objectives usually contain at least the following elements:

● The desired level of profitability
● Business boundaries
  – What kind of products will be sold to what kinds of markets (marketing)
  – What kind of facilities will be developed (operations, R&D, information systems, distribution, etc.)
  – The size and character of the labour force (personnel)
  – Funding (finance)
● Other corporate objectives, such as social responsibility, corporate image, stock market image, employer image, etc.

Such a corporate plan, containing projected profit and loss accounts and balance sheets, being the result of the process described below, is more likely to provide long-term stability for a company than plans based on a more intuitive process and containing forecasts which tend to be little more than extrapolations of previous trends.

From Figure 1.9, it can be seen that key account planning fits firmly within what is generally known as the marketing domain in the centre circle.

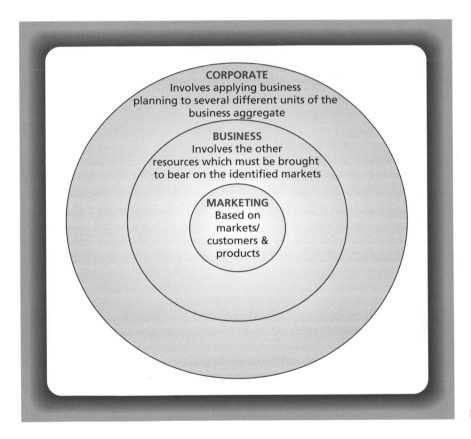

CORPORATE
Involves applying business planning to several different units of the business aggregate

BUSINESS
Involves the other resources which must be brought to bear on the identified markets

MARKETING
Based on markets/ customers & products

Figure 1.9

■ How key account planning fits in with marketing planning, corporate planning, and other functions

First of all, it is necessary to position marketing planning firmly within the context of strategic planning generally. Strategic decisions are concerned with:

● the long-term direction of the organisation, as opposed to day-to-day management issues;

- defining the scope of the organisation's activities in terms of what it will and will not do;
- matching the activities of the organisation to the environment in which it operates, so that it optimises opportunities and minimises threats;
- matching the organisation's activities to its resource capacity, be it finance, manpower, technology, or skill levels.

Whilst marketing planning is based on markets, segments, and products, corporate planning involves other resources that have to be brought to bear on the identified markets.

Marketing itself is a process for: defining markets; quantifying the needs of the customer groups (segments) within these markets; determining the value propositions to meet these needs; communicating these value propositions to all those people in the organisation responsible for delivering them and getting their buy-in to their role; playing an appropriate part in delivering these value propositions to the chosen market segments; and monitoring the value actually delivered.

For this process to be effective, we have also seen that organisations need to be consumer/customer driven.

A map of this process is shown in Figure 1.10. This process is clearly cyclical, in that monitoring the value delivered will update the organisation's understanding of the value that is required by its customers. The cycle is predominantly an annual one, with a marketing plan documenting the output from the "understand value" and "determine value proposition" processes, but equally changes throughout the year may involve fast iterations around the cycle to respond to particular opportunities or problems.

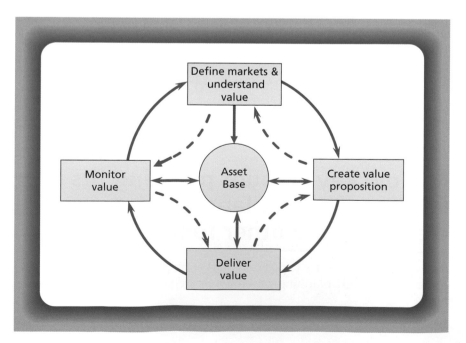

Figure 1.10
Map of the marketing process.

It is well known that not all of the value proposition delivering processes will be under the control of the marketing department, whose role varies considerably between organisations.

The marketing department is likely to be responsible for the first two processes, "understand value" and "determine value proposition", although even these need to involve numerous functions, albeit co-ordinated by specialist marketing personnel. The "deliver value" process is the role of the whole company, including, for example, product development, manufacturing, purchasing, sales promotion, direct mail, distribution, sales, and customer service. The marketing department will also be responsible for monitoring the effectiveness of the value delivered.

The various choices made during this marketing process are constrained and informed not just by the outside world, but also by the organisation's asset base. Whereas an efficient new factory with much spare capacity might underpin a growth strategy in a particular market, a factory running at full capacity would cause more reflection on whether price should be used to control demand, unless the potential demand warranted further capital investment. As well as physical assets, choices may be influenced by financial, human resources, brand and IT assets, to name just a few.

Thus, it can be seen that the first two boxes are concerned with strategic marketing planning processes (in other words, developing market strategies), whilst the third and fourth boxes are concerned with the actual delivery in the market of what was planned and then measuring the effect.

Our research at Cranfield has clearly shown that superior performance is linked to marketing plans with the following characteristics:

1　Homogenous market segment definition
2　Segment-specific propositions
3　Strategy uniqueness
4　Strength leverage and weakness minimization
5　Creation of internal and external synergies
6　Provision of tactical guidance
7　Alignment to objectives
8　Alignment to market trends
9　Appropriate resourcing
10　Clear basis of competition

As will be demonstrated later in this book, it is highly unlikely that excellent key account strategies will make up for ill thought-out marketing strategies, hence ill thought-out corporate strategies.

The strategic planning process is illustrated in Figure 1.11 (start at "J" – "January"). It is clear from this that ▶ **key account** planning must take place at the same time as, or even before, draft plans are prepared for a strategic business unit.

If this is not clear, let us give an example of a supplier's company servicing the needs of a national health service. It will be seen from Figure 1.12

▶ **DEFINITION** ◀

A key account is a major customer considered by the supplying company to be of strategic importance to the achievement of its own objectives. Hence, such a customer is singled out for special treatment.

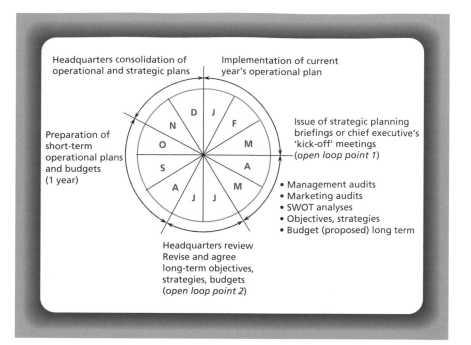

Figure 1.11
Strategic and
operational
planning – timing.

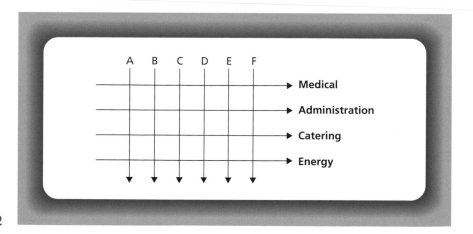

Figure 1.12

that there are four "markets" within hospitals to be served. These are Medical, Administration, Catering, and Energy.

There will be a number of key accounts, or hospital groups, referred to here as hospital groups A, B, C, D, etc. Each of these hospital groups may well have their own key account manager who has to plan for them.

Thus, for example, the key account manager for Hospital A has to prepare a draft plan across all four "markets" and this would clearly be a key input to the planning process.

■ The position of key account planning in strategic marketing planning

As a general principle, planning should start in the market where the customers are. Indeed, in anything other than small organisations, it is clearly absurd to think that any kind of meaningful planning can take place without committed inputs from those who operate where the customers are. Figure 1.13 shows a hierarchy of strategic planning, starting with key account planning. Thus, the planning process shown in Figure 1.11 would start with plans for individual key accounts.

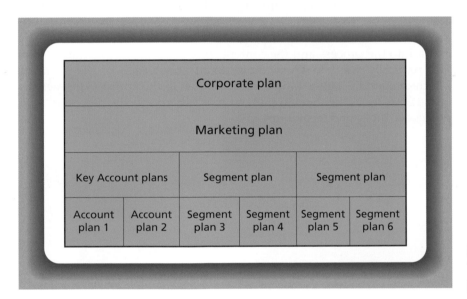

Figure 1.13
The planning process.

Conclusion

Research[1] into the efficacy of strategic plans for marketing and key accounts has shown that such plans, when well conceived and executed, make a significant contribution to commercial success, the main effects being:

- the systematic identification of emerging opportunities and threats;
- preparedness to meet change;
- the specification of sustainable competitive advantage;
- improved communications between different functions and their managers;

[1] For evidence, see McDonald, M. (2007). "Strategic Marketing Planning: Theory and Practice" in Baker, M. (ed.) *The Marketing Book*, Butterworth-Heinemann, Oxford, 2007.

- reduction of conflicts between individuals and departments;
- the commitment of key departments and individuals to delivering the value promised to customers;
- more appropriate allocation of scarce resources;
- a more market- and customer-focused orientation across the organization; and
- better, sustainable financial performance.

If the reader still entertains any doubts about the superior performance that will result from the preparation of effective strategic plans for key accounts, this, alas, is not the book for them.

If, however, the reader either is convinced, or still has an open mind, then please continue. Those managers who want to cut straight to the chase, as it were, may prefer to go straight to Chapter 14, which provides the templates that will constitute an excellent strategic key account plan. The reason for this approach is very straightforward. World class key account managers need to be pragmatic. It is the nature of the job. By going into the process and the contents of a key account plan, managers will naturally want to know more detail about each of the elements referred to, and Chapter 14 will point readers to the appropriate sections of the book to enable them to find out more about specific processes, sub-processes, tools, and techniques.

CHAPTER 2

Which key accounts need a strategic plan

■ Introduction

Although most of the people reading this book will be key account managers or aspiring key account managers, it is nonetheless important to ensure that unnecessary planning is avoided. Some key accounts will require the full treatment described in Chapter 14, whereas others will require little more than forecasts and budgets. This chapter is in three parts. Part one describes briefly a classification system for key accounts, having first described what a key account is; the second part describes how world class customers segment, define, and target their own markets; and the third part describes a key account classification system which is now in fairly broad use globally, having been promulgated for over 10 years by the Key Account Best Practice Research Club at Cranfield.

PART 1

■ What is a key account? How to select them and define them

Key accounts are customers in a business-to-business market identified by selling companies as of strategic importance.

This doesn't mean all large customers, of course. A quick glance at Figure 2.1 indicates a very rough split between customers in a typical database.

From this it can be seen that in most cases the bulk of accounts will be either small medium enterprises (SMEs) or larger, mid-sized accounts, with only a few very large, powerful customers.

The first question most companies get the wrong answer to is "How many key accounts should we have?" One global telecommunications company claimed to have a thousand! But, as will be seen just from the amount of data alone that has to be collected (see Chapter 3) in order to prepare a plan which aligns the supplier's resources with the customer's, it will never be possible to have more than at most, 20 or thereabouts. At one stage, DHL Worldwide had only 18 integrated key accounts globally, and each of these made more revenue and profit than any country managing director.

A little thought about our own private lives will confirm that whilst we each have hundreds of "friends" (from school, university, work, sports, etc.), we have the capacity for real love, warmth, and intimacy with only a few, maybe five or six. In the case of companies, all of whom have limited resources for R&D, IT, HR, logistics, etc., it would be impossible to commit them to more than a handful of projects in carefully selected key accounts.

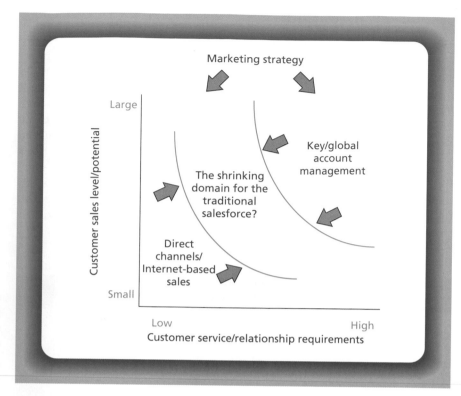

Figure 2.1
The critical new interfaces for sales (copyright Professor Nigel Piercy reproduced with his kind permission).

The criteria for selecting which accounts should go into a company's key account programme are not set in concrete, but should obviously take account of the potential for growth in future time periods. So, in the main, they will be large and powerful. But frequently there are grounds for including smaller, more influential customers on the basis of the prestige that attaches itself to all their suppliers, or on the basis of future growth. For example, neither Virgin nor Microsoft would have been in many suppliers' key account programmes 30 years ago.

Even then, however, it isn't easy. Consider the different structures shown in Figure 2.2. Multinationals often have several subsidiary companies around the world, sometimes with the same name, sometimes with different names.

It is clearly inefficient to have several independent key account managers dealing with one group buyer, who can often take advantage of the lack of integration and coordination on the part of the supplier. This often results in lower prices as a result of the buying company's superior knowledge about overall purchases from the supplying company's different units. So, the first task of the supplying company is to define precisely the form of the customer. If the customer prefers each of its subsidiaries to buy independently, so be it. But if not, sellers beware! Figure 2.3 shows how DHL deals with this situation.

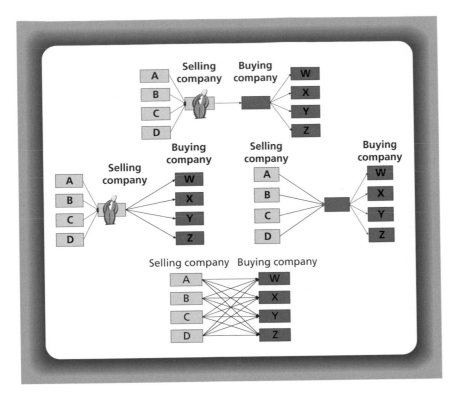

Figure 2.2
Define the customer.

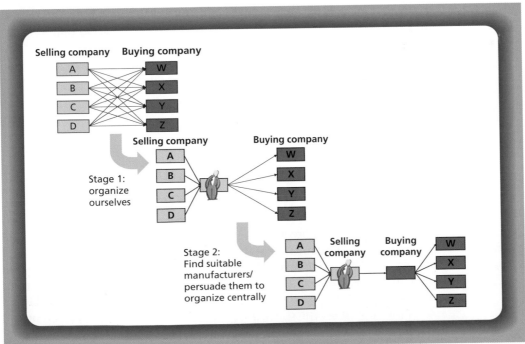

Figure 2.3
Case study: DHL and manufacturers.

Table 2.1 indicates another danger for the supplier in defining the business of a customer. In this particular case, this supplier thought it had 100% of the customer's business, but on taking account of the lines provided by its own sister companies, it quickly realized that it was not as important to the customer as it had imagined, as it had only 17% of the customer's wallet for this particular category of goods.

Table 2.1 Defining the customer's "wallet"

How does the customer view the spend?

Purchases	Share of wallet (%)
Incontinence pads £100 k	100
Over the counter (OTC) incontinence products £250 k	40
All incontinence products (OTC and ethical) £350 k	29
All products for the elderly £600 k	17

Check the purchase budget group

To conclude this section:

- Do not include too many customers in your key account programme.
- Do not put in it only customers you already have good relationships with.
- Take account of potential growth in your selection.
- Understand the buying preferences of the customer (i.e. centralized or decentralized).
- Understand the customer's own category definitions.

Classifying key accounts: How to understand their differences

Once selected, it will be obvious when examining the list that they are all different in size, organizational structure, culture, requirements, behaviour, and so on. Also, your own relationships will range from non-existent, to poor, to average, to very close; and these differences must be taken account of before even thinking about preparing strategic accounts for them. Figure 2.4 shows a well accepted way of classifying key accounts based on our 10 years of research at Cranfield University School of Management's Key Account Management Best Practice Research Club.

Each one of these relationship types is now described in more detail. Figure 2.5 shows an exploratory, pre-trading phase.

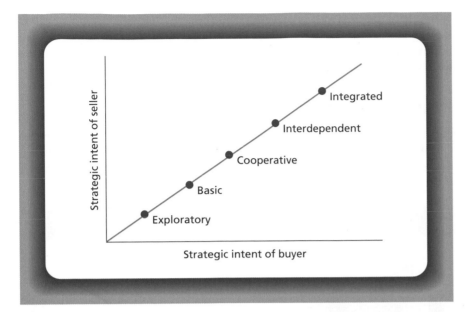

Figure 2.4
The relational development model (adapted from a model developed by Millman, A.F. and Wilson, K.J. (1994). "From Key Account Selling to Key Account Management").

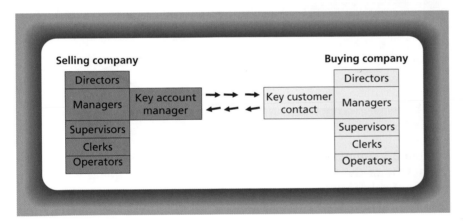

Figure 2.5
Exploratory KAM (Cranfield University School of Management, 1996).

As can be seen from Table 2.2, a lot of careful exploratory work needs to take place before committing serious resources to this kind of potential key account.

Table 2.2 Exploratory KAM

- Pre-trading
- Customer potentially qualifies as key account
- Both sides exploring
- Signalling important
- Seller needs to be patient and prepared to invest
- Reputations critical

In particular, it is at this phase that the supplier should decide whether he really wishes to invest a lot of his own resources in finding out more about this potential account. The methodology for carrying out this exploratory investigation is provided in the next chapter.

Basic KAM

Figure 2.6 illustrates a familiar "bow tie" type of relationship, which the Cranfield research shows to be the most common. It is a bit like the docking of a space station and a space craft – not very safe and easily prised apart if the slightest thing goes wrong.

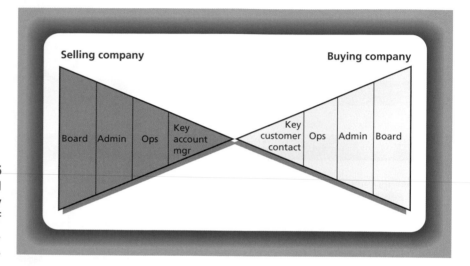

Figure 2.6
Basic KAM
(Cranfield University School of Management, 1996).

Table 2.3 summarizes the main characteristics of such basic relationships. One of the main causes for such relationships going wrong is a change of either buyer or key account manager.

Table 2.3 Basic KAM
● Transactional: emphasis on efficiency
● Driven by price, success measured by price
● Probably multisourcing
● Easy to exit
● Single point of contact
● Business relationship only
● Very little information sharing
● Reactive rather than proactive
● Probably low common interest
● Organization suits selling company
● Reward structure of key accounts managers paramount
● Small chance of growing business
● Can be stable state or trial stage

In many ways, this stage is similar to the exploratory stage described above and the supplier will need a lot more information about the account before deciding whether to invest further to build the relationship.

Cooperative KAM

This is the second most common kind of key account management (KAM) relationship, which is shown diagrammatically in Figure 2.7.

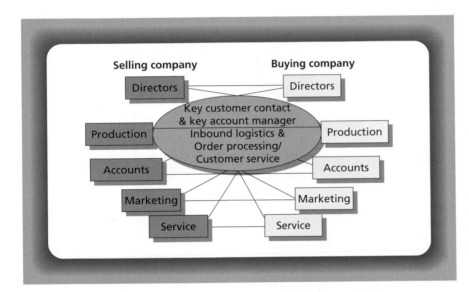

Figure 2.7
Cooperative KAM
(Cranfield University
School of
Management,
1996).

From this it can be seen that many interdisciplinary relationships have developed between the selling company and the buying company. The major problem is that, whilst the supplying company believes it is being customer-centric, no charges are made for the added services being rendered and frequently there is little structured organization of such relationships by the key account manager. The result of this is that often heavy additional costs are built up that are not charged for and such relationships frequently make a loss, as can be seen from Figure 2.8 from the Cranfield Research. This shows that, on average, it was only cooperative relationships that made a negative contribution.

There are, however, other unintended consequences. Either the buying company takes advantage of the largesse of the supplier because they are not paying for all the added benefits, or they become irritated with the lack of organized structure in the several relationships and demand better processes. If, however, the key account manager isn't empowered to take this kind of action back in their own company, the supplier is often dropped in favour of a supplier who has a key account manager with real authority. Table 2.4 summarizes the cooperative main characteristics of a relationships.

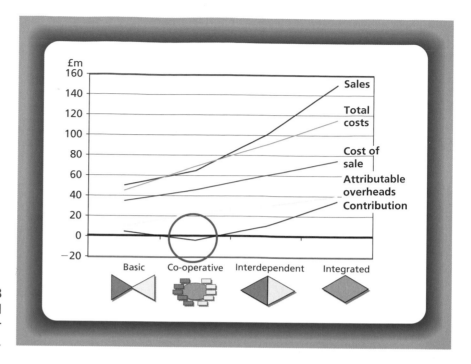

Figure 2.8
Relationships and the customer profitability trap.

Table 2.4 Cooperative KAM

- Selling company adds value to relationship
- Based on assumption/experience of delivery performance
- May be preferred supplier
- Exit not particularly difficult
- Multifunction contacts
- Relationship power still mainly with buyer
- Organization mainly standard
- Limited visits to customer
- Limited information sharing
- Forecasting rather than joint strategic planning
- Not really trusted by customer

It will be understood from this that the cooperative phase of KAM is potentially extremely dangerous and in our experience, many key accounts fall into this category. Suppliers should, therefore, either move them forward to a stronger relationship by investing in them, or gradually move them back to a more transactional relationship, described here as basic.

Interdependent KAM

Figure 2.9 illustrates the well-known "diamond" relationships in KAM. In this type of relationship, interdepartmental relationships are properly

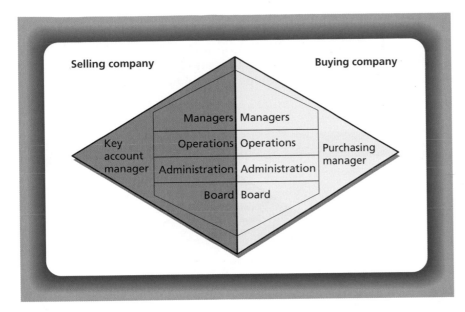

Figure 2.9
Interdependent
KAM (Cranfield
University School of
Management,
1996).

organized by the buyer and the supplier's key account manager, although it will be observed that there is still a dividing line separating the two organizations.

The characteristics of interdependent relationships are shown in Table 2.5, from which it can be seen that, whilst both organizations are very close, the supplying company can still be dropped, albeit with some inconvenience, but not with really serious consequences.

Table 2.5 Interdependent KAM

- Both acknowledge importance to each other
- Principal or sole supplier
- Exit more difficult
- Larger number of multifunctional contacts
- Developing social relationships
- High volume of dialogue
- Streamlined processes
- High level of information exchange, some sensitive
- Better understanding of customer
- Development of trust
- Proactive rather than reactive
- Prepared to invest in relationship
- Wider range of joint and innovative activity
- Joint strategic planning, focus on the future
- Opportunity to grow business

Integrated KAM

Integrated KAM relationships, as illustrated in Figure 2.10, are the rarest of all relationships and, during the 10 years of research at Cranfield, only about 20 such genuine relationships were found.

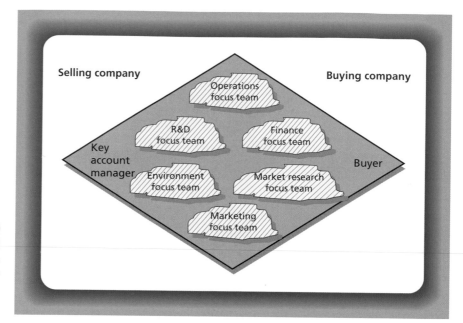

Figure 2.10
Integrated KAM
(Cranfield University
School of
Management,
1996).

Open book accounting for example, is a characteristic on the part of both supplier and customer and total trust is enjoyed between them. Often cost reductions are shared and added values are also shared, benefiting both parties equally. A mutual interdependence makes it virtually impossible for either party to drop the other, as both are as one, creating value in the market place.

Another characteristic illustrated in Figure 2.10 is the existence of many interdisciplinary joint long-term projects. From this it will be obvious that only a handful of relationships can ever be like this because of limited specialist resources on both sides.

Figure 2.11, from the European Institute of purchasing (reproduced here with their kind permission), shows in summary form the impact on suppliers who do not have such an "inside track". Seventy five per cent of project costs are determined at the R&D stage, whilst 90% are determined at the prototype stage. This leaves only 10% – usually price considerations – for suppliers bidding at such a late stage.

The characteristics of integrated relationships are summarized in Table 2.6.

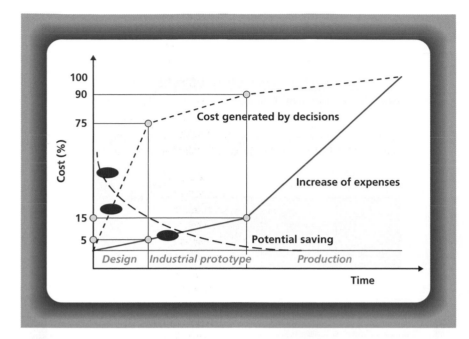

Figure 2.11
Impact of an
upstream action.

Table 2.6 Integrated KAM

- Real partnership: complementary, mutually dependent
- Few in number
- Sole supplier, poss handling secondary suppliers
- High exit barriers, exit it traumatic
- Individual organizations subsidiary to team socially
- Dedicated, cross-boundary functional/project teams
- Open information sharing on sensitive subjects
- Transparent costing systems
- Assumption of mutual trustworthiness, at all levels
- Abstention from opportunistic behaviour
- Lowered protection against opportunism
- Joint long-term strategic planning
- Better profits for both

Mini Case

Case 1

Figure 2.12 shows Porter's value chain (described in detail in Chapter 3) for a manufacturing organization. For 3M's integrated key accounts, at any point in time, they have several major joint projects with the customer's R&D, inbound logistics, operations, outbound logistics, sales and marketing, and after sales service. The joint learning from such state-of-the-art companies keeps them continuously ahead of competitors and ensures long-term, stable, and profitable relationships.

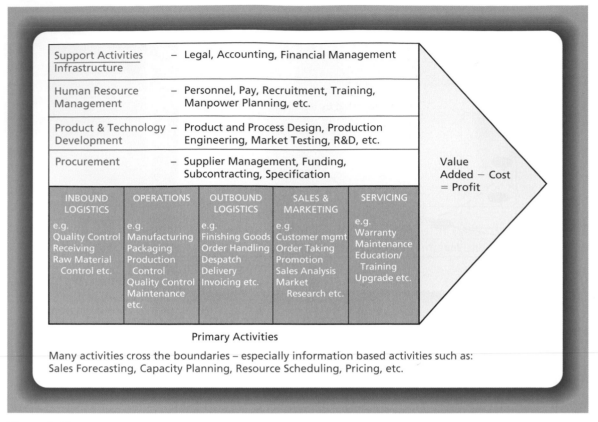

Figure 2.12
Porter's value chain.

Disintegrating KAM

Relationships can, of course, go sour, just as in a marriage. Table 2.7 shows the main causes. It is interesting to note that it is rarely for price reasons. Our

Table 2.7 Disintegrating KAM

- Occurs at any level
- Rarely caused by price problems
- Often change in key personnel
- Key account manager's approach or lack of skills
- Failure to forge multilevel links
- Breach of trust
- Prolonged poor performance against agreed programme
- Changing market positions
- Changing culture, organization, ownership, role
- Complacency
- Financial disappointment

research at Cranfield has shown that two of the most frequent reasons are a lack of skills on the part of the key account manager and breach of trust.

Companies who persist in promoting excellent sales people into key account roles without training them in the kind of general management skills required and who then compound their error by rewarding them purely on how much they sell, are a constant source of irritation and annoyance to sophisticated customers who want to develop profitable relationships rather than being "sold to" all the time. Breach of trust is another frequent cause of upset.

Mini Case

Case 2

The Chairman of one major multinational supplier to the car and building industries blithely announced at the company's annual general meeting that their growth in profits had come largely from lower raw material costs. It doesn't take too much imagination to understand why, the following day, this company's phones were red hot with irate customers who hadn't been told about this and who felt they had been ripped off by this supplier!

PART 2

■ How world class companies classify and target their own markets

Introduction

In the KAM planning templates in Chapter 14, it is implicit that any key account manager wishing to win the trust of a targeted key account must endeavour to understand the customer's business as if they actually were employed by them. This is because, if the intention is to create advantage for the customer rather than just helping them to avoid disadvantage, which is what most other suppliers can do, probably at a lower price, then the supplying company needs to have an in-depth understanding of the customer's business – in particular what they are tying to achieve in their own market place against their competitors.

The methodology by which world class companies classify and target their own markets should be read carefully by key account managers, for three reasons – firstly, for any customer that doesn't do this properly, any attempt on the part of the key account manager to help them do it will be much appreciated; secondly, by understanding the customer's commercial priorities, key account managers will be better able to appreciate ways in which their own company can create advantage for the customer; and thirdly, because exactly the same methodology (but using different variables) will be used for identifying and targeting key accounts.

It can easily be understood that a business should define its markets in such a way that it can ensure that its costs for key activities will be competitive. Or, alternatively, it should define the markets it serves in such a way that it can develop specialized skills in servicing those markets and, hence, overcome a relative cost disadvantage. Both, of course, have to be related to a company's distinctive competence.

However, the approach developed in the late 1960s by the Boston Consulting Group is justly criticized for relying on two single factors, that is to say relative market share and market growth, neither of which explain business success on their own.

To overcome this difficulty and to provide a more flexible approach, General Electric and McKinsey jointly developed a multifactor approach employing the same fundamental ideas as the Boston Consulting Group. They used industry attractiveness and business strengths as the two main axes and constructed these dimensions from a number of variables. Using these variables and some scheme for weighting them according to their perceived importance, businesses were classified into one of nine cells in a three-by-three matrix. Thus, the same purpose is served as in the Boston matrix (comparing investment opportunities among businesses), but with the difference that multiple criteria are used. These criteria vary according to circumstances, but often include those shown in Figure 2.13.

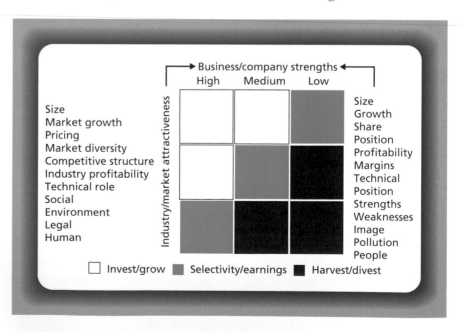

Figure 2.13
A nine-box DPM.

However, it is not necessary to use a nine-box matrix and many managers prefer to use a four-box matrix similar to the Boston box. Indeed this is the author's preferred methodology as it seems to be more easily understood by and useful to practicing managers.

The four-box directional policy matrix (DPM) is given in Figure 2.14. Here, the circles represent sales into a market or segment and, in the same

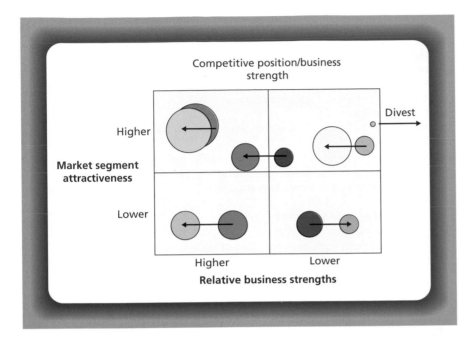

Figure 2.14
A four-box DPM.

way as in the Boston matrix, each is proportional to that segment's contribution to overall turnover.

The difference in this case is that rather than using only two variables, the criteria which are used for each axis are totally relevant and specific to each company using the matrix. This shows:

- markets/segments categorized on a scale of attractiveness to the firm;
- the firm's relative strengths in each of these markets/segments.

The specific criteria to be used should be decided by key executives using the device, but a generalized list for the vertical axis is given in Table 2.8.

It is advisable to use no more than five or six factors; otherwise the exercise becomes too complex and loses its focus. Read on, however, before selecting these factors, as essential methodological instructions on the construction of a portfolio matrix follow.

An example of a completed matrix is given in Figure 2.15, which shows a portfolio completed for an agrochemical company. It indicates the size and direction of the company's main segments now and in 3 years' time.

How world class companies set marketing objectives and strategies

The general marketing procedures which lead to the setting of marketing objectives flow, or course, from the portfolio analysis described above and revolve around the following logical decisions:

1 *Maintain*: This usually refers to the "cash cow" type of product/ market and reflects the desire to maintain competitive positions (bottom left quadrant in Figure 2.15).

Table 2.8 Factors contributing to market attractiveness

Market factors
Size (money units or both)
Size of key segments
Growth rate per year: total segments
Diversity of market
Sensitivity to price, service features, and external factors
Cyclicality
Seasonality
Bargaining power of upstream suppliers
Bargaining power of downstream suppliers

Financial and economic factors
Contribution margins
Leveraging factors, such as economies of scale and experience
Barriers to entry or exit (both financial and non-financial)
Capacity utilization

Technological factors
Maturity and volatility
Complexity
Differentiation
Patents and copyrights
Manufacturing process technology required
Competition
Types of competitors
Degree of concentration
Changes in type and mix
Entries and exits
Changes in share
Substitution by new technology
Degrees and types of integration

Socio-political factors in your environment
Social attitudes and trends
Laws and government agency regulations
Influence with pressure groups and government representatives
Human factors, such as unionization and community acceptance

2   *Improve*: This usually refers the "star" type of product/market and
    reflects the desire to improve the competitive position in attractive
    markets (top left quadrant in Figure 2.15).

3   *Harvest*: This usually refers to the "dog" type of product/market and
    reflects the desire to relinquish a competitive position in favour of
    short-term profit and cash flow (bottom right quadrant in Figure 2.15).

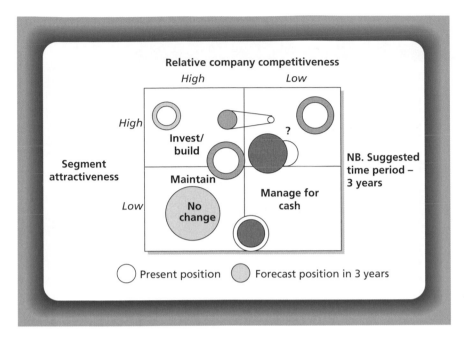

Figure 2.15
Portfolio analysis:
DPM.

4 *Exit*: This also usually refers to the "dog" type of product/market and
sometimes the "question mark" and reflects a desire to divest because
of a weak competitive position or because the cost of staying in it
is prohibitive and the risk associated with improving its position is
too high.

5 *Enter*: This usually refers to a new business area.

The strategy guidelines suggested by the different positions in a DPM are
summarized in Figure 2.16.

However, great care should be taken not to follow slavishly any set of
"rules" or guidelines related to those suggested here. These guidelines are
included more as checklists of questions which should be asked about
each major product in each major market before setting marketing objectives and strategies. In addition, the use of pejorative labels such as "dog",
"cash cow", and so on should be avoided if possible.

It is at this stage in the planning process that the circles (representing
the segments) in the DPM can be relocated (where applicable) to show
their relative size and position in 3 years' time. This can be done to show,
first, where they will be if the company takes no action and, second, where
they should ideally be. These latter positions will of course become the
marketing objectives.

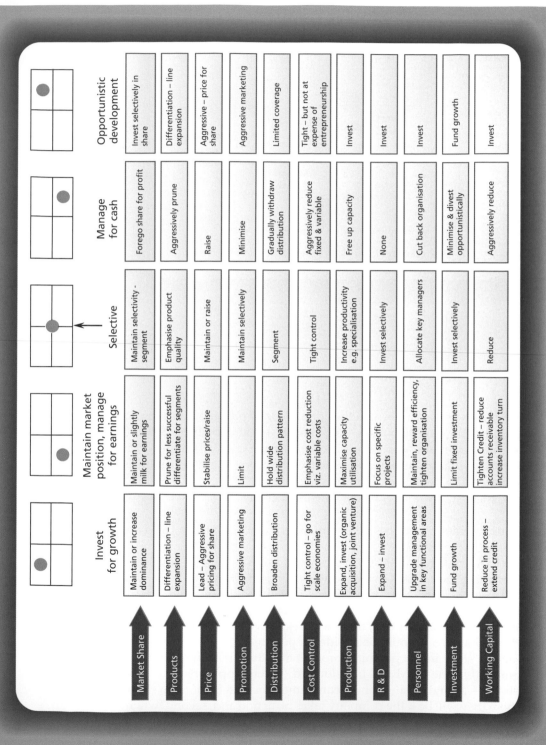

Figure 2.16
Strategy guidelines suggested for different positioning on the DPM

PART 3

■ Classifying target key accounts using a similar methodology

We have seen in outline, the process by which an organization's objectives and strategies can be totally market driven. This is only possible if market segments/markets are first identified and then categorized both according to the potential of each for growth in profit over some designated period of time and according to the organization's competitive capabilities in meeting customer needs in each segment/market.

Inevitably, this means that there will always be part of our market in the "low-potential/low strength" quadrant and it is therefore possible that some key accounts within such segments will also fall in this quadrant, as well as in the other three quadrants.

Before carrying out the next phase of analysis, it is worth considering this point very seriously, for clearly it will be the key accounts in the "high-potential/high-strength" segments which we should be targeting for our primary growth focus. We should also bear in mind that key accounts in the "low-potential/high-strength" quadrant also need targeting as a major activity in order to protect our current business. In addition, we need to consider key accounts in those segments located in the "high-potential/low-strength" quadrant, for these represent opportunities for future revenue streams. By definition, this means that any key accounts in the "low-potential/low-strength" quadrant should be the last to command our attention given our scarce resources.

Nonetheless, we still need a methodology for classifying key accounts irrespective of which quadrant they fall in. The next section introduces a method called "KAM portfolio analysis" and explains in detail how it should be done.

■ KAM portfolio analysis

Introduction

Portfolio analysis is simply a means of assessing a number of different key accounts, first according to the potential of each in terms for achieving the organization's objectives and, second, according to the organization's capability for taking advantage of the opportunities identified.

An adapted version of the DPM, portfolio analysis offers a detailed framework which can be used to classify possible competitive environments and their respective strategy requirements. It uses several indicators in measuring the dimensions of "account attractiveness" on one hand and "company capabilities" (relative to competitors) on the other. These indicators can be altered by management to suit the operating conditions of particular industrial sectors. The outcome of using portfolio analysis is the diagnosis of an organization's situation and strategy options relative to its position with respect to these two composite dimensions.

The purpose of the following guidelines is to obtain the maximum value out of this methodology.

Preparation

Prior to commencing portfolio analysis, the following preparation is advised:

1 Data/information profiles should be available for all key accounts to be scored (see Chapter 3).
2 Define the time period being scored. A period of 3 years is recommended.
3 Ensure sufficient data are available to score the factors (where no data are available, this is not a problem as long as a sensible approximation can be made for the factors).
4 Ensure up-to-date sales forecasts are available for all products/services plus any new products/services.

Analysis team

In order to improve the quality of scoring, it is recommended that a group of people from a number of different functions take part, as this encourages the challenging of traditional views through discussion.

Two key definitions

▶ **Key account attractiveness** is a measure of the potential of the key account for yielding growth in sales and profits. It is important to stress that this should be an objective assessment of key account attractiveness using data external to the organization. The criteria themselves will, or course, be determined by the organization carrying out the exercise and will be relevant to the objectives the organization is trying to achieve.

▶ **Business strength/position** is a measure of an organization's actual strengths in each key account, that is to say the degree to which it can take advantage of a key account opportunity. Thus, it is an objective assessment of an organization's ability to satisfy key account needs relative to competitors.

▶ **D E F I N I T I O N** ◀

Key account attractiveness is a measure of the potential of the key account for yielding growth in sales and profit.

▶ **D E F I N I T I O N** ◀

Business strength/position is a measure of an organization's actual strengths in each key account and it will differ according to each key account.

Twelve steps to producing the KAM portfolio (each of these steps will be explained in more detail later)

Step 1 Define the key accounts which are to be used during the analysis.
Step 2 Define the criteria for key account attractiveness and allocate weights out of a hundred for each.

Step 3   Define the parameters for size, growth profit potential, and "soft factors".

Step 4   Score the relevant key accounts out of 10 on the attractiveness factors and multiply the scores by the weights to achieve a total weighted score.

Step 5   Position the key accounts on the vertical axis.

Step 6   Define the critical success factors (from the customer's point of view) for each key account and the weight for each out of a hundred.

Step 7   Score your organization's performance out of 10 on each critical success factor relative to competitors, and multiply the scores by the weights to achieve a total weighted score.

Step 8   Position key accounts on the horizontal axis in the portfolio.

Step 9   Position the key accounts on the box assuming no change to current policies. That is to say a forecast should be made of the future position of the key accounts (this step is optional).

Step 10 Redraw the portfolio to position the key accounts where the organization wants them to be in, say, 3 years time. That is to say the objectives they wish to achieve for each key account.

Step 11 Set out the strategies to be implemented to achieve the objectives.

Step 12 Check the financial outcomes resulting from the strategies.

Let us now consider each step in turn.

Step 1: List the population of key accounts which you intend to include in the KAM portfolio

As stated earlier in this chapter, the list can include key accounts with which you have no business yet or accounts which are currently small or entrepreneurial, but which have the potential to become big.

To do this, it is suggested that a preliminary categorization be done according to size or potential size. Thus, if there were, say, 100 key accounts, the preliminary categorization might resemble Figure 2.17.

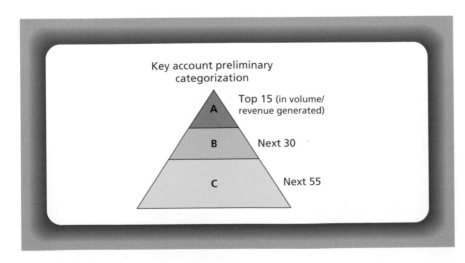

Figure 2.17
Example of an outcome of preliminary categorization (© Professor Malcolm McDonald, Cranfield School of Management).

It is important not to use the methodology which follows on all 100 accounts at once, as the criteria for each group may need to be different. The following methodology should, in the example shown, be carried out as three separate exercises A, B, and C, but for the purpose of this book, we are considering only the top 15 or 20 accounts.

Step 2: Define key account attractiveness criteria and weights for each

Attractiveness definition: This is a combination of a number of factors which can usually be summarized under three headings: growth rate, accessible volume or value, and profit potential. Each of these headings will possess a degree of importance to the organization which should be calculated as follows:

1 *Growth*: The average annual growth rate of revenue spent on the relevant goods or services by that key account (the percentage growth 2007 over 2006 *plus* the percentage growth 2008 over 2007 *plus* the percentage growth 2009 over 2008 divided by three). If preferred, the compound growth rate could be used.

▶ **DEFINITION** ◀

Accessible volume or value is the total spend of the key account in $t + 3$ less revenue impossible to access, regardless of investment made.

2 ▶ *Accessible volume or value*: An attractive key account is not only large – it can also be accessed. One way of calculating this is to estimate the *total* spend of the key account in $t + 3$ (year three) *less* revenue impossible to access, *regardless of investment made*. Alternatively, the total spend can be used, which is the most frequent method as it does not involve any managerial judgement to be made which could distort the truth. *The former method is the preferred method.*

▶ **DEFINITION** ◀

Profit potential is the margins available to any competitor.

3 ▶ *Profit potential*: This is much more difficult to deal with and will vary considerably according to industry. One way of assessing the profit potential is to make an estimate of the margins available to any competitor.

"Soft factors"

Naturally, growth, size, and profit will not encapsulate the requirements of all organizations.

It is then possible to add another heading, such as "soft factors", "risk", or "other" to the aforementioned three factors (growth rate, accessible volume or value, and profit potential).

The following are the factors most frequently used to determine "soft" account attractiveness factors:

- Regular flow of work – stability
- Strategy match
- Prompt payment
- Opportunity for cross-selling
- Ease of doing business
- Status/reference value
- Hub of network/"focal" company in a network

- Important to a sister company
- Requirement for global coverage
- Requirement for a single point of total responsibility
- Requirement for strategic alliances
- Requirement to manage complex issues (e.g. industrial relations and multiwork forces)
- Abdication (customer hands over total responsibility)
- Customer needs financial guarantees
- Client looking to work with a listed company
- Requirement to innovate on repetitive type work
- Blue-chip customer capable of meeting your financial security requirements (top 100 company)

Attractiveness considerations: Try to keep the total list of factors to five or less (including "soft" factors, otherwise the calculations become cumbersome and trivial).

In addition, once agreed, under no circumstances should key account attractiveness factors be changed unilaterally, otherwise the attractiveness of your key accounts is not being evaluated against common criteria and the matrix becomes meaningless. However, the scores will be specific to each key account.

It is also important to list the key accounts that you intend to apply the criteria before deciding on the criteria themselves, since the purpose of the vertical axis is to discriminate between more and less attractive key accounts. The criteria themselves must be specific to the population of key accounts and must not be changed for different key accounts in the same population.

Now allocate weights to each attractiveness factor, as shown in the example below.

Example:

Factors	Weight
Growth rate	30
Accessible volume or value	15
Profit potential	40
Soft factors	15

Note: The weightings need to be considered very carefully, as in some cases, volume may be more important than profit potential.

Step 3: Define the parameters for size, growth, profit potential, and "soft factors". This will obviously depend on the company doing this exercise, but the example below shows how this can be done. This example also shows attractiveness factors and weightings for each

Example:

Key account attractiveness factors	10–7	6–4	3–0	X weight
Volume/value	>10 m	1–10 m	<1 m	15
Growth/potential	>20%	5–20%	<5%	30
Profit potential	>25%	10–25%	<10%	40
"Soft" factors	Good	Medium	Poor	15
				100

Step 4: Score each key account

Score each key account on a scale of 1–10 against the attractiveness factors and multiply the score by the weight. This will provide a ranking list for the attractiveness axis from low to high.

Step 5: Position the key account on the vertical axis

The example below illustrates this step.

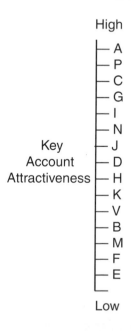

Step 6: Define business strength/position and relative weights

This is a measure of an organization's actual strengths in each key account and it will differ according to each key account.

These critical success factors will usually be a combination of an organization's relative strengths versus competitors' in connection with customer-facing needs, that is to say those things which are required by the customer. They can often be summarized as:

- product requirements,
- price requirements,
- service requirements,
- promotion requirements.

Step 7: Score critical success factors

This simple example shows that, whilst competitors A and B beat us on price, we are still better than they are, at satisfying this customer's needs, as we are superior on service which is more important to the customer.

A method for doing these calculations properly is given in Chapter 3.

The example below shows how this can be done for *each* key account.

Key account attractiveness requirements				
Requirements	Weight	US	Comp A	Comp B
Products	15	8 × 15	7 × 15	6 × 15
Price	20	6 × 20	8 × 20	9 × 20
Service	60	9 × 60	5 × 60	4 × 60
Price	5	5 × 5	8 × 5	9 × 5
Total weighted score		805	585	515

An easy way to do this is to decide the actual stage of the relationship (i.e. *basic* to *integrated*) in order to find the position on the horizontal axis.

1 *Exploratory*: You do not currently do business with this account.
2 *Basic*: You have some transactional business with this account.
3 *Cooperative*: You have regular business with this account and may well be a preferred supplier, but you are only one of many suppliers and pricing is still important.
4 *Interdependent*: You have multifunctional, multilevel relationships, but the customer could still exit if necessary.
5 *Integrated*: You have multifunctional, multilevel relationships, your systems are interlinked and exit for both parties would be difficult.

Figure 2.18 shows how this can be quantified.

It is recommended that the more robust method outlined in the example above be used in preference to this quicker method.

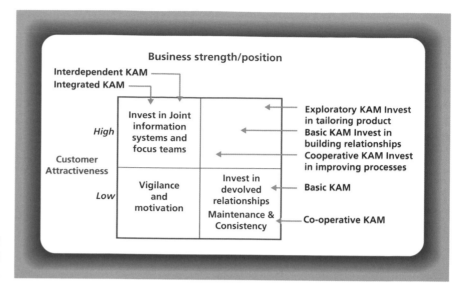

Figure 2.18
Portfolio analysis
matrix.

Step 8: Produce the portfolio analysis

The portfolio analysis should produce a matrix which resembles Figure 2.19.

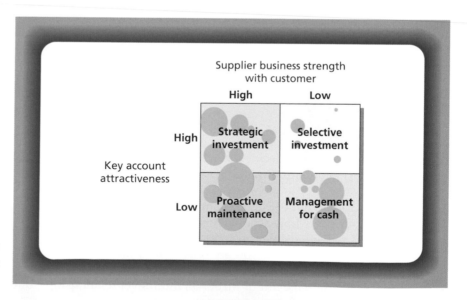

Figure 2.19
The key account
portfolio.

There are likely to be key accounts in all four boxes. It is advisable to list the names of the accounts, one per line, in order of their position on the vertical and horizontal axes.

Enter two figures next to each account name on each line:

● your current sales;
● the total available sales over 3 years (to any competitor).

Figure 2.20 is a real example from an insurance company, with the figures disguised to protect anonymity.

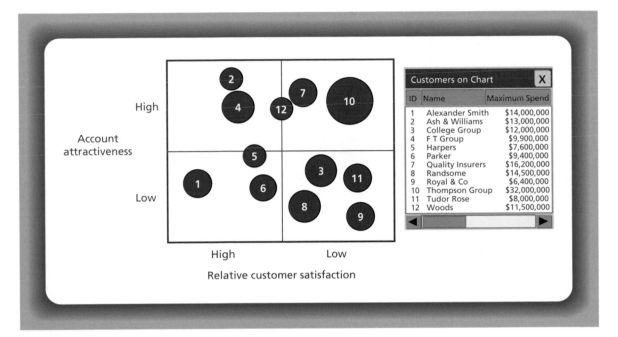

Figure 2.20
Insurance company DPM.

Step 9: Produce a forecast matrix (optional)

The analysis should position the key accounts on the horizontal axis where they are projected to be 3 years from now, *assuming no change to your current policies.*

The key accounts can only move *horizontally*, either to the left or to the right, because you have already taken account of potential future growth on the vertical axis.

Now enter a new figure for your *forecast* sales for each account, assuming no change in your current polices.

The first time you complete this analysis, it is unlikely that the forecast position will be satisfactory.

This step is not obligatory, but is useful for spurring Directors into action if it portrays a deteriorating position overall.

Step 10: Produce a matrix showing the objectives position

This analysis should position each key account on the horizontal axis showing the *objectives* position in 3 years time of each one.

Accounts can either stay in their current box, move to the right, or move to the left.

Enter a new figure for your *objectives* for sales against each key account.

Step 11: Outline the objectives and strategies for each key account for the next 3 years

Finally, a strategic plan for each key account should be produced. It should outline the objectives and strategies for each one.

Table 2.9 sets out more specific guidelines for setting objectives for each of the key accounts in each of the four boxes.

It will be observed that each box has a "label". These labels can be changed but should *not* be changed to derogatory or oversimplified names such as "gold", "silver", "bronze", "A", "B", "C", "D", etc.!! Also, key account objectives and strategies are defined in detail in Chapter 7.

Table 2.9 Strategic plan for each key account

Category	Description
Strategic customers	Very important customers, but the relationship has developed still further, to the level of partnership. The relationship is "win–win", both sides have recognized the benefits they gain from working together.
	Customers buy not on price but on the added value derived from being in partnership with the supplier.
	The range of contacts is very broad and joint plans for the future are in place.
	Products and services are developed side-by-side with the customer. Because of their large size and the level of resource which they absorb, only a few customers fall into this category.
Status customers	Very important customers (in terms of value).
	Commit to security of supply and offer products and services which are tailored to the customer's particular needs.
	Price is less important in the customer's choice of supplier.
	Both parties have some goals in common.
	The two organizations have made some form of commitment to each other.
	Invest as necessary in these customers in order to continue the business relationship for mutual advantage, but do not over invest.
Star customers	Price is still a major factor in the decision to buy but security of supply is very important and so is service.
	Spend more time with some of these customers and aim to develop a deeper relationship with them in time.
Streamline customers	These customers usually want a standard product, "off the shelf".
	Price is the key factor in their decision to buy.
	The relationship is helpful and professional, but transactional.
	Do not invest large amounts of time in the business relationship at this stage.

Step 12: Check the financial outcomes from the strategies

Cost out the actions which comprise the stated strategies in all boxes other than the bottom right-hand box. There may be circumstances for those in which a strategic plan should be produced for some of them, but generally speaking, forecasts and budgets should be sufficient, as it is unlikely that the supplying company will ever trade on terms other than low prices.

For an explanation, see the mini case below.

Mini Case

Case 3

Consider Figure 2.19. Please pay particular attention to the large key account circle in the bottom right-hand box. The following is a true story about a global paper company for whom the authors were doing some KAM consultancy.

A main board director was bemoaning the fact that one of the world's biggest media companies – hence a massive user of paper – was putting its paper order out to tender and was determined to accept the two lowest price bids. It was then to drop all other suppliers. The authors quickly established that to lose such a big customer would be a blow to profitability, as all its mill fixed costs would remain the same, without this customer.

So the authors advised the paper company to bid the lowest price in order to win the contract, then to withdraw all support other than that specified in the contract. In this case, clearly, sending a key account manager on regular visits and offering other services would have been a waste of resources, as it was clear that this particular customer didn't want a close relationship with any supplier and was obsessed with lowest price, so making it virtually impossible for any supplier to make much profit.

It is accounts such as these, usually in the bottom right-hand box, which are unattractive and driven by price alone that do not justify strategic key account plans. Such plans are only justified if the supplying company believes there is a real opportunity to move them to a more favourable position in the portfolios.

CHAPTER 3

How to collect information in order to understand the needs of the key accounts prior to preparing strategic plans for them

Summary

Research at Cranfield has shown that those organizations which invest resources in detailed analysis of the needs and processes of their key accounts fare much better in building long-term profitable relationships. We have termed this stage *pre-planning*. Armed with a detailed knowledge of the customer's business, it is more likely that the supplier can discover ways of helping them create advantages in their marketplace.

■ Introduction

We saw the basis on which key accounts should be defined and selected in Chapter 2. This was summarized diagrammatically and is repeated here as Figure 3.1.

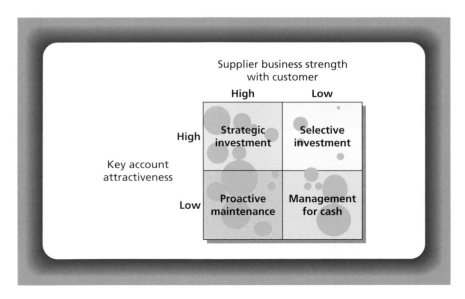

Figure 3.1
A four-box directional policy matrix.

The purpose of this chapter is to provide a set of specific and detailed procedures for key account analysis prior to producing a strategic plan for each key account selected as being worthy of focused attention by the key account manager.

An overview of the total process, which we have called the business partnership process, is given in Figure 3.2.

Steps 1 and 2 should ideally be carried out by "headquarters" personnel; otherwise there is the danger of several key account managers all duplicating the same tasks.

It should be clear by now that all segments in a market are not equally attractive to the supplying company. Hence, given scarce resources, a key account in a really attractive segment must be more important than a

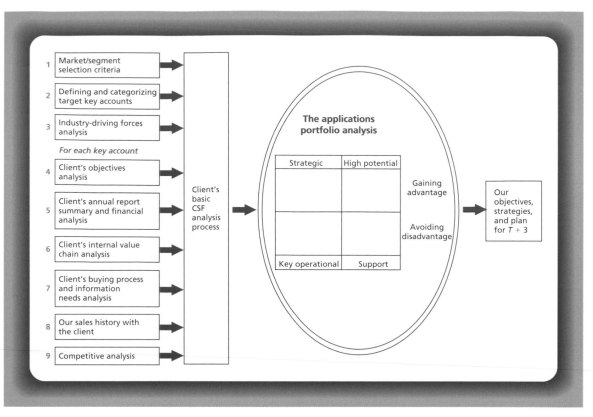

Figure 3.2
Business partnership process.

key account of similar potential in a less attractive segment. It is best, however, if the politics of this, along with step 2 – defining and categorizing key accounts – are left to other senior managers in the supplier's organization.

Steps 1 and 2 will be dealt with in Chapter 4. This chapter is devoted to describing each of the remaining steps involved in key account pre-planning, beginning with step 3.

■ Key account analysis pre-planning

Before it is possible to plan for key accounts, a detailed analysis of each key account must be undertaken by each individual key account manager and their team, somewhat in the manner of conducting a marketing audit. This is step 3 in Figure 3.2.

Step 3: Industry-driving forces analysis

Figure 3.3 shows an overall picture of the kind of analysis that needs to be carried out in order to understand key accounts better and, in particular, the environment in which they are operating today.

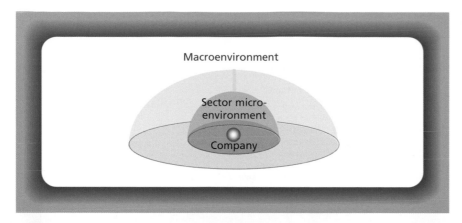

Figure 3.3
Macroenvironment.

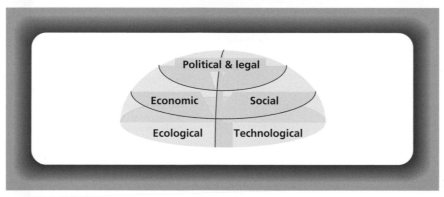

Figure 3.4
Macroenvironment
influences: STEEP.

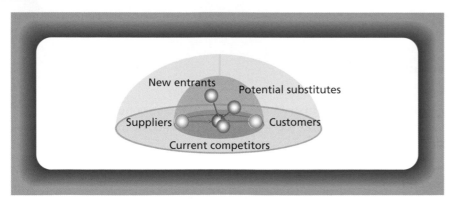

Figure 3.5
Microenvironment
influences.

Figure 3.4 shows some of the detail that needs to be understood about the political/legal, economic, social, ecological, and technical environment in which key accounts operate. A template to summarize these external influences will be provided in Chapter 14.

Figure 3.5 shows the microenvironmental influences affecting key accounts. These will now be expanded on.

Step 3 is known as Porter's industry Five Forces analysis. It is taken from Porter's book *Competitive Strategy* and has been of enormous value to generations of managers since its appearance in 1980. It is shown in summary form in Figure 3.6.

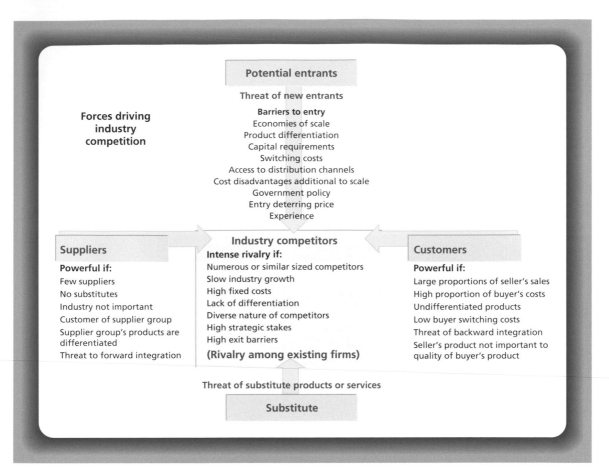

Figure 3.6
Forces driving industry competition.

Put simply, any industry has a number of competitors (located in the centre of the figure) and the relative performance of these competitors is determined by recognizable forces:

● Potential entrants
● Customers
● Potential substitute products and services
● The power of suppliers

The words in Figure 3.6 aptly describe the implications of each of the four outside forces on the competitors and it is clear that all competitors in a sector or industry will be affected by these driving forces.

This analysis is obviously best assisted by someone in central support services, perhaps marketing, as there is little point in a number of key account managers in the same industry all spending their time conducting the same analysis. If this is not practicable, then the job will indeed have to be done be individual key account managers for their own sectors.

It must be stressed, however, that such an analysis is a pre-requisite for the individual account analysis described later, as it provides key account managers with a deep analysis of their customers' industry and how it works and affects their performance.

Some forms are provided in Chapter 14 for the key account manager to summarize in a relevant way the outcome of Porter's Five Forces analysis in terms of the opportunities and threats that face the customer.

It should also be stressed here that steps 4–9 are all concerned with the analysis/diagnosis stage which must be completed by each key account manager before preparing a strategic plan for each key account.

Step 4: Customer's objectives analysis

The exercise given in Figure 3.7 should be completed for each key account being targeted. It can be seen that the intention is to take the industry-driving forces analysis and apply it specifically to an individual account in order to understand better what advantages and disadvantages it has. The main reason for doing this is to help the supplier understand ways in which its products or services may enable the client to exploit advantages and minimize disadvantages.

It is not the intention to complete this document as if it were a proforma. Each heading is intended merely to act as a trigger for some powerful conclusions about the client's competitive situation. This information will be used along with the further information to be gathered in steps 5–9.

Step 5: Customer's annual report summary and financial analysis

Figure 3.8 enables a summary to be made of a careful reading and analysis of a customer's published annual report. Even if there is not a formal report published for the shareholders (say, e.g., if your client is a subsidiary or division of a larger company), the directors do nonetheless tend to produce internal reports and newsletters which can be used instead.

Such documents can be a major source of information on what the customer believes to be the major issues facing them, their achievements and their objectives and strategies – in other words, their hopes for the future.

It is always possible to extract valuable information which can be used in helping a supplier understand how their organization might be of assistance. This information can now be put alongside the information gleaned from the previous objectives analysis summary.

Figure 3.9 focuses on the financial affairs of the customer and concerns information which can also be obtained from annual reports and other published sources. At first sight, this might appear to be some way removed from the reality of selling goods and services to a major account.

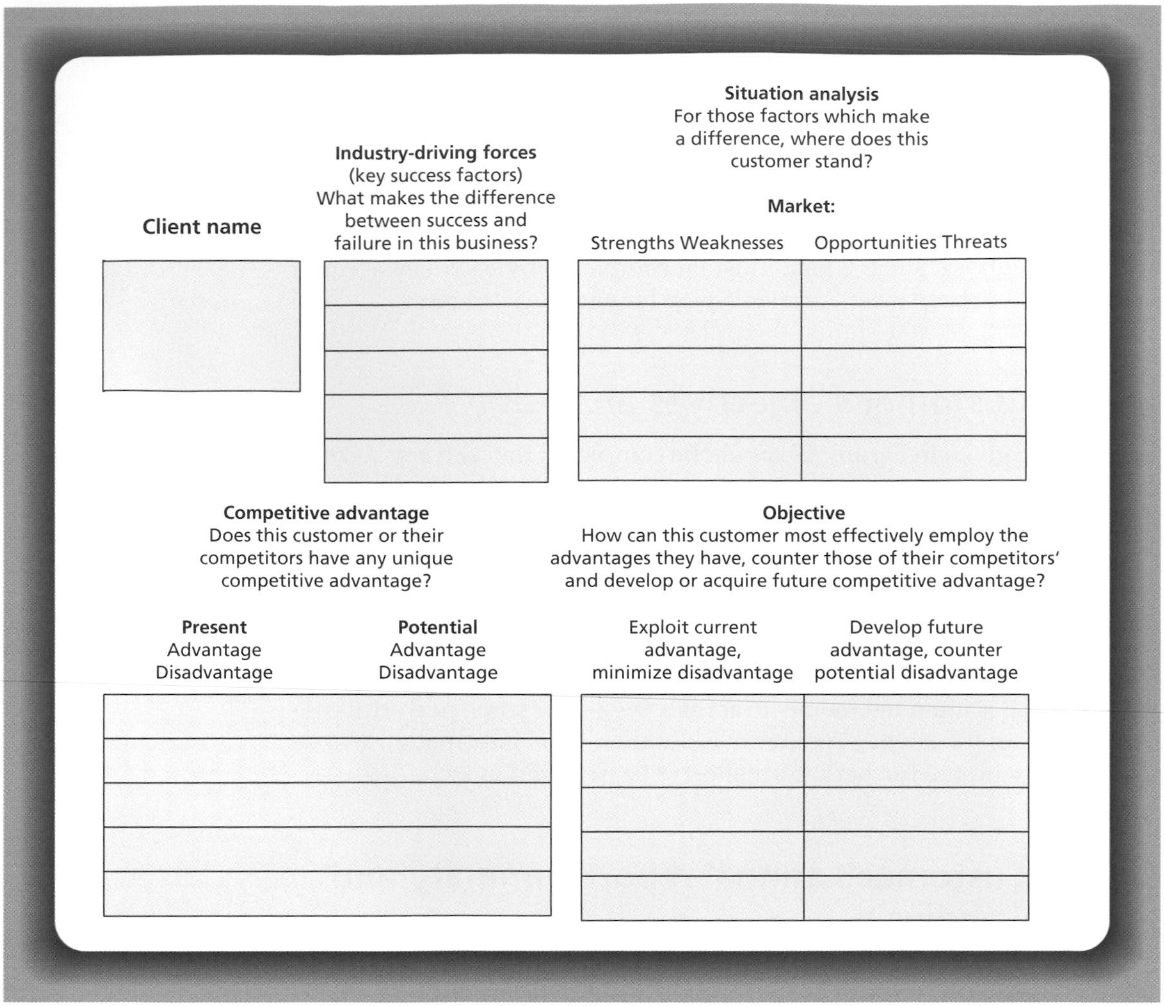

Situation analysis
For those factors which make
a difference, where does this
customer stand?

Industry-driving forces
(key success factors)
What makes the difference
between success and
failure in this business?

Client name

Market:

Strengths Weaknesses   Opportunities Threats

Competitive advantage
Does this customer or their
competitors have any unique
competitive advantage?

Objective
How can this customer most effectively employ the
advantages they have, counter those of their competitors'
and develop or acquire future competitive advantage?

Present	**Potential**		**Exploit current**	**Develop future**
Advantage	Advantage		advantage,	advantage, counter
Disadvantage	Disadvantage		minimize disadvantage	potential disadvantage

Figure 3.7
Objectives analysis exercise (industry-driving forces).

However, a little thought will reveal that most organizations today are acutely aware of their financial performance indicators:

- Current ratios
- Net profit margins
- Return on assets
- Debtor control
- Asset turnover

The purpose of the analysis contained in Figure 3.9 is to make the supplier acutely aware of the financial issues faced by the customer and to encourage the explanation of whether any of the supplier's products and services could improve any of these ratios.

1 Major achievements	_____
	_____
	_____
2 Major problems/Issues	_____
	_____
	_____
3 Objectives	_____
	_____
	_____
4 Strategies	_____
	_____
	_____
5 Conclusions/Opportunities	_____
	_____
	_____

Figure 3.8
Annual report
summary.

It will be obvious that any supplier who has taken the trouble to work out what impact its products and services have on the customer's bottom line will be preferred to a potential supplier who focuses only on product features.

Step 6: Client's internal value chain analysis

Figure 3.10 illustrates an organization's internal value chain as popularized by Professor Michael Porter in his book on competitive strategies which was referred to earlier. It is assumed that readers are familiar with this concept. The value chain is introduced here as an invaluable tool in understanding how a major account actually functions. The bottom level shows bought-in goods or services entering the organization, passing through operations, and then moving out to their markets through distribution, marketing, and sales and service. Sitting above these core processes are organizational support activities such as human resource management, procurement, and so on.

Financial ratio indicator	Formula	Source				Company standing	Industry standing	Does it appear as though improvement is needed?		Are there any initial thoughts about how our organization's products/services can help?
		Annual report						Yes	No	
Current ratio	Current assets / Current liabilities									
Net profit margin	Net profit / Net sales									
Return on assets	Net profit / Total assets									
Collection period	Debtors less bad debts / Average day's sales									
Stock turnover	Cost of goods sold / Stock									

Description of indicators		
	Current ratio	Measures the liquidity of a company – does it have enough money to pay the bills?
	Net profit margin	Measures the overall profitability of a company by showing the percentage of sales retained as profit after taxes have been paid. If this ratio is acceptable, there probably is no need to calculate the Gross profit or Operating profit margins.
	Return on assets	Evaluates how effectively a company is managed by comparing the profitability of a company and its investments.
	Collection period	Measures the activity of debtors. Prolonged collection period means that a company's funds are financing customers and not contributing to cash flow of the company.
	Stock turnover	Evaluates how fast funds are flowing through Cost of goods sold to produce profit. If stock turns over faster, it is not in the plant as long before it is saleable as a product.

Figure 3.9
Financial analysis.

Investigating how a major account actually manages these core activities can be a substantial task for a key account team, involving, as it does, an in-depth understanding of the detailed processes of the customer. This could include, for example, understanding what happens when a supplier's goods and services are delivered, where they are stored, how they are handled, how they are moved, how they are unpacked, how they are used, and so forth. The purpose of such a detailed analysis is to explore what issues and problems are faced by the customer with a view to resolving them through improvements and innovations.

Figure 3.11 is a very simple illustration of some of these issues and how they could be improved, thus representing sources of differentiation in the value chain.

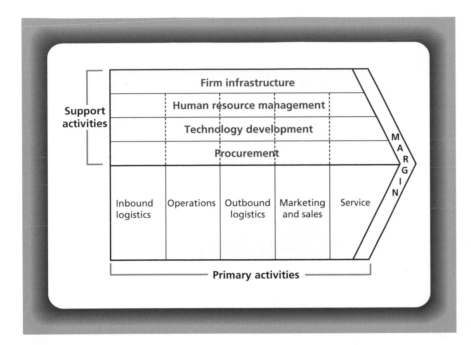

Figure 3.10
The value chain.

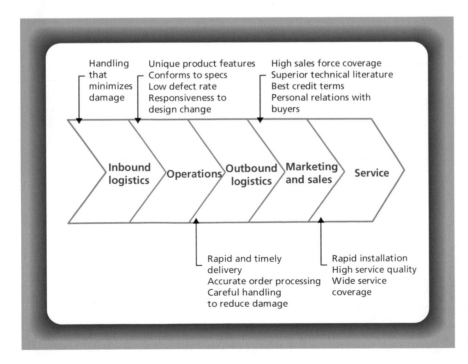

Figure 3.11
Sources of differentiation in the value chain.

For readers operating in a service environment, Figure 3.12 gives an example of how Porter's value chain can be adapted – in this case, for the financial services industry.

For service companies such as IFAs this version may be more appropriate. For each key account, list ways in which you can use your resources/skills (e.g. E-commerce) to improve their value chain, by reducing their costs, by avoiding costs, or by creating value for their customers.

		Reducing cost	Creating value
Infrastructure	– Legal, Accounting, Financial Management		
Human resource management	– Personnel, Pay, Recruitment, Training, Manpower Planning, etc.		
Product and technology development	– Product and Process Design, Market Testing, R&D, etc.		
Procurement	– Supplier Management, Funding, Subcontracting, Specification		

Recognize exchange potential	Initiate dialogue	Exchange information	Negotiate/ Tailor	Commit	Exchange value	Monitor	
							Reducing cost
							Creating value

Figure 3.12
Internal value chain: service companies, e.g. IFAs (© Professor Malcolm McDonald).

All information emanating from this analysis can be usefully summarized using a format similar to that shown in Figure 3.13. From this, it can be seen that there are four general headings of customer benefits:

1 Possibilities for increased revenue for the customer
2 Possibilities for cost displacement
3 Possibilities for cost avoidance
4 Intangible benefits

Another way of looking at this is to identify the methods of gaining competitive edge through value in use:

1 *Reduce the life cycle/Alter the cost mix*: Customers are often willing to pay a considerably higher initial price for a product with significantly lower post-purchase costs.

Tangible benefits	Product solution	Analysis and comment
Increased revenue		
Increased sales volume		
Enhanced product line		
Cost displacement		
Reduced labour costs		
Reduced equipment costs		
Reduced maintenance costs		
Lowered stock costs		
Reduced energy costs		
Cost avoidance		
Reduced new personnel requirement		
Eliminate planned new equipment		
Intangible benefits		
Customer good will		
Improved decision-making		

Figure 3.13
Value chain analysis summary.

2 *Expand value through functional redesign*: For example, a product which increases the user's production capacity or throughput, a product which enables the user to improve the quality or reliability of his or her end-product, a product which enhances end-use flexibility, or a product which adds functions or permits added applications.

3 *Expand incremental value by developing associated intangibles*: For example, service, financing, and "prestige".

Mini Case

Case 1 – Value chain analysis for a packaging company

An international chemical company undertook this investigation process using a novel method. They organized a 2-day event for eight senior people from different functions in a large packaging company. These executives included marketing people, a health and safety executive, an environmental specialist, a logistics manager, a manufacturing manager, and a couple of directors! These executives were matched by equivalent managers and directors from the supplying company. An independent consultant was asked to chair the 2-day event.

The purpose of the event, which was held in a neutral location, was to investigate ways in which the several goods and services of the supplying company were received, used, and perceived by the customer. This enquiry was obviously only possible because of the good relationships already enjoyed by the supplier.

While it took a few hours for the independent moderator to break down the natural barriers to honest and open communication, the event had a major impact on the processes and attitudes of the supplier. For example, at one stage the customers were asked to go into a syndicate room and write down all the things they did not like or found inadequate in the supplying company. The sheer size of the list and the contents so shocked the supplier that it immediately agreed to set up a number of functional and cross-functional working groups comprising executives from both sides in order to study how cost-effective improvements could be made.

All issues were investigated openly and honestly, ranging from the strategic issues faced by the customer in its industry to very tactical issues concerned with processes. The end-result was a dramatically improved relationship which led to substantial benefits to both sides.

It is not suggested that this is the only way to discover the kind of detailed information outlined in Figure 3.13. In many cases, much patience is required over considerable periods of time and the effectiveness and efficiency with which this investigative task can be carried out will be a function of how good and deep the existing relationships are.

Nonetheless it is difficult to see how improvements can be made without a thorough understanding of the customer's systems and processes.

The list of possibilities for improvement of the supplier is now growing quite considerably. However, there are still more aspects of the business which need to be analysed.

Step 7: The customer's buying process

Figure 3.14 outlines the buying process for goods and services. In the remainder of this section, it will be assumed that the supplier is selling a service, although the same process applies equally well to products.

Selling to an organization can be a complex process because it is possible for a number of different people to become involved at the customer end. Although theoretically only one of these is the buyer, in practice he or she

Customer Analysis Form

Salesperson ——————————
Products ——————————
——————————
Date of analysis——————————
Date of reviews——————————

Customer ——————————————————
Address ——————————————————
———————————— Telephone number ————————

	Buy class	New buy	Straight re-buy	Modified re-buy

Member of Decision Making Unit (DMU)	Production	Sales & Marketing	Research & Development	Finance & Accounts	Purchasing	Data Processing	Other
Buy Phase Name							
1 Recognizes need or problem and works out general solution							
2 Works out characteristics and quantity of what is needed							
3 Prepares detailed specification							
4 Searches for and locates potential sources of supply							
5 Analyses and evaluates tenders, plans, products							
6 Selects supplier							
7 Places order							
8 Checks and tests products							

Factors for consideration	1 price	4 back-up service	7 guarantees and warranties
	2 performance	5 reliability of supplier	8 payment terms, credit, or discount
	3 availability	6 other users' experience	9 other, e.g. past purchases, prestige, image, etc.

Figure 3.14
Buying process for goods and services (adapted from Robinson, J., Farris, C.W. and Wind, Y. (1967). *Industrial Buying and Creative Marketing*, Allyn and Bacon).

might not be allowed to make a decision to purchase until others with technical expertise or hierarchical responsibility have given their approval.

The personal authority of the buyer will to a large extend be governed by the following factors:

1 *The cost of the service*: The higher the cost, the higher up in the organization the purchasing decision will be made (see Table 3.1). Please note that, although the level of expenditure figures will have increased substantially during the past 23 years, the table is included because it is indicative of a hierarchy of purchasing authority.
2 *The "newness" of the service*: The relative novelty of the service will pose an element of commercial risk for an organization. A new and untried proposition will require support from a senior management level, whereas a routine, non-risky service can be handled at a lower level.
3 *The complexity of the service*: The more complex the service offered the more technical the implications which have to be understood within

Table 3.1 Responsibility for financial expenditure

Level of expenditure	Level at which decision is taken (%)			
	Board (collective)	Individual Director	Departmental Manager	Lower management or clerical
Over £50,000	88	11	2	–
Up to £50,000	70	25	4	Less than 0.5
Up to £5000	29	55	14	2
Up to £2500	18	54	24	4
Up to £500	4	31	52	14

Source: "How British Industry Buys", a survey conducted by Cranfield School of Management for *The Financial Times*, January 1984. Although this survey is over 23-years old, our recent research at Cranfield indicates that the percentages are still approximately right.

the client company. Several specialist managers might be required to give their approval before the transaction can be completed.

All those involved in the buying decision are known as the decision-making unit (DMU) and it is important for the key account manager to identify the DMU in the customer company. Table 3.2 provides some research findings which demonstrate how rarely sales people reach all component members of the DMU.

Table 3.2 Buying influences by company size

Number of employees	Average number of buying influences (the DMU)	Average number of contacts made by salesperson
0–200	3.42	1.72
201–400	4.85	1.75
401–1000	5.81	1.90
1000 plus	6.50	1.65

Source: *Marketing Plans*, 6th Edition, Butterworth-Heinemann, Oxford, 2007.

A useful way of anticipating who would be involved in the decision-making processes in a company is to consider the sales transaction from the buyer's point of view. It has been recognized that the process can be split into a number of distinct steps known as "buy phases". These buy phases will be followed in most cases, particularly for major purchases. It will be obvious that at stages beyond the *cooperative* key account management

(KAM) stage, the incumbent supplier will have an inside track and, hence, an advantage, throughout the process. In many cases, customers do not even bother to put their proposed purchase requirements out to tender, preferring to deal with their current trusted partner.

■ Buy phases

(This section of the text owes much to the original research conducted by the Marketing Science Institute in the USA under the guidance of Patrick J. Robinson.)

1 *Problem identification*: A problem is identified or anticipated and a general solution worked out. For example, the marketing planning department finds that it has inadequate information about sales records and costs. It needs better information made available on the computer.
2 *Problem definition*: The problem is examined in more detail in order to grasp the dimensions and, hence, the nature of the ultimate choice of solution. Taking our earlier example of the international chemical company further, investigation showed that the supplier's original software system was not devised with the customer's current marketing planning requirements in mind. A new system was required which can also provide the option for the inclusion of other new data.
3 *Solution specification*: The various technical requirements are listed and a sum of money is allocated to cover the cost of investing in new software.
4 *Search*: A search is made for potential suppliers, in this case those with the capability of devising a "tailor-made" system to meet the above requirements.
5 *Assessment*: Proposals from interested suppliers are assessed and evaluated.
6 *Selection*: A supplier is selected and final details are probably negotiated prior to the next step.
7 *Agreement*: A contract/agreement is signed.
8 *Monitoring*: The service is monitored in terms of meeting installation deadlines and performance claims.

If we happened to be running a computer programming service to industry, we could deduce from the buying process that the DMU at this company might well contain the following people: a marketing planner, a sales director, a sales office manager, the company computer specialist, the company accountant, the company secretary, and perhaps even the managing director, depending on the nature of the contract and the buyer. Sometimes the buyer might be one of those already listed and not exist as a separate role.

We could also speculate with some certainty that each of these people would need to be satisfied about different aspects of the efficiency of our service and we would need to plan accordingly.

For now, it is enough to recognize that, when selling to an organization, the person with the title of buyer is often unable to make important decisions of his/her own. Although he/she can be a useful cog in the company's purchasing machine, he/she is often not a free agent.

Pressures on the buyer

When we purchase something for the home, we know from our own experience how difficult it can sometimes be. Even if we are buying only a carpet, we have to agree whether or not it should be plain or patterned, what colour, what price, what quality, and so on. Even seemingly straightforward considerations like these are clouded by issues such as whether the neighbours or relatives will think we are copying them or whether we are being too chic or too outrageous. The buying decision-makers in a typical company are faced with a greater multitude of pressures which come from two directions: from outside the company (external pressures) and from inside the company (internal pressures).

External pressures

External pressures can be many and varied and may involve important issues such as the following:

1 *The economic situation*: What will be the cost of borrowing? Are interest rates likely to rise or fall? Is it a good time to invest in a new service now? Is the market decline really over or should we wait for more signals of recovery?

2 *Political considerations*: How will government fiscal policy affect our business or that of our customers? Will proposed legislation have an impact on either us or our markets?

3 *Technology*: How are we as a company keeping up with technological developments? How does this new proposal rate on a technological scale? Is it too near the frontiers of existing knowledge? How long will it be before a whole new phase of technology supersedes this investment?

4 *Environmental considerations*: Will this new service be advantageous to us in terms of energy conservation or pollution control? Does it present any increase in hazards to our workforce? Will we need more room to expand? Is such room available?

5 *The business climate*: How do our profit levels compare with those of companies in general and those in our type of business in particular? Are there material cost increases in the pipeline which could reduce our profits? Is the cost of labour increasing?

Any one of these external issues could put pressure on the buying decision-maker – and this is only half the picture.

Internal pressures

Another set of pressures evolve from within the company itself such as the following:

1 *Confused information*: It is often difficult to obtain the correct information to support a buying decision. Either the information does not exist or it has not been communicated accurately from the specialist department. Sometimes it is not presented in a convenient form and this leads to confusion and misunderstanding.

2 *Internal politics*: The relative status of individuals or departments can sometimes hinder the buying process. Personal rivalries or vested interests can create difficulties about priorities or standards. The "politics" might entail non-essential people being involved in the decision-making process, thereby elongating the communication chain and slowing down decision-making.

3 *Organizational*: How the company is organized can affect the efficiency of its buying process. It is essential for everyone within the company to be aware of their role and the level of authority if they are to perform effectively.

Personal pressures

Buyers can be pressurized by a number of personal matters, some real, others imagined. They might be unsure about their role or how their colleagues accept their judgement. They might lack experience in the buying role and be unsure of how to conduct themselves. They might prefer a quiet life and therefore be against change, preferring to continue transactions with tried and tested suppliers – even if it can be clearly demonstrated that there are advantages in changing them. They might be naturally shy and not enjoy first meetings. They might find it difficult to learn new information about technical developments or the special features of your particular service.

> All of these pressures, both external and internal, have a profound bearing on the behaviour of the buyer and, if the account manager is to relate to the buyer, he/she must try to understand them.

By way of summarizing this section on business-to-business selling, it can be demonstrated that the successful account manager needs to be aware of all these things when approaching a buyer acting on behalf of an organization. All of the following elements need to be known and understood:

● The relative influence of the buyer in the context of the particular product or service being offered.
● What constitutes the DMU in the buying company.
● How the buying process works.
● The pressures on the buying decision-maker.

With this information, the account manager is in a better position to plan his/her work and to adopt appropriate conduct when face-to-face with the buying decision-maker(s). Exactly how this information should be used will be covered later in this chapter.

■ Buy classes

Whether or not the account manager is selling to an individual or to an organization, the decision-making processes of the prospects can be divided into what are termed "buy classes". There are three types of *buy class*.

1 *New buy*: In effect, all the foregoing discussion has focused on the new buy category. It is here that those people who make up the DMU are fully exercised as the buy phases unfold. In the new buy class, the needs of all decision-makers must be met and influenced by the key account manager. Not surprisingly, this takes time and so it is not unusual for a lengthy period to elapse between the initial discussion and contract closure.

2 *Straight rebuy*: Once the salesperson has had the opportunity of demonstrating how the service can help the customer, further purchases of the service do not generally require such a rigorous examination of all of the buy phases. In fact, should the customer merely wants a repeat purchase of the same service, then their only concerns are likely to be about issues such as whether the price has been held to the same level as before, whether the standard of the service has changed, and whether it can be provided at a specific time. Such issues can generally be resolved by negotiation with the buyer.

3 *Modified rebuy*: Sometimes a modification of the product or service might be necessary. It might be that the supplier wants to update the product or service and provide better performance by using different methods or equipment. Alternatively, it could be the customer who calls for some form of modification from the original purchase. Whatever the origin, all or some of the buy phases will have to be reexamined and again the key account manager will have to meet with and persuade and satisfy the relevant members of the DMU.

There are often advantages for an account manager in trying to change a straight rebuy into a modified rebuy. They are twofold:

1 A modified rebuy reactivates and strengthens the relationship with the various members of the customer's DMU.
2 The more closely a supplier can match its service to the customer's needs (and remember this matching only comes about as a result of mutual learning, as communication and trust develop between the supplier and the customer), the more committed the customer becomes to the product or service.

The higher the commitment the customer has to the particular product or service and the supplier, the more difficult it becomes for competitors to break in.

Identifying the decision-maker

Recognizing that there is a DMU is an important first step for the account manager but, having done this, it is essential to identify who actually has the power to authorize the purchase. No matter how persuasive the arguments for buying your service, if you are not reaching the key decision-maker then all your efforts could well be in vain. Identifying this person is too important to be left to chance and yet many account managers fail to meet with them. Sometimes they just have not done enough research about the company to obtain an accurate picture of its character and key concerns. It is important that the account manager researches the company sufficiently in order to obtain a thorough understanding of its operations, personnel, and priorities.

> Alternatively, many account managers prefer to continue liaising with their original contacts in the client company, the ones with whom they feel comfortable and have come to regard as friends, rather than to extend their network to include more influential client representatives. Because many purchase decision-makers will hold senior positions, the thought of meeting them somehow seems a daunting prospect, particularly to complacent or ill-prepared account mangers.

Yet many of these fears are groundless. There is no evidence that senior executives set out to be deliberately obstructive or use meetings to expose the account manager's possible inadequacies. In fact, quite the opposite appears to be true.

Certainly, the decision-makers will be busy people and so will want discussion to be to the point and relevant. At the same time, they will be trying to get the best deal for their company and it is only natural that they should.

Step 8: Your sales history with the client

Figure 3.15 shows a very simple analysis of the supplier's sales over a designated period of time working with the customer. The purpose is merely to summarize the business history, share, and prospects with this customer.

Step 9: Competitive comparison and competitor strategy

Figure 3.16 shows one of a number of possible ways of establishing how well the suppliers are meeting the customer's needs in comparison with your competitors. It is obviously better if this is done using evidence obtained from independent market research, but providing the analysis suggested in this chapter is carried out thoroughly and with diligence, it should be possible to complete this part of the analysis internally with sufficient accuracy.

Your sales history with the client					
Products		T-2	T-1	T-0	Trend
Customer volume (total)					
Your volume					
Your share volume					
Your share value					
Sales analysis					
Products		T-2	T-1	T-0	Trend
	Val				
	Vol				
	%				
	Val				
	Vol				
	%				
	Val				
	Vol				
	%				
	Val				
	Vol				
	%				
	Val				
	Vol				
	%				
Comments					

Figure 3.15
Sales analysis and history.

Competitive comparison				
	Importance rating	You	Competitor 1 2 3	Implications
Product quality				
Product range				
Availability				
Delivery				
Price/discounts				
Terms				
Sales support				
Promotion support				
Other				

Importance rating	**Rating**
(by customer)	(customer view)
A – very important (essential)	1 – consistently/fully meets needs
B – important (desirable)	2 – meets needs inconsistently
C – low importance	3 – fails to meet needs

Competitor's strategy	
Competitor	Strategy
1.	
2.	
3.	

Figure 3.16
Competitive comparison and competitor strategy.

Some people prefer to carry out this analysis using a more traditional (strengths, weaknesses, opportunities, and threats or SWOT) format as given in Figure 3.17.

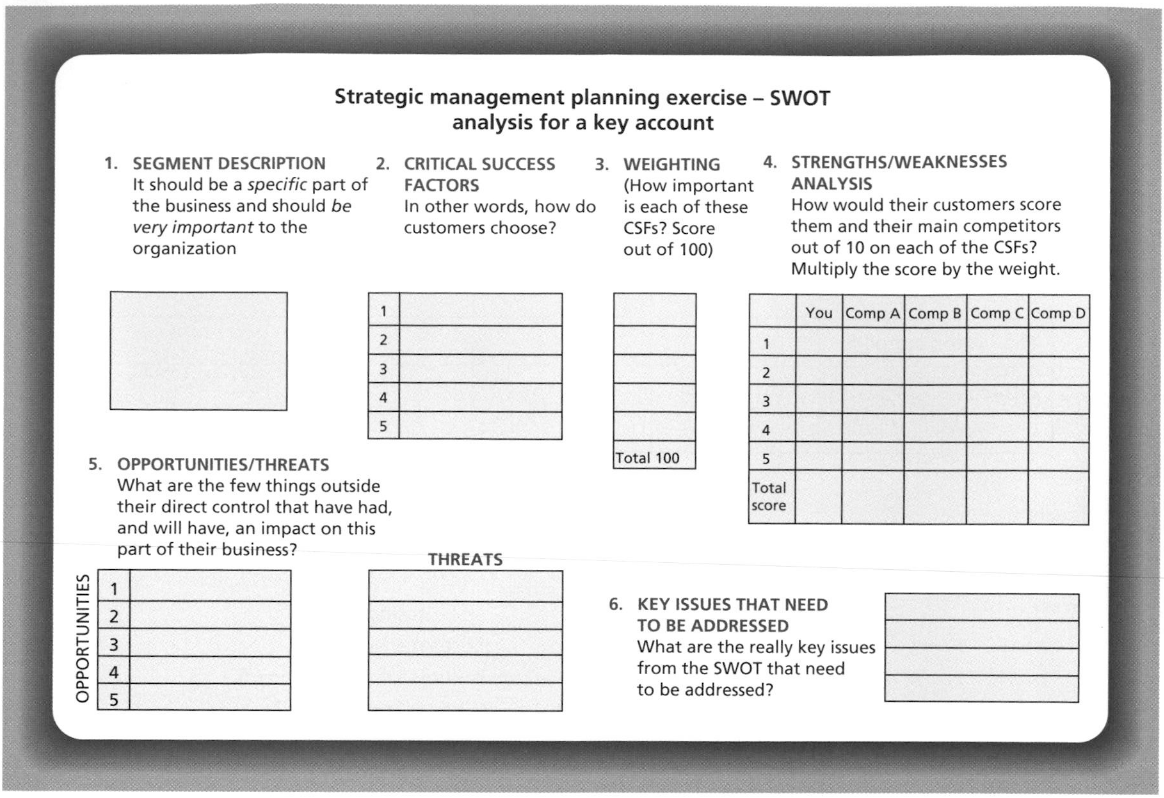

Figure 3.17
Strategic marketing planning exercise SWOT analysis.

The main point of course is that any organization hoping to get and keep business with a major account needs to provide superior customer value and this can only be achieved by comparisons with the best that competitors have to offer.

■ Next steps

The painstaking key account analysis is now compete and a number of customer critical success factors (CSFs) will have been accumulated, together with specific ways in which the supplier's products or services and processes can help.

Figure 3.18 describes a useful way of categorizing the supplier's business solutions and approaches to the customer prior to producing a strategic marketing plan for the customer.

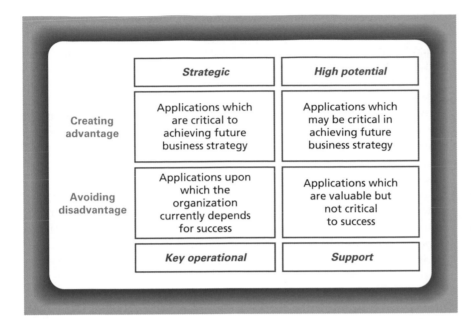

Figure 3.18 The applications portfolio (adapted from Professor Chris Edwards, Cranfield School of Management and used with his kind permission).

The applications portfolio comprises four quadrants. The quadrants at the bottom left and right are labelled "Avoiding disadvantage". While the meaning of this label might be self-evident, it is nonetheless worth providing an example of this category.

Take, for instance, a bank considering buying automatic teller machines (ATMs) for use by customers outside bank opening hours. Not having ATMs would clearly place the bank at a disadvantage. However, having them does not give the bank any advantage either. The majority of commercial transactions fall into this category.

The bottom left quadrant represents key operational activities, such as basic accounting, manufacturing and distribution systems. The bottom right quadrant might include activities such as producing Powerpoint slides for internal presentations.

In contrast, the top two quadrants represent a real opportunity for differentiating a supplier's offering by creating advantage for the customer. The top right quadrant might be beta testing a product, service, or process prior to making a major investment in launching it for the customer.

Mini Case

Case 2 – Gaining advantage

A classic example of a high potential application was Thompson's computer systems in the leisure/holiday market where the company was able to place its own holidays at the head of all travel agents' lists.

This latter point cannot be stressed enough. The whole point of gathering so much information about the key account is to work out ways in which the supplier can create advantage for the customer. Anything else is likely to be decided on price.

The reality of commercial life is that most of what any organization does falls into the avoiding disadvantage category. However, leading companies adopt a proactive business approach. They work hard at developing products, services, and processes designed to deliver advantage for their major accounts, for it is clear that creative customer-focused suppliers will always be preferred over those who merely offer "me too" products and trade only on price.

The KAM Best Practice Research Club at Cranfield has strong evidence to suggest that, once such an audit on a key account has been completed, if it is presented formally to senior managers in the account, the response is extremely favourable and, further, that additional confidential information is likely to be provided by the customer to enable the supplier to prepare a strategic marketing plan.

Finally, referring back to Figure 3.2, it will be clear that all these data and information collected using the tools described in this chapter (described as "CSFs" in Figure 3.2) can be used to populate the templates provided in Chapter 14 – in other words, to prepare a strategic plan for a key account.

The next chapter explains how to understand the marketing process of your key accounts and follows on logically from this chapter on understanding their needs.

CHAPTER 4

How to understand the marketing processes of your key accounts: Strategic marketing planning

Summary

This chapter explores how key accounts prepare their strategies for their markets (marketing planning). It will help considerably in understanding how they operate and the ways in which the supplier can help.

Although we have already outlined some of these processes in Chapter 1, they are dealt with more fully here. Those readers who are already fully familiar with the complexities of strategic marketing planning can move directly to Chapter 5, although we do recommend that the contents of this chapter are read and digested by those who want to understand their key accounts.

In order to explore the complexities of developing a strategic marketing plan, this chapter is written in two parts. The first describes the strategic marketing planning process itself and the key steps within it. It also deals with implementation issues and barriers to marketing planning. Understanding these barriers will be very useful for suppliers.

The second part provides a tried and tested method for evaluating the strategic marketing plans of your key accounts. If you are fortunate enough to see a copy of their strategic plans, using this method will be easy. If you have only limited information to go on, this methodology will still be useful to you.

PART 1

■ Introduction

Research into the efficacy of formalized marketing planning has shown that marketing planning can make a significant contribution to commercial success. The main effects within organizations are:

- the systematic identification of emerging opportunities and threats;
- preparedness to meet change;
- the specification of sustainable competitive advantage;
- improved communication among executives;
- reduction of conflicts between individuals and departments;
- the involvement of all levels of management in the planning process;
- more appropriate allocation of scarce resources;
- consistency of approach across the organization;
- a more market-focused orientation across the organization.

However, although it can bring many benefits, a strategic marketing plan is mainly concerned with competitive advantage – that is to say, establishing, building, defending, and maintaining it.

In order to be realistic, it must take into account the organization's existing competitive position, where it wants to be in the future, its capabilities, and the competitive environment it faces. This means that the marketing planner must learn to use the various available processes and techniques which help to make sense of external trends and to understand the organization's traditional ways of responding to these.

However, this poses a problem regarding which are the most relevant and useful tools and techniques, for each has strengths and weaknesses and no individual concept or technique can satisfactorily describe and illuminate the whole picture. As with a jigsaw puzzle, a sense of unity only emerges as the various pieces are connected together.

What is agreed, however, is that strategic marketing planning presents a useful process by which an organization formulates its strategies, *providing it is adapted* to the organization and its environment.

■ The role of marketing

As we stated in Chapter 1, marketing is a process for: defining markets; quantifying the needs of the customer groups (segments) within these markets; determining the value propositions to meet these needs; communicating these value propositions to all those people in the organization responsible for delivering them and getting their buy-in to their role; playing an appropriate part in delivering these value propositions to the chosen market segments; and monitoring the value actually delivered.

For this process to be effective, we have also seen that organizations need to be consumer/customer driven.

As a reminder, we repeat here as Figure 4.1 the "map" shown as Figure 1.10 in Chapter 1.

Input to this process will commonly include:

● The corporate mission and objectives, which will determine which particular markets are of interest
● External data such as market research
● Internal data which flow from ongoing operations

Also, it is necessary to define the markets the organization is in, or wishes to be in, and how these divide into segments of customers with similar needs. The choice of markets will be influenced by the corporate objectives as well as the asset base. Information will be collected about the markets, such as the market's size and growth, with estimates for the future.

The map is inherently cross-functional. "Deliver value", for example, involves every aspect of the organization, from new product development through inbound logistics and production to outbound logistics and customer service.

The map represents best practice, not common practice. Many aspects of the map are not explicitly addressed by well-embedded processes, even in sophisticated companies.

Also, the map is changing. One-to-one communications and principles of relationship marketing demand a radically different sales process from that traditionally practised. Hence, exploiting new media such as the

Internet requires a substantial shift in thinking, not just changes to information technology (IT) and hard processes. An example is illuminating:

Marketing managers at one company related to us their early experience with a website which was enabling them to reach new customers considerably more cost-effectively than their traditional sales force. When the website was first launched, potential customers were finding the company on the web, deciding the products were appropriate on the basis of the website, and sending an email to ask to buy. So far so good. But, stuck in a traditional model of the sales process, the company would allocate the "lead" to a salesperson, who would phone up and make an appointment perhaps 3 weeks hence. The customer would by now probably have moved on to another online supplier who could sell the product today, but those that remained were subjected to a sales pitch which was totally unnecessary, the customer having already decided to buy. Those that were not put off would proceed to be registered as able to buy over the web, but the company had lost the opportunity to improve its margins by using the sales force more judiciously. In time the company realised its mistake: unlike those prospects which the company identified and contacted, which might indeed need "selling" to, many new web customers were initiating the dialogue themselves, and simply required the company to respond effectively and rapidly. The sales force was increasingly freed up to concentrate on major clients and on relationship building.

In Chapter 1, we put marketing planning into the context of marketing and other corporate functions, so we can now turn specifically to the marketing planning process, how it should be done, and what the barriers are to doing it effectively. We are, of course, referring specifically to the first two boxes in Figure 4.1.

■ The marketing planning process

Most managers accept that some kind of procedure for marketing planning is necessary. Accordingly, they need a system which will help them think in a structured way and also make explicit their intuitive economic models of the business. Unfortunately, very few companies have planning systems which possess these characteristics. However, those that do tend to follow a similar pattern of steps.

Figure 4.2 illustrates the several stages that have to be gone through in order to arrive at a marketing plan. This illustrates the difference between

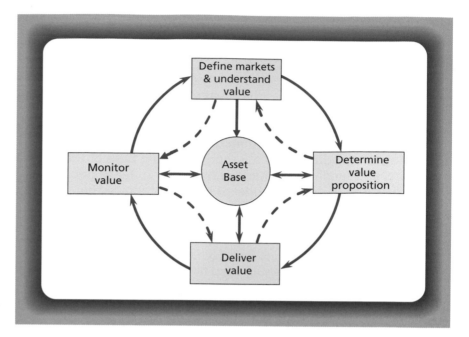

Figure 4.1
Map of the marketing process.

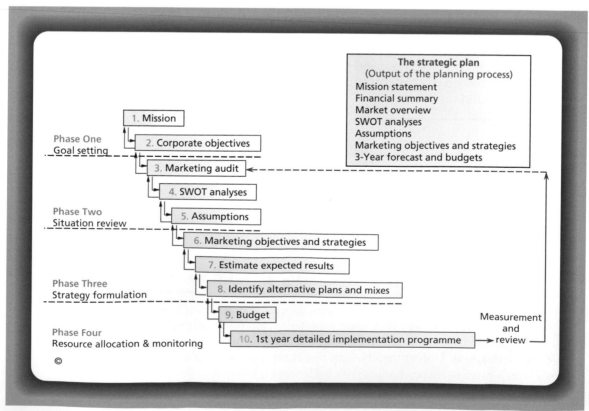

Figure 4.2
The 10 steps of the strategic marketing planning process.

the *process* of marketing planning and the actual plan itself, which is the *output* of the process, discussed later in this chapter.

Each of the process stages illustrated in Figure 4.2 will be discussed in more detail in this chapter. Each of these steps may have to be gone through more than once before final programmes can be written.

Where marketing planning has failed, it has generally been because companies have placed too much emphasis on the procedures themselves and the resulting forecasts, rather than on generating information useful to and consumable by management. But more about reasons for failure will be discussed later. For now, let us look at the marketing planning process in more detail, starting with the mission statement.

Step 1: Mission statement

Figure 4.2 shows that a strategic marketing plan should begin with a mission or purpose statement. This is perhaps the most difficult aspect of marketing planning for managers to master, because it is largely philosophical and qualitative in nature. Many organizations find their different departments, and sometimes even different groups in the same department, pulling in different directions, often with disastrous results, simply because the organization hasn't defined the boundaries of the business and the way it wishes to do business.

Here, we can see two levels of mission. One is a *corporate* mission statement, the other is a lower level or *purpose* statement. But there is yet another level, as shown in the following summary:

Type 1: "Motherhood" – usually found inside annual reports designed to "stroke" shareholders. Otherwise of no practical use.

Type 2: The real thing. A meaningful statement, unique to the organization concerned, which "impacts" on the behaviour of the executives at all levels.

Type 3: This is a "purpose" statement (or lower level mission statement). It is appropriate at the strategic business unit, departmental or product group level of the organization.

The following is an example of a meaningless, vapid, motherhood-type mission statement, which most companies seem to have. They achieve nothing and it is difficult to understand why these pointless statements are so popular. Employees mock at them and they rarely say anything likely to give direction to the organization. We have entitled this example "The generic mission statement", and they are to be avoided.

The Generic Mission Statement

Our organization's primary mission is to protect and increase the value of its owners' investments while efficiently and fairly serving the needs of its customers [...insert organization name...] seeks to accomplish this in a manner that contributes to the development and growth of its employees, and to the goals of countries and communities in which it operates.

The following should appear in a mission or purpose statement, which should normally run to no more than one page:

● Role or contribution
● Profit (specify), or
● Service, or
● Opportunity seeker

Business definition – define the business, preferably in terms of the *benefits* you provide or the *needs* you satisfy, rather than in terms of what you make.

Distinctive competences – these are the essential skills/capabilities resources that underpin whatever success has been achieved to date. Competence can consist of one particular item or the possession of a number of skills compared with competitors. If, however, you could equally well put a competitor's name to these distinctive competences, then they are not distinctive competences.

Indications for the future

● What the firm *will* do
● What the firm *might* do
● What the firm will *never* do

Step 2: Setting corporate objectives

It is worth repeating here briefly what we stated in Chapter 1 about corporate objectives.

Corporate objectives usually contain at least the following elements:

> ● The desired level of profitability
> ● Business boundaries
>   – What kind of products will be sold to what kinds of markets (marketing)
>   – What kinds of facilities will be developed (operations, R&D, information systems, distribution, etc.)
>   – The size and character of the labour force (personnel)
>   – Funding (finance)
> ● Other corporate objectives, such as social responsibility, corporate image, stock market image, employer image, etc.

Such a corporate plan, containing projected profit and loss accounts and balance sheets, being the result of the process described above, is more likely to provide long-term stability for a company than plans based on a more intuitive process and containing forecasts which tend to be little more than extrapolations of previous trends. This process is further summarized in Figure 4.3, which reiterates Figure 1.9 in Chapter 1.

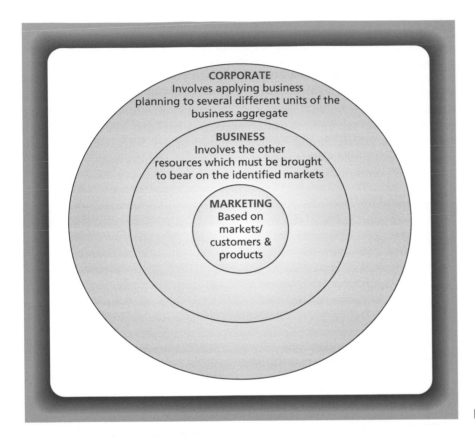

Figure 4.3

Step 3: The marketing audit

Any plan will only be as good as the information on which it is based, and the marketing audit is the means by which information for planning is organized. There is no reason why marketing cannot be audited in the same way as accounts, in spite of its more innovative, subjective nature. A marketing audit is a systematic appraisal of all the external and internal factors that have affected a company's commercial performance over a defined period.

Given the growing turbulence of the business environment and the shorter product life cycles that have resulted, no one would deny the need to stop at least once a year at a particular point in the planning cycle to try to form a reasoned view of how all the many external and internal factors have influenced performance.

Sometimes, of course, a company will conduct a marketing audit because it is in financial trouble. At times like these, management often attempts to treat the wrong symptoms, most frequently by reorganizing the company. But such measures are unlikely to be effective if there are more fundamental problems which have not been identified. Of course, if the company survived for long enough, it might eventually solve its problems through a process of elimination. Essentially, though, the argument is that the problems have first to be properly defined. The audit is a means of helping to define them.

Two kinds of variables

Any company carrying out an audit will be faced with two kinds of variables. There is the kind over which the company has no direct control, for example economic and market factors. Second, there are those over which the company has complete control, the operational variables, which are usually the firm's internal resources. This division suggests that the best way to structure an audit is in two parts, external and internal. Table 4.1 shows areas which should be investigated under both headings. Each should be examined with a view to building up an information base relevant to the company's performance.

Table 4.1 Conducting an audit

External audit	Internal audit
Business and economic environment	Own company
Economic political, fiscal, legal, social, cultural, technological	Sales (total, by geographical location, by industrial type, by customer, by product)
Intra-company	
The market Total market, size, growth, and trends (value volume)	Market shares
	Profit margins, costs
Market	Marketing
characteristics, developments, and trends; products, prices, physical distribution, channels, customers, consumers, communication, industry practices	information research
	Marketing mix
	variables, product management, price, distribution, promotion, *operations and resources*
Competition	
Major competitors	Key strengths and weaknesses
Size	
Market share coverage	
Market standing and reputation	
Production capabilities	
Distribution policies	
Marketing methods	
Extent of diversification	
Personnel issues	
International links	
Profitability	

Many people mistakenly believe that the marketing audit should be some kind of final attempt to define a company's marketing problems, or, at best, something done by an independent body from time to time to ensure that a company is on the right track. However, many highly successful companies, normal information and control procedures and marketing research throughout the year, start their planning cycle each year with a formal, audit-type process, of everything that has had an important influence on marketing activities. Certainly, in many leading consumer goods companies, the annual self-audit approach is a tried and tested discipline.

Objections to line managers doing their own audits usually centre on the problem of time and objectivity. In practice, a disciplined approach and thorough training will help. But the discipline must be applied from the highest to the lowest levels of management, if the tunnel vision that often results from a lack of critical appraisal is to be avoided.

Where relevant, the marketing audit should contain life cycles for major products and market segments, for which the future shape will be predicted using the audit information. Also, major products and markets should be plotted on some kind of matrix to show their current competitive position.

The next question is: What happens to the results of the audit?

Some companies consume valuable resources carrying out audits that produce very little in the way of results. The audit is simply a database, and the task remains of turning it into intelligence, that is, information essential to decision making.

Step 4: Market overview

This step which appears prominently in the actual strategic marketing plan should spell out clearly:

- What the market is;
- How it works;
- What the key decision-making points are;
- What the segments are.

Market definition is fundamental to success and must be made in terms of need sets rather than in product/service terms. Thus, Gestetner failed by defining its markets as "duplicators" and IBM almost failed by defining its market as "mainframes". In financial services, a pension is a product, not a market, as many other products can satisfy the same or similar needs. Table 4.2 lists hypothetical markets in the financial services sector.

Table 4.2 Some market definitions (personal market)	
Market	**Need**
Emergency Cash ('Rainy Day')	Cash to cover an undesired and unexpected event often the loss of/damage to property).
Future Event Planning	Schemes to protect and grow money which are for anticipated and unanticipated cash calling events (eg. Car replacement/repairs, education, weddings, funerals, health care)
	(Continued)

Table 4.2 (Continued)	
Asset Purchase	Cash to buy assets they require (eg. Car purchase, house purchase, once-in-a-lifetime holiday).
Welfare Contingency	The ability to maintain a desired standard of living (for self and/or dependants) in times of unplanned cessation of salary.
Retirement Income	The ability to maintain a desired standard of living (for self and/or dependants once the salary cheques have ceased.
Wealth Care and Building	The care and growth of assets (with various risk levels and liquidity levels).
Day-to-Day Money Management	Ability to store and readily access cash for day-to-day requirements.
Personal Financial Protection and Security from Motor Vehicle Incidents	Currently known as car insurance.

Figures 4.4 and 4.5 show the marketing books market in the UK. Figure 4.4 shows the market "mapped" solely as marketing books. Figure 4.5 shows the market mapped in terms of the broader market definition of knowledge promulgation, from which it can be seen that new competitors and distribution channels come into play. Thinking and planning like this certainly had a dramatic effect on the marketing strategy of the major publisher involved.

Figure 4.6 is a generic market map, which shows how a market works from suppliers to users and, like a balance sheet, it must "balance", in the sense that if five million radiators are made or imported, five million radiators must be distributed, five million radiators must be installed, and the decision about which radiators are to be installed must be made by someone. It is the purpose of the market map to spell all this out quantitatively.

It is at key decision points that market segmentation should take place. A segment is a group of customers or consumers that share the same (or approximately the same) needs. This step is crucial, for it is upon the key segments from the market map that SWOT (Strengths, Weaknesses, Opportunities, and Threats) analyses should be completed.

Market segmentation

Most organizations' different market segments will contain a number of key accounts. Before proceeding to categorize key accounts, analyse their needs and set objectives and strategies for them; it is necessary to ensure that you have the clearest understanding of how their market works, what their key segments are, and where you can exert the most influence on

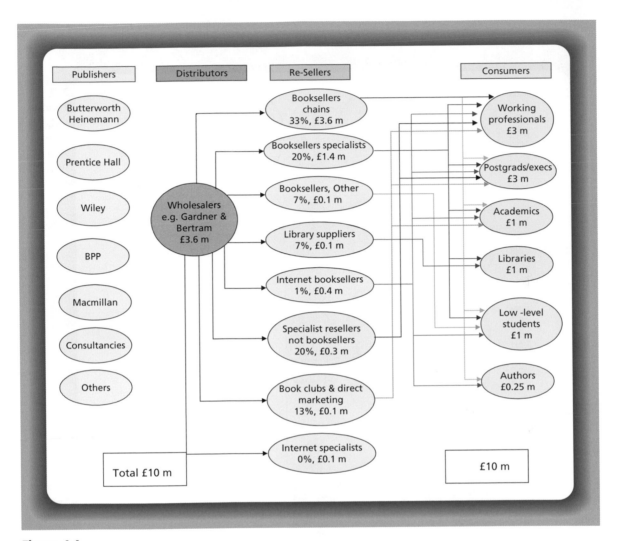

Figure 4.4

decisions about what is bought and from whom. This is essential knowledge, for it will provide the backdrop against which plans for key accounts are evaluated and eventually controlled. Indeed, it would be fair to say that an appreciation of market segmentation is an essential criterion for effective key account management (KAM).

"The good thing about being mediocre is you are always at your best". Someone once said this to us about corporate life. Imagine getting your sales force up at five every morning to go out and kill for "We are really mediocre!" The reason no one has ever heard of Alexander the Mediocre is that he was mediocre and was not Alexander the Great. So what makes any of us think that making mediocre offers to customers is ever going to have anything but mediocre results?

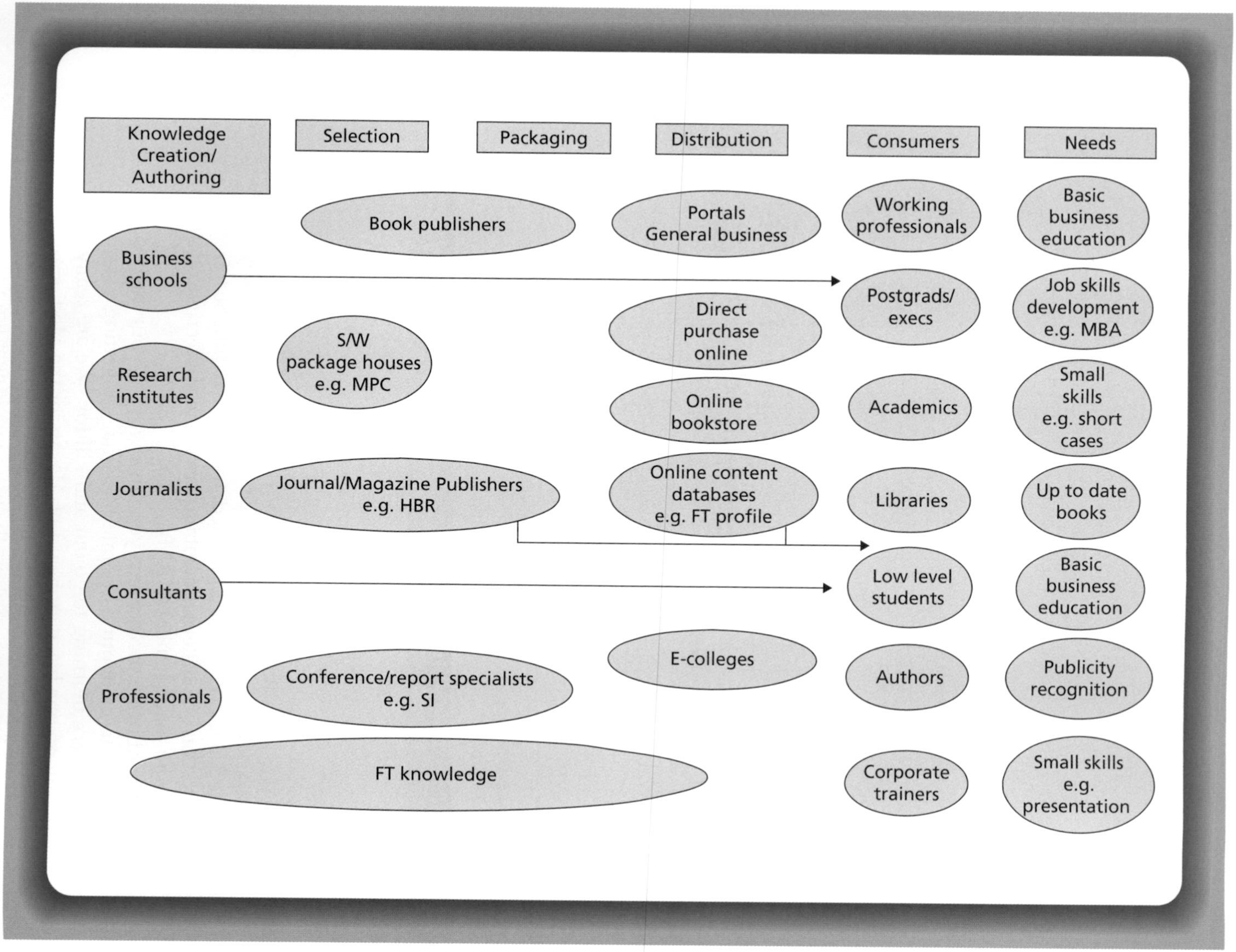

Figure 4.5

The diagram is organized into five columns labeled left to right:

Knowledge Creation/Authoring
- Business schools
- Research institutes
- Journalists
- Consultants
- Professionals
- FT knowledge

Selection
- Book publishers
- S/W package houses e.g. MPC
- Journal/Magazine Publishers e.g. HBR
- Conference/report specialists e.g. SI

Packaging

Distribution
- Portals General business
- Direct purchase online
- Online bookstore
- Online content databases e.g. FT profile
- E-colleges

Consumers
- Working professionals
- Postgrads/execs
- Academics
- Libraries
- Low level students
- Authors
- Corporate trainers

Needs
- Basic business education
- Job skills development e.g. MBA
- Small skills e.g. short cases
- Up to date books
- Basic business education
- Publicity recognition
- Small skills e.g. presentation

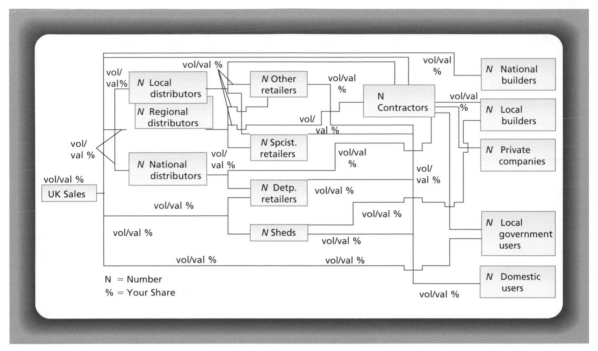

Figure 4.6
Market mapping (including the number of each customer type)

Taking this theme a stage further, we can ask ourselves what sort of company would make a commodity out of bread, fertilizer, glass, chlorine, potatoes, or mobile phones, for example?

By way of an answer, ask whether anyone can "taste" the difference between Castrol GTX and any other manufacturer's oil or between Alfa Laval Steel, SKF Bearings, Intel Microprocessors, and so on. Yet these great companies are dealing with low differentiation products in mainly mature markets.

INSIGHT

So, what is the secret of success?

As we have already stated, a review of the work of a number of gurus, such as Sir Michael Perry, Tom Peters, and Phillip Kotler, reveals a striking similarity between what they consider to be the key elements of world-class marketing:

● a profound understanding of the market
● market segmentation and selection
● powerful differentiation, positioning, and branding
● effective marketing planning processes
● long-term integrated marketing strategies.

While this is not the complete list, it is interesting to note the order of the elements listed here. We find it remarkable because, even in 2007, so many companies are messing about with their brands without really understanding their market and how it is segmented or their competitive position. Indeed, "What shall we do with our brand?" is one of the most recurrent questions and, while it is easy to understand why, branding being the glamorous part of marketing, it is intensely irritating when the questioners know so little about their markets.

INSIGHT   Let us explain what we mean. We frequently run workshops for the boards of strategic business units. Before we start the workshop, we ask the directors to write a list, in order of priority, of their key target markets. Often they write down their products, such as pensions or mainframe computers. Rarely is there any sensible grasp of the meaning of the word "market". So, they fail the first test. The second part of the exercise is to write down their sources of differential advantages against each key target market listed. When these senior people fail such an elementary test, it is clear that their organization is either in or heading towards trouble.

We recently came across one insurance company which prided itself on its market segmentation. On questioning, however, its segments turned out to be *sectors*, which explained why it had little or no differentiation and was competing mainly on price. Indeed, this is one of the most commonly observed misconceptions about market segmentation. Everyone knows that a segment is a group of customers with the same or similar needs and that there are many different purchase combinations within and across sectors, yet companies still persist in confusing sectors with segments.

Perhaps the most frequent mistake, however, is a priori segmentation, which is largely the result of the vast amount of prescriptive literature on the subject of segmentation.

All books state that there are several bases for segmentation, such as demographics, socio-economics, geography, usage, psychographics, geo-demographics, life style, and so on, and the literature is replete with proponents of one or more of these. Not all (as socio-economics criteria) behave the same. Nor do all 18–24-year-old women (demographics) behave the same. Nor do all the people who live in the same street (geo-demographics) behave the same. Yet these are the silly labels attached to so-called segments by about 85% of companies, so no wonder they fail to achieve any kind of differential advantage against their competitors. However, this is to miss the point completely, for in any market there is only one correct segmentation. One hundred percent of goods and services are made, distributed, influenced, and used and the purchase combinations which result are a fact, not a figment of someone's imagination. The task is to understand the market structure, how it works, and what the actual segments are at different junctions in the market.

At each of these key junctions, segmentation is not only possible, but necessary.

It is here that the process becomes quite complicated, for the trick is to make an exhaustive list of all the different purchase combinations which take place at each junction. This entails listing what is bought (to include applications, features, where, when, and how products or services are bought), together with the associated descriptors (who buys what). This will often produce somewhere between 30 and 80 different purchase combinations or what we term *micro-segments*. However, the reality is that these micro-segments do indeed represent what actually happens in the market.

The next step, which is to specify the benefits that each of these micro-segments seek by buying what they buy in the way they do, is crucial. It is often here that external market research is necessary.

It is now simply a question of using one of the many software packages available to cluster micro-segments with similar requirements. Clusters are given a dimension of size by adding the volumes or values represented by each micro-segment. It is our experience that most markets can be broken down into 10 or less segments. The only remaining task is to ensure that our offers meet the requirements of each segment and that we, as suppliers, are organized to sell, deliver, and support the appropriate value propositions.

One thing is abundantly clear from our detailed segmentation work: price is rarely the prime motivator in the way people buy. The following case history will illustrate the point.

Mini Case

Case 1 – How ICI used market segmentation to its advantage

ICI Fertilizers went through a severe loss-making period during the late 1980s as the market matured and foreign competitors entered the market with cheap imports. Prices and margins fell to disastrous levels. However, the company had the perspicacity to go through the segmentation process described here and discovered seven relatively distinct segments of farmers, only one of which was price sensitive. This segment represented only 10% of the market, not 100%, as had been previously thought. One segment was highly technological in its approach, while another was more influenced by the appearance of crops. Yet another was loyal to merchants. Yet another was loyal to brands. Each segment was given a name and its needs were researched in depth. Products were developed and offers were made to match the precise needs of the individual segments, while the company and its processes were reorganized in order to ensure that the appropriate value could be delivered. ICI Fertilizers became an extremely profitable company in an industry whose own governing body had officially designated fertilizer as a commodity!

Hopefully, this heartening story of creative segmentation leading to sustained profitability in a mature and generally unprofitable industry will encourage key account managers to think carefully about segmentation for their own key accounts as a way of helping them understand ways in which they may be able to create value for them. The market segmentation process described here is summarized in Figure 4.7.

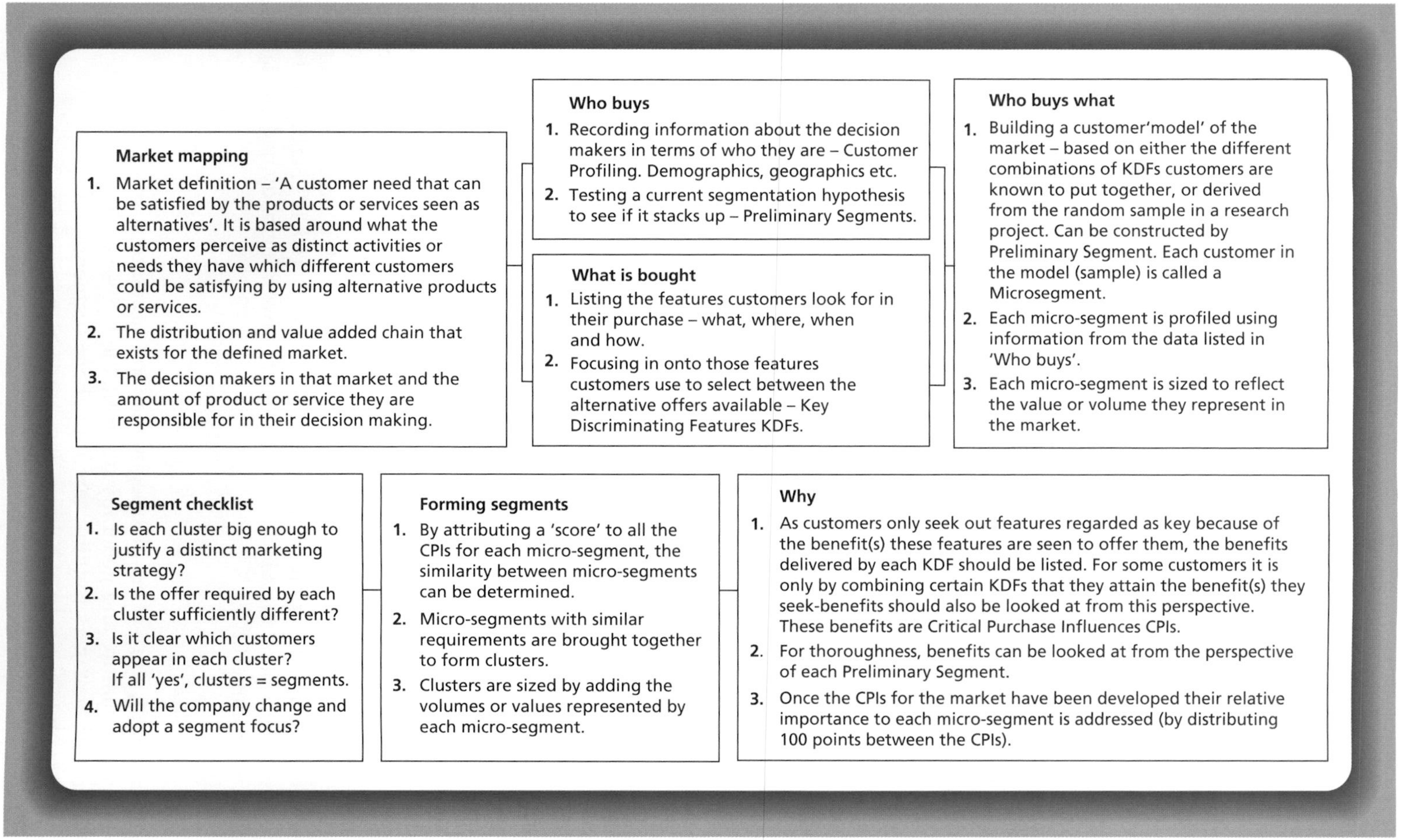

Market mapping

1. Market definition – 'A customer need that can be satisfied by the products or services seen as alternatives'. It is based around what the customers perceive as distinct activities or needs they have which different customers could be satisfying by using alternative products or services.
2. The distribution and value added chain that exists for the defined market.
3. The decision makers in that market and the amount of product or service they are responsible for in their decision making.

Who buys

1. Recording information about the decision makers in terms of who they are – Customer Profiling. Demographics, geographics etc.
2. Testing a current segmentation hypothesis to see if it stacks up – Preliminary Segments.

What is bought

1. Listing the features customers look for in their purchase – what, where, when and how.
2. Focusing in onto those features customers use to select between the alternative offers available – Key Discriminating Features KDFs.

Who buys what

1. Building a customer'model' of the market – based on either the different combinations of KDFs customers are known to put together, or derived from the random sample in a research project. Can be constructed by Preliminary Segment. Each customer in the model (sample) is called a Microsegment.
2. Each micro-segment is profiled using information from the data listed in 'Who buys'.
3. Each micro-segment is sized to reflect the value or volume they represent in the market.

Segment checklist

1. Is each cluster big enough to justify a distinct marketing strategy?
2. Is the offer required by each cluster sufficiently different?
3. Is it clear which customers appear in each cluster? If all 'yes', clusters = segments.
4. Will the company change and adopt a segment focus?

Forming segments

1. By attributing a 'score' to all the CPIs for each micro-segment, the similarity between micro-segments can be determined.
2. Micro-segments with similar requirements are brought together to form clusters.
3. Clusters are sized by adding the volumes or values represented by each micro-segment.

Why

1. As customers only seek out features regarded as key because of the benefit(s) these features are seen to offer them, the benefits delivered by each KDF should be listed. For some customers it is only by combining certain KDFs that they attain the benefit(s) they seek-benefits should also be looked at from this perspective. These benefits are Critical Purchase Influences CPIs.
2. For thoroughness, benefits can be looked at from the perspective of each Preliminary Segment.
3. Once the CPIs for the market have been developed their relative importance to each micro-segment is addressed (by distributing 100 points between the CPIs).

Figure 4.7
Market Segmentation process – Summary.

Why market segmentation is vital in key account planning

In today's highly competitive world, few companies can afford to compete only on price for the product has not yet been sold that someone, somewhere, cannot sell cheaper – apart from which, in many markets it is rarely the cheapest product which succeeds anyway. What this means is that we have to find some way of differentiating ourselves from the competition and the answer lies in market segmentation.

The truth is that very few companies can afford to be "all things to all people". The main aim of market segmentation as part of the marketing planning process is to enable a business concern to target its effort at the most promising opportunities. However, what is an opportunity for firm A is not necessarily an opportunity for firm B. So a firm needs to develop a typology of the customer or segment it prefers, for this can be an instrument of great productivity in the marketplace.

The whole point of market segmentation is that a firm must either:

- define its markets broadly enough to ensure that its costs for key activities are competitive or
- define its markets in such a way that it can develop specialized skills in serving them to overcome a relative cost disadvantage.

Both strategies have to be related to a firm's distinctive competence and to that of its competitors.

Correct market definition is crucial for the following:

- Share measurement
- Growth measurement
- The specification of target customers
- The recognition of relevant competitors
- The formulation of marketing objectives and strategies

To summarize, the objectives of market segmentation are as follows:

- To help determine marketing direction through the analysis and understanding of trends and buyer behaviour.
- To help determine realistic and obtainable marketing and sales objectives.
- To help improve decision making by forcing managers to consider the available options in depth.

A clear and comprehensive understanding of their market, how it works, how it breaks down into natural segments, and the specific nature of the unique value sought by each of these segments will obviously give key account managers a significant advantage in building long-term relationships with their customers.

Step 5: SWOT analyses

The only remaining question is: What happens to the results of the audit? Some companies consume valuable resources carrying out audits that bring very little by way of actionable results.

Indeed, there is always the danger that, at the audit stage, insufficient attention is paid to the need to concentrate on analysis that determines which trends and developments will actually affect the company. Whilst the checklist demonstrates the completeness of logic and analysis, the people carrying out the audit should discipline themselves to omit from their audits all the information that is not central to the company's marketing problems. Thus, inclusion of research reports or over-detailed sales performance histories by product which lead to no logical actions whatever only serve to rob the audit of focus and reduce its relevance.

Since the objective of the audit is to indicate what a company's marketing objectives and strategies should be, it follows that it would be helpful if some format could be found for organizing the major findings. One useful way of doing this is in the form of a number of SWOT analyses. A SWOT is a summary of the audit under the headings, internal strengths, and weaknesses as they relate to external opportunities and threats.

A SWOT should be conducted for each segment that is considered to be important in the company's future. These SWOT analyses should, if possible, contain just a few paragraphs of commentary focusing on *key* factors only. They should highlight internal *differential* strengths and weaknesses vis-á-vis competitors and *key* external opportunities and threats. A summary of reasons for good or bad performance should be included. They should be interesting to read, contain concise statements, include only relevant and important data, and give greater emphasis to creative analysis.

To summarize, carrying out a regular and thorough marketing audit in a structured manner will go a long way towards giving a company knowledge of the business, trends in the market, and where value is added by competitors, as the basis for setting objectives and strategies.

Later in this chapter, a more detailed method for carrying out a SWOT is explained.

Step 6: Assumptions

There are certain key determinants of success in all companies about which assumptions have to be made before the planning process can proceed.

Let us now return to the preparation of the marketing plan. If we refer again to the marketing planning process, and have completed our marketing audit and SWOT analyses, assumptions have to be written now. There are certain key determinants of success in all companies about which assumptions have to be made before the planning process can proceed.

This is really a question of standardizing the planning environment. For example, it would be no good receiving plans from two product managers, one of whom believed the market was going to increase by 10%, while the other believed the market was going to decline by 10%.

Examples of assumptions might be given as follows.

With respect to the company's industrial climate, it is assumed that:

1 Industrial overcapacity will increase from 105% to 115% as new industrial plants come into operation.
2 Price competition will force price levels down by 10% across the board.
3 A new product in the field of x will be introduced by our major competitor before the end of the second quarter.

Assumptions should be few in number, and if a plan is possible irrespective of the assumptions made, then the assumptions are unnecessary.

Step 7: Marketing objectives and strategies

The next step in marketing planning is the writing of marketing objectives and strategies, the key to the whole process.

An *objective* is what you want to achieve. A *strategy* is how you plan to achieve your objectives.

Thus, there can be objectives and strategies at all levels in marketing. For example, there can be advertising objectives and strategies and pricing objectives and strategies.

However, the important point to remember about marketing objectives is that they are about *products* and *markets* only. Common sense will confirm that it is only by selling something to someone that the company's financial goals can be achieved, and that advertising, pricing, service levels, and so on are the means (or strategies) by which we might succeed in doing this. Thus, pricing objectives, sales promotion objectives, advertising objectives, and the like should not be confused with marketing objectives.

Marketing objectives are simply about one, or more, of the following:

● Existing products for existing markets
● New products for existing markets
● Existing products for new markets
● New products for new markets

They should be capable of measurement, otherwise they are not objectives. Directional terms such as "maximize", "minimize", "penetrate", "increase", etc. are only acceptable if quantitative measurement can be attached to them. Measurement should be in terms of some, or all, of the following: sales volume, sales value, market share, profit, and percentage penetration of outlets (e.g. to have 30% of all retail outlets stocking our product by year 3).

Marketing strategies are the means by which marketing objectives will be achieved and generally are concerned with the four Ps, as follows:

Product	The general policies for product deletions, modifications, additions, design, branding, positioning, packaging, etc.
Price	The general pricing policies to be followed by product groups in market segments.
Place	The general policies for channels and customer service levels.
Promotion	The general policies for communicating with customers under the relevant headings, such as advertising, sales force, sales promotion, public relations, exhibitions, direct mail, etc.

Step 8: Estimate expected results and identify alternative plans and mixes

Having completed this major planning task, it is normal at this stage to employ judgement, analogous experience, field tests, and so on, to test out the feasibility of the objectives and strategies in terms of market share, costs, profits, and so on. It is also normally at this stage that alternative plans and mixes are considered, if necessary.

Step 9: The Budget

In a strategic marketing plan, these strategies would normally be costed out approximately and, if not practicable, alternative strategies would be proposed and costed out until a satisfactory solution could be reached. This would then become the budget. In most cases, there would be a budget for the full 3 years of the strategic marketing plan, but there would also be a very detailed budget for the first year of the plan which would be included in the 1-year operational plan.

It will be obvious from all of this that not only the setting of budgets becomes much easier, but the resulting budgets are more likely to be realistic and related to what the *whole* company wants to achieve, rather than just one functional department.

The problem of designing a dynamic system for budget setting, rather than the "tablets of stone" approach, which is more common, is a major challenge to the marketing and financial directors of all companies.

The most satisfactory approach would be for a marketing director to justify all marketing expenditure from a zero base each year against the tasks he/she wishes to accomplish. A little thought will confirm that this is exactly the approach recommended in this chapter. If these procedures are followed, a hierarchy of objectives is built up in such a way that every item of budgeted expenditure can be related directly back to the initial corporate financial objectives. For example, if sales promotion is a major means of achieving an objective in a particular market, when sales promotional items appear in the programme, each one has a specific purpose which can be related back to a major objective.

Doing it this way not only ensures that every item of expenditure is fully accounted for as part of a rational, objective, and task approach, but also that when changes have to be made during the period to which the plan relates, these changes can be made in such a way that the least damage is caused to the company's long-term objectives.

> The incremental marketing expense can be considered to be all costs that are incurred after the product leaves the factory, *other than* costs involved in physical distribution, the costs of which usually represent a discrete subset.

There is, of course, no textbook answer to problems relating to questions such as whether packaging should be a marketing or a production expense, and whether some distribution costs could be considered to be marketing costs. For example, insistence on high service levels results in high inventory carrying costs. Only common sense will reveal workable solutions to issues such as these.

Under *price,* however, any form of discounting that reduces the expected gross income, such as promotional discounts, quantity discounts, royalty rebates, and so on, as well as sales commission and unpaid invoices, should be given the most careful attention as incremental marketing expenses.

Most obvious incremental marketing expenses will occur, however, under the heading promotion, in the form of advertising, sales salaries and expenses, sales promotional expenditure, direct mail costs, and so on. The important point about the measurable effects of marketing activity is that anticipated levels should be the result of the most careful analysis of what is required to take the company towards its goals, while the most careful attention should be paid to gathering all items of expenditure under appropriate headings. The healthiest way of treating these issues is a zero-based budgeting approach.

Step 10: First year detailed implementation programme

In a 1-year tactical plan, the general marketing strategies would be developed into specific sub-objectives, each supported by more detailed strategy and action statements.

A company organized according to functions might have an advertising plan, a sales promotion plan, a pricing plan, and so on.

A product-based company might have a product plan, with objectives, strategies, and tactics for price, place, and promotion as necessary.

A market or geographically based company might have a market plan, with objectives, strategies, and tactics for the 4Ps as necessary.

Likewise, a company with a few major customers might have customer plans.

Any combination of the above might be suitable, depending on circumstances.

> A written strategic marketing plan is the backdrop against which operational decisions are taken. Consequently, too much detail should be avoided. Its major function is to determine where the company is, where it wants to go, and how it can get there. It should be distributed on a "need to know" basis only. It should be used as an aid to effective management. It cannot be a substitute for it.

■ What should appear in a strategic marketing plan?

A written marketing plan is the backdrop against which operational decisions are taken.

Consequently, too much detail should be avoided. Its major function is to determine where the company is, where it wants to go, and how it can get there. It lies at the heart of a company's revenue-generating activities, such as the timing of the cash flow and the size and character of the labour force. What should actually appear in a written strategic marketing plan is shown in Table 4.3. This strategic marketing plan should be distributed only to those who need it, but it can only be an aid to effective management. It cannot be a substitute for it.

It will be obvious from Table 4.3 that not only does budget setting become much easier and more realistic, but the resulting budgets are more likely to reflect what the whole company wants to achieve, rather than just one department.

The problem of designing a dynamic system for setting budgets is a major challenge to the marketing and financial directors of all companies. The most satisfactory approach would be for a marketing director to justify all marketing expenditure from a zero base each year against the tasks to be accomplished. If these procedures are followed, a hierarchy of objectives is built in such a way that every item of budgeted expenditure can be related directly back to the initial financial objectives.

For example, if sales promotion is a major means of achieving an objective, when a sales promotion item appears in the programme, it has a specific purpose which can be related back to a major objective. Thus, every item of expenditure is fully accounted for.

Marketing expense can be considered to be all costs that are incurred after the product leaves the "factory", apart from those involved in physical distribution. When it comes to pricing, any form of discounting that reduces the expected gross income – such as promotional or quantity discounts, overrides, sales commission, and unpaid invoices – should be

Table 4.3 What should appear in a strategic marketing plan

1   Start with a mission statement.
2   Next, include a financial summary which illustrates graphically revenue and profit for the full planning period.
3   Now do a market overview: Has the market declined or grown? How does it break down into segments? What is your share of each? Keep it simple. If you don't have the facts, make estimates. Use life cycles, bar charts, and pie charts to make it all crystal clear.
4   Now identify the key segments and do a SWOT analysis for each one: Outline the major external influences and their impact on each segment. List the key factors for success. These should be less than five. Give an assessment of the company's differential strengths and weaknesses compared with those of it competitors. Score yourself and your competitors out of 10 and then multiply each score by a weighting factor for each critical success factor (e.g. CSF 1 = 60, CSF 2 = 25, CSF 3 = 10, CSF 4 = 5).
5   Make a brief statement about the key issues that have to be addressed in the planning period.
6   Summarize the SWOTs using a portfolio matrix in order to illustrate the important relationships between your key products and markets.
7   List your assumptions.
8   Set objectives and strategies.
9   Summarize your resource requirements for the planning period in the form of a budget.

given the most careful attention as marketing expenses. Most obvious marketing expenses will occur, however, under the heading of promotion, in the form of advertising, sales salaries and expenses, sales promotion, and direct mail costs.

The important point about the measurable effects of marketing activity is that anticipated levels should result from careful analysis of what is required to take the company towards its goals, while the most careful attention should be paid to gathering all items of expenditure under appropriate headings. The healthiest way of treating these issues is through zero-based budgeting.

We have just described the strategic marketing plan and what it should contain. The tactical marketing plan layout and content should be similar, but the detail is much greater, as it is for 1 year only.

PART 2

The following marketing plan assessment methodology was developed over a 5-year period of research by Dr. Brian Smith at Cranfield University School of Management. It is, therefore, robust and we commend it to you in attempting to assess the quality of the marketing strategies of your key account.

Strategic Marketing Planning Quality Test

by
Dr. Brian Smith
Cranfield School of Management

Effective Marketing Strategies Contain

A definition of one or more target market *segments*

A definition of the value proposition for each segment

And have properties of

- Guiding tactical activity for the operational plan
- Meeting customer needs
- Leveraging strengths
- Minimising weaknesses
- Enabling synergy
- Allowing for competitors' strategy
- Allowing for macro-environmental trend implications
- Meeting our business objectives
- Being achievable with the resources allocated
- Differing sufficiently from competitors

Strategy Quality - Score Sheet

	Marketing Strategy	Notes
1. Segments		
2. Actions		
3. Competitive Advantage		
4. Synergy		
5. Competitors		
6. Customer Needs		
7. Competitors' Strategies		
8. External Changes		
9. Weaknesses		
10. Strengths		
11. Meet Objectives		
12. Resources		
Total		

Strategy test 1

- Our marketing strategy makes it clear what markets or parts of the market we will concentrate our efforts on
  - If your strategy attacks all of your market sector (e.g retail groceries, super-conducting magnets) equally = 0
  - If your strategy is focused by "descriptor group" (e.g. ABC1s, Large firms, SMEs etc.) = 1
  - If your strategy attacks needs-based segments (e.g. efficacy focused customers with high ego needs) = 2
  - If you don't know = -1

Strategy test 2

- Our marketing strategy makes clear what tactical actions fit with the marketing strategy and which do not
  - If your strategy allows complete freedom of action = 0
  - If your strategy allows a high degree of freedom of action = 1
  - If your strategy makes most of your action plan decisions for you = 2
  - If you don't know = -1

Strategy test 3

- Our marketing strategy clearly defines our intended competitive advantage in the target market segments
    - If there is no strong and supported reason why the customer should choose you = 0
    - If there is a reason the customer should buy from you but no strong proof = 1
    - If you can state clearly the reason the customer should buy from you and not the competitor and substantiate that reason = 2
    - If you don't know = -1

Strategy test 4

- Our marketing strategy allows synergy between the activities of the different parts of the organisation
    - If the strategy is a compromise of what each department is capable of = 0
    - If the strategy uses the strengths of only one or two departments = 1
    - If the strategy uses the best strengths of all departments = 2
    - If you don't know = -1

Strategy test 5

- Our marketing strategy is significantly different from that of our competitors in our key market segments
    - If we attack the same customers with the same value proposition = 0
    - If we attack the same customers OR use the same value proposition =1
    - If we attack different customers with a different value proposition = 2
    - If you don't know = -1

Strategy test 6

- Our marketing strategy recognises and makes full allowance for the needs and wants of our target customers
    - If you only meet the basic functional needs (e.g. safety, regulation, efficacy) =0
    - If you also meet the higher functional needs (e.g. efficiency, service, price) = 1
    - If you also meet the emotional and ego needs (e.g. brand, confidence) = 2
    - If you don't know = -1

Strategy test 7

- Our marketing strategy recognises and makes full allowance for the strategies of our competitors
    - If you are ignoring the competitors' strategy = 0
    - If you are allowing for some of the competitors' strategy = 1
    - If you are allowing for all of the competitors' strategy = 2
    - If you don't know = -1

Strategy test 8

- Our marketing strategy recognises and makes full allowance for changes in the business environment that are beyond our control, such as technological, legislation or social change
    - If your strategy is designed for today's conditions = 0 your strategy allows for one or two changes (e.g technology or demographics) = 1
    - If your strategy considers the combined effects of all the external factors = 2
    - If you don't know = -1

Strategy test 9

- Our marketing strategy either avoids or compensates for those areas where we are relatively weak compared to the competition
  - If you have taken little or no account of your relative weaknesses = 0
  - If you are trying to fix your relative weaknesses = 1
  - If your strategy means that your relative weaknesses don't matter = 2
  - If you don't know = -1

Strategy test 10

- Our marketing strategy makes full use of those areas where we are relatively strong compared to the competition
  - If you have taken little or no account of your relative strengths = 0
  - If you are trying to use your relative strengths = 1
  - If your strategy means that your relative strengths become more important = 2
  - If you don't know = -1

Strategy test 11

- Our marketing strategy, if successfully implemented, will meet all the objectives of the organisation
  - If your strategy, fully & successfully implemented, does not deliver your financial or non-financial objectives = 0
  - If your strategy, fully & successfully implemented, delivers only your financial objectives = 1
  - If your strategy, fully & successfully implemented, delivers your financial & non-financial objectives = 2
  - If you don't know = -1

Strategy test 12

- The resources available to the organisation are sufficient to implement the marketing strategy successfully
  - If you have neither the tangible nor the intangible resources to implement the strategy = 0
  - If you have only the tangible or the intangible resources, but not both = 1
  - If you have both the tangible and the intangible resources needed to implement the strategy = 2
  - If you don't know = -1

How did you score?

- 18-24 - Well done! (are you sure?)
  - Can I buy some shares?
- 12-17 - You will succeed
  - If your competition is weak!
- 6-11 - You will survive
  - If your competition is weak!
- Less than 6
  - Oh dear, it was nice knowing you

The assessment method is given in the form of a questionnaire, but the important thing to remember is that, even if the key account's strategic plan gets a low score (i.e. it is not very effective), this presents you with an opportunity for helping your customer.

Tables 4.4, 4.5, and 4.6 summarize Smith's doctoral research and make interpretation of the quantitative assessment easier to understand.

Table 4.4 Market share risk profile

●	Target market definition	The marketing strategy has a higher probability of success if the target is defined in terms of homogeneous segments and is characterized by utilizable data
●	Proposition specification	If the proposition delivered to each segment is different from that delivered to other segments and addresses the needs which characterized the target segment
●	SWOT alignment	If the strengths and weaknesses of the organization are independently assessed and the choice of target and proposition leverages strengths and minimizes weaknesses
●	Strategy uniqueness	If choice of target and proposition is different from that of major competitors
●	Anticipation of market change	If changes in the external microenvironment and macroenvironment are identified and their implications allowed for

Table 4.5 What do most marketing strategies look like?

1	Do they define true segments? or descriptor groups	1	No, only products, channels,
2	Does it have segment-specific propositions?	2	No, it is a single offer tweaked by sales
3	Is it SWOT aligned?	3	No, it simply lists factors
4	Does it anticipate the future?	4	No, they don't see the combined implications of market changes
5	Is it unique?	5	No, it's often the same thing to the same people in the same way for about the same price

Table 4.6 The risks of weak strategies

1	If you don't define true segments	1	Resources are wasted on customers that can't be won
2	If you don't have segment-specific propositions	2	The proposition is not differentiated and becomes commoditized
3	If it isn't SWOT aligned	3	The company fails to use all its competencies and neglects weaknesses
4	If it fails to anticipate the future	4	The proposition and target reflect yesterday's market
5	If it is not unique	5	The company goes head on with its competitors and the biggest wins

CHAPTER 5

Assessing forecast revenues and the future profitability of key accounts

Following the detailed review in Chapter 3 of how to analyse key accounts, the purpose of this chapter is to build on the analysis by focusing on the real potential of key accounts for enhancing the supplier's profitability.

In this chapter, we challenge the usual notions of profit. First, we will look at historic profit, which is the usual measure key account managers use to value their key accounts. We will show how historic profit can be calculated and its (limited) practical applications in the management of key accounts. Then, we will introduce the concept of customer lifetime value, the future value of a key account. We will demonstrate how this can be calculated and discuss some of the difficulties. One of the issues with the estimation of customer lifetime value is the time value of money, and this problem will be explained.

However, not all of the value of a key account relationship comes from the obvious and measurable financial aspects of the relationship. There is value in a key account management (KAM) relationship that arises from the relationship itself, rather than through transactions. This chapter includes a short discussion of the relationship value of key accounts and explores how key account managers can capture that relationship value.

Finally, we add a useful discussion on the link between KAM and shareholder value, looking at how both sides benefit from a KAM relationship and how those benefits can be managed.

■ Fast track

- Measuring product profitability, rather than customer profitability, can focus the company on short-term product sales rather than on long-term value creation through key account relationships.
- Customer profitability is measured as the revenues less product costs and costs to serve that the company received from the customer in the previous year.
- Customer profitability analysis is a useful tool for establishing how dependent the company is on a few key customers, and for understanding how long it might take for new customers to become profitable. However, it measures a single period in the past, which might be misleading as a guide to the future.
- Customer lifetime value measures the stream of future profits or cash flow from a customer over the remaining lifetime of the relationship. It is a valuable tool for the development of key account objectives and strategies.
- To calculate customer lifetime value, key account managers must understand the concept of the time value of money.
- Value is also gained from customers in other ways, such as referrals, references, innovation, and learning. The KAM plan should consider how these other sources of value will be obtained.

■ Introduction

Marketing's role in creating shareholder value is under closer scrutiny than ever before. More and more organizations are asking questions about the payback on their marketing activities. It is no longer enough just to have memorable advertizing or close customer relationships. Increasingly, marketing managers have to consider the financial justification for their marketing or customer plans, and have to defend these plans to their senior managers. In turn, those senior managers are tasked to deliver profits or shareholder value.

For some years now, there has been an extensive debate amongst marketers about the returns to marketing and whether marketing creates or destroys value. The beginnings of this debate can be traced back to a comment attributed (in the UK) to Lord Leverhulme and (in the US) to John Wanamaker:

> Half the money I spend on advertizing is wasted.
>   The trouble is, I don't know which half.

Whoever first said it, this quote is a powerful illustration of the problem: How can a company be sure that its marketing creates a positive return on investment?

Until recently, most companies have taken a product profitability approach to measuring performance. In the product profitability approach, individual products or product lines are examined and the profitability of each is calculated separately. The direct costs of production are attributed to the relevant product, and indirect costs such as marketing and sales costs are allocated according to some proportional method. The product profitability approach has the great advantage of relative simplicity. Many companies are in fact organized along product lines, with separate production lines, marketing teams, or even business units.

> Focusing on product profitability can jeopardize efforts to build long-term relationships with customers.

The danger with a product profitability focus is that companies become overly focused on product development and product sales, rather than on building long-term relationships with customers. The profit made on individual product sales becomes more important than the bigger picture. It might, for example, be better for the company to sell one product or service at a loss in order to make follow-on sales of many other products or services provided by other business units. The first business unit, however, might well refuse to make the initial, unprofitable sale.

More generally, companies that are overly focused on product profitability find it difficult to think about the overall relationship with a customer. This can be annoying for the customer, inefficient for the supplier, and possibly even damage the overall relationship. Think, for example, about the bank that lends you several hundred thousand pounds to buy a new house and then goes on sending current account statements to your old address. In this case, nobody "owns" the relationship with the customer. The customer is made to feel that they are of little importance to the supplier and that the supplier's only interest is in selling more and more products.

Why measuring the value of customers is important

In recent years, there has been a shift in emphasis in marketing in general and in the measurement of value in particular. Rather than focusing on the profitability of particular products, companies are becoming increasingly interested in the profitability of customers.

There are a number of reasons for this change in emphasis from products to relationships. In mature markets, with slower growth and higher levels of supply relative to demand, the right strategy for business success is not customer acquisition but customer retention. It costs at least five times as much time, effort, and money to acquire a new customer as to keep an existing customer. As a result, the service element in most transactions has increased dramatically. Customer expectations about service have increased. Business-to-business, suppliers have responded to these customer demands by "solution selling", offering service, support, training, and assistance as part of the sales package.

As more research into profitability has been carried out, and as the business model has shifted towards service solutions, it has become clear that post-production costs are increasingly influential in determining profitability. In other words, many businesses find that it is not the cost of making something that is the most important cost for them, but the cost of the sales, marketing, and customer service support. It has also become clear that these costs vary, sometimes considerably, by customer. As companies develop KAM, this trend is increasing. KAM itself is an expensive service element; it is vital that companies think carefully about which customers they offer KAM to, and what level of service they deliver to which key account. To make these kinds of decisions, companies need to think about customer profitability and customer lifetime value, not just product profitability.

> Profitability is heavily influenced by post-production costs, namely, the cost of sales, marketing, and customer service support.

The message for business is that it is not just the transaction that is important; it also matters to *which customer* the sale is.

Customer profitability analysis

As companies start to consider the value of their customer relationships, they usually begin with ▶ **customer profitability** analysis. Customer profitability analysis is the calculation of the historic profit (or, more often, the contribution before overheads) of a customer during a preceding period, usually a year.

> ▶ **DEFINITION** ◀
>
> Customer profitability is a "snapshot" of the profit or contribution from a customer during a previous period.

The calculation usually takes the form of customer revenue less product costs and costs to serve. Customer-specific overheads may also be taken into account. For true customer profitability, overheads may be allocated, but most marketers are interested primarily in relative customer profitability so, for reasons of simplicity, the calculation often omits overheads. Thus, customer profitability analysis should strictly be referred to as customer contribution analysis.

Four pieces of information are needed to calculate key account profitability:

- Revenues from that customer during the period.
- Costs of the products purchased by the customer.
- Costs to serve the customer.
- Customer-specific overheads (if applicable).

Calculating customer revenues

The basic calculation of customer revenues is the number of each type of product that the customer bought during that period, multiplied by the product price (Table 5.1).

Table 5.1 Basic customer revenue calculation

Product	Quantity purchased in period (A)	Price (B) (€)	Revenues (A × B) (€)
Product A	1	100	100
Product B	3	50	150
Product C	10	20	200
Product D	10	5	50
Product...			
		Total customer revenues:	500

Although the basic customer revenue calculation looks straightforward, there are some points that need to be borne in mind.

Most of the information to complete Table 5.1 can be obtained from the invoices raised to the customer over the year. However, column A (product quantities) could be misleading if some of the products were subsequently returned. This information can be obtained from credit notes.

A trickier problem concerns the data in column B (price). It is the realized price that matters, and this may be very different from the list price or from the invoice price (Table 5.2).

Table 5.2　Calculating realized price	
List price	€100
Discounts	(5)
Invoice price	€95
Rebates	(1)
Payment terms	(1)
Credit/claims	(3)
Delivery/freight costs	(5)
Realized price	€85

As Table 5.2 shows, even the invoice price may not reflect the actual amount received. Sometimes the customer will receive rebates for volume. There may also be payment terms which give customers additional discounts if they pay early.[1] Product problems or returns might lead to credit notes and/or claims. Finally, customers may negotiate price deals if they collect products, or if they alter delivery arrangements; and delivery costs will differ between key accounts who want a single delivery to a central depot, and those who want multiple deliveries to multiple sites. All of these factors should be taken into account before establishing the realized price that will be used to calculate customer revenues.

When calculating key account revenues, key account managers should be especially careful if they are collating invoice data from several countries or business units. The information included and not included on customer invoices can vary between different business units, even within the same company. This is illustrated by the case of the packaging manufacturer.

> Realized price (the price the company actually receives) should be used wherever possible to calculate customer revenues. Invoice prices can be deceptive.

Using customer invoice data with care: the case of the packaging manufacturer

PackCo* is a manufacturer of paper packaging materials. It has identified a number of key accounts which are big global companies with operations ranging from the US

* This example is based on a real company, although some details have been changed or removed for reasons of commercial confidentiality.

---

[1] Early payment discounts may be considered as a finance expense by the accountants. However, they should be treated as a price reduction for customer profitability analysis purposes.

through Europe and Latin America. The key account managers at PackCo draw customer revenue information from invoice data in each of these three main regions. However, it has recently become clear that there are important differences between the information included on the invoices. The KAM team asked the Finance Director to summarize the differences in invoicing. His summary is shown below:

US	Europe	Latin America
PackCo list price	PackCo list price	PackCo list price
Customer-negotiated price	*Customer-negotiated price*	Agent-negotiated discount
	Product mix discount	*Customer-negotiated price*
Agent-negotiated discount	*Invoice price*	Special offer on one product
Agent fee	Free goods supplied	Other discounts
Logistics discount	Loyalty discount	Campaign discount
Repalletizing fee	Special offer discount	Clearance discount
Lead time discount	Delivery credit	Quantity discount
Loyalty discount	Loyalty discount	*Invoice price*
Trade advertized discount	Campaign discount	Customer-specific discount
Environmental charge	Other discounts	Product mix discount
Invoice price	*Realized price*	Loyalty discount
Other discounts		Co-load discount
Realized price		*Realized price*

The Finance Director's summary shows how complex this company's relationship is with its global key accounts. Not only are there multiple discounting structures, there are also different campaigns and special offers to be taken into account and, in Latin America, there is a relationship with the distributor as well as the customer. In this example, the invoice price in the US is fairly close to the realized price; however, the invoice price in Europe and Latin America may give a very misleading picture of key account revenues.

Calculating direct product or service costs

Service costs are one of the largest and also fastest-growing areas of cost for most companies.

The direct costs of a product or service are the costs that are directly linked to the manufacture of that product or delivery of that service. If the product was not manufactured or the service was not delivered, the direct costs would not be incurred. Where the manufacture of physical products is concerned, direct product costs are usually taken to be the direct costs of production divided by the number of items produced. Usually, property costs (the cost of offices and factories, etc.) are not regarded as part of direct costs, although raw materials and labour costs would be considered to be direct costs of production. For service businesses, direct costs will largely comprise people costs.

There is no clear line between direct and indirect costs, and the treatment of some types of cost varies between companies. For example, when considering the direct costs associated with a key account, it is important to consider the treatment of items such as logistics and order processing.

Some companies treat logistics costs as part of direct product costs; others treat logistics as indirect costs. Similarly, in some companies the order processing is considered as a production or operations function and the associated costs are subsumed into direct product costs; other companies would consider order processing to be part of administration or customer service, and treat the costs as indirect costs. Key account managers are advised to discuss the composition of direct cost numbers with their finance department or operations managers.

Table 5.3 lists some of the cost areas that might be included in the calculation of product costs.

Table 5.3 Elements of direct costs	
Manufacturers	**Service businesses**
Order processing	Order processing
Raw materials	People/time costs (including the
Processing costs	costs of subcontractors)
Technical service/consultancy	Technical service/consultancy
Special grades/sizes	
Special finishing	
Packaging	
Customer-specific equipment costs	
Logistics	

Calculating indirect costs

Indirect costs are the "service surround" costs that a supplier incurs. Typically, the indirect costs are incurred whether or not the product or service is actually manufactured or delivered. Indirect costs are essential to the management of the relationship, but are not necessarily related to a specific product or transaction.

Indirect costs are sometimes referred to as "Sales, Administration, and General" or SAG costs. As we have seen, customer-specific logistics costs may also be included. The SAG cost or service costs for many businesses are not just one of the largest areas of cost, but also one of the fastest growing. This is particularly so for KAM, where the cost of the key account manager or KAM team will form a considerable part of the SAG costs.

As well as being a substantial cost area, and one that has a major impact on customer profitability, indirect costs also vary considerably from key account to key account. Some key accounts buy in a very efficient manner: order placed quickly in large order quantities, centralized delivery, standard product, finishing or packaging, etc. Other key accounts have very detailed non-standard requirements, or they use up a lot of sales or service time.

> The leader of a KAM team at a leading European business-to-business insurance company said:
>
> You get some customers who want their hands held for every single process and that can end up taking hours and hours of extra work... The fact of the matter is, we don't really want to have one person who sits there and "hand-holds" somebody unless that particular customer is so valuable to us, that it makes it worth that expenditure of resource.

There are two approaches to calculating indirect costs: standard costs, and activity-based costing (ABC).

Standard costs

Standard costs are the typical costs for performing a repeated operation. They are used in calculating customer profitability where the cost item is small but the same item recurs frequently, such as raising invoices or credit notes, sending statements, or writing letters. The standard cost of an item can be calculated by considering a set of activities, such as writing a batch of letters, and then dividing the total cost by the number of letters in that batch to give an average cost per letter. The standard cost does not necessarily reflect the actual cost of writing a particular letter, but it is an approximation and accurate enough on smaller items. Standard costs can be obtained from the finance director.

Once the standard cost is known, all that the key account manager has to do is to find out how many letters, invoices, credit notes, and statements were sent to the key account during the period and multiply the number sent by the standard cost of each (Table 5.4).

Table 5.4 Using standard costs

Item	Standard cost (€)	Number of items sent to key account during period	Total item cost (€)
Letter	20	4	80
Invoice	40	10	400
Credit note	50	1	50
Statement	10	12	120
		Total	*650*

Standard costs are used for smaller, repetitive operations. Where the cost elements are larger or more varied, standard costing could give a misleading view and some form of ABC will be preferred.

Activity-based costing

ABC looks at the actual costs associated with performing certain tasks or delivering services. The activity-based cost is calculated as the number of days (or hours) a manager spends on a task, multiplied by the pay rate per working day (or hour) for a manager of that grade. The underlying philosophy of ABC is the notion of cost drivers – in this case, time spent and pay rate.

ABC approaches are widely used by professional services firms such as lawyers and accountants. ABC is useful in these cases because the activities that lawyers and accountants undertake can vary greatly, so standard costs would not be appropriate. Moreover, the hourly rate can be specific to the individual, if required. It is much more expensive to use the senior partner's time than that of the office junior. It is worth noting that the key account manager's role is also very varied and, therefore, where a key account manager's time has to be divided between several key accounts, some form of ABC would be appropriate.

Full ABC projects are complex and sophisticated, and provide very detailed and accurate information. However, for most practical KAM purposes, a simpler form of activity-based approach is more than adequate. Two examples of simple activity-based approaches are given in the following box.

Simple activity-based approaches

A financial services company which had only introduced KAM a year ago decided it wanted a "quick and dirty" view of the costs of its KAM operation to make sure that costs were not getting out of hand. On the face of it, this was a complex KAM operation with five KAM team members and a number of administrators looking after 18 key accounts. To his relief, the business unit director quickly discovered that the staff involved fell into three pay grades – administrator, key account manager, and senior manager. He was able to work out the approximate day rate for each role. Then, he asked some administrators, the key account managers, and the senior manager to keep a diary of where they were spending their time. They were asked to note down major activities and chunks of time – days and half-days spent in meetings or on client visits, for example. After 3 months, the diaries were analysed. By focusing on the big chunks of cost, this director was quickly able to attribute about 80% of his SAG costs to specific clients. The director also used standard costs to allocate the costs of writing letters, basic account administration, and raising standard client contracts.

A small software company had recently been spun off from its parent company in a management buy-out. Most of the business still came from the former parent company, but the company had some success in attracting a limited number of new accounts. The management team was anxious to ensure the correct balance of activity between managing the relationship with the parent company, managing new key accounts, and working on customer acquisition activities. This was a very IT-literate company and so it used data from electronic diaries, combined with a staff survey, to create a spreadsheet showing what percentage of their time the managers were spending on a variety of duties. Each quarter the managers were sent an email listing the proportions of time they had previously reported and asking them to update the record. This system was moderately expensive of time and effort to set up, but was very quick for the managers to update. Consequently, the response rate to the quarterly questionnaire was very high. The tracking system meant that the quality of activity-based data improved over time.

Technology can be used to help identify where the key account manager spends his/her time.

The example of the software company shows that technology can support the key account manager in his/her efforts to allocate costs. For example, many call centre management software packages incorporate a feature that allows for the tracking of both inbound and outbound calls. This feature can be used to allocate the costs of desk-based account managers or support staff between the clients they service. Similarly, some Sales Force Automation IT packages can provide data about where sales people spend their time.

Types of indirect costs

There are several types of indirect costs. The main types that a key account manager should consider when calculating the profitability of a key account are shown in Table 5.5.

Table 5.5 Indirect costs and calculation method

Indirect cost	Calculation method
Sales costs	Simple activity based (diary based) or IT-generated activity based
Administration costs (desk-based account management, letters, statements, raising contracts, credit notes, etc.)	A mixture of standard and IT-generated activity based
KAM	Simple activity based (diary based) or IT-generated activity based
Other marketing (during and after-sales service, technical support, training)	Simple activity based (diary based) or IT-generated activity based
Product development/technical	Simple activity based (diary based)

> ### An important note about indirect costs and customer profitability
>
> Where the costs are considerable and where they vary by customer, such as sales or KAM costs, it is *a very bad idea* simply to allocate them proportional to the volume of goods the customer purchases, or proportional to revenues. Allocating costs by volume or revenue will understate the relative profitability of customers who buy efficiently (those who require little handholding) and overstate the relative profitability of demanding customers. This method, which is seductively simple and therefore more widely used than it should be, could result in a company acquiring disproportionate numbers of less profitable and very demanding key accounts.

Customer-specific overheads

To complete the calculation of customer profitability, a key account manager needs to consider whether there are any customer-specific overheads.

The overheads of a business are the central costs that the company incurs to be in business, but which are not directly or indirectly related to the sale of goods or services. Some examples of overhead costs are: heating, lighting, rent and rates, other premises costs, head office costs, IT costs, and HR costs.

Strictly, the true calculation of customer profitability would require a key account manager to allocate *all* business costs, including overhead costs, to a customer. Indeed, many attempts that companies have made to implement customer profitability analysis have failed because of the difficulty of allocating overheads to customers. For practical customer management purposes, allocating overheads to individual customers is a step too far.

However, there is one exception to the rule that overhead costs can be disregarded in customer profitability analysis. The exception is where the acquisition of a new key account would result in additional overheads or, put another way, where there are customer-specific overheads. Some examples of customer-specific overheads might be a supplier who maintains a branch office within a key account's premises, or a supplier who manages customer-specific stock in a dedicated area of the warehouse. Customer-specific overheads should be included in the calculation of customer profitability.

> Customer-specific overheads should be included in the calculation of customer profitability.

Calculating customer profitability

A completed calculation of customer profitability is shown in Table 5.6.

Table 5.6 The calculation of customer profitability

Period = $t-1$	Customer A	Customer B
Revenue	500	500
Less: Product costs	(350)	(280)
Less: Costs to serve (sales, KAM, logistics, customer-specific admin)	(50)	(30)
Less: Customer-specific overheads (stock held for customer, branch at customer site)	(5)	–
Customer profit	95	190

Table 5.6 shows a sample customer profitability analysis for customers A and B, which are both key accounts of this company and had revenues last year $(t-1)$ of €500,000. This, however, is where the similarity ends. Customer A purchased a higher proportion of bespoke products, so the direct product costs for customer A were €350,000 compared to €280,000 for customer B. A was a more demanding customer than B, requiring more pre- and after-sales support, so that the indirect costs to serve A were €50,000 compared to €30,000 for B. Finally, A's contract provided for a small amount of customer-specific stock, which led to a customer-specific overhead cost of €5000. So, customer A generated €95,000 for the supplier last year. This compares to €190,000 from customer B. This supplier makes twice as much money from B as from A, a result that is not apparent from contemplating their revenues. This example also illustrates the dangers of allocating indirect costs proportional to revenues or volumes rather than working out what the actual activity-based costs were. In fact, B is a much more attractive key account than A, and the key account team might consider trying to attract more customers like B.

Uses and limitations of customer profitability analysis

If business units do not communicate with one another, companies may fail to identify large customers and may treat them, inappropriately, as though they were small customers.

One of the key uses of customer profitability analysis is to focus the organization on customers and to kick-start the process of understanding the value of the relationship. As such, it is an important tool in implementing KAM. Too many companies manage large customers as though they were a series of small customers, because the relationship is managed by individuals and business units which do not communicate. Some suppliers are astonished when they discover that other parts of their business are making (sometimes competing) offers to the same customer. Still more embarrassing for suppliers is when it is the customer who points this out to them. Smart customers may even play different parts of the same supplier off against one another. In other cases, the customer is not given the importance it deserves because nobody has ever examined the total value of that customer across the whole business.

Another application of customer profitability analysis is that analysing the costs to acquire a customer (sales, marketing, and KAM costs in particular) is useful in thinking about the breakeven period on the costs of customer acquisition. In some key account situations the cost of customer acquisition is considerably higher than the year by year profits. So, a customer has to be retained for more than a year, and possibly for several years, in order to generate a positive return on the costs and efforts invested in acquiring them. Knowing how much it costs to acquire a new customer and how long it takes for a new customer to break even on the costs of acquiring them is useful strategic input into key account manager decisions about the proportion of time they spend on customer acquisition versus retention.

A third use of customer profitability analysis relates to supplier dependency and the degree to which a very few customers are generating the majority of a supplier's profits. Most of us are familiar with the adage that 80% of the revenues come from 20% of the customers, also known as the 80:20 or Pareto rule. But the 80:20 rule also applies to customer profitability. An early example was US heating wire manufacturer, Kanthal. The company carried out a detailed customer profitability analysis and discovered that it had, not an 80:20, but a 225:20 customer profitability skew:

Kanthal's 225:20 customer profitability analysis

20% of customers = 225% of profits
70% of customers = breakeven
10% of customers = *minus* 125% of profits

"The Kanthal customers generating the greatest losses were among those with the largest sales volume…. You can't lose large amounts of money on a small customer."

Cooper and Kaplan, *Harvard Business Review* (May–June 1991)

Clearly, Kanthal could use its detailed information about the very profitable and the very unprofitable customers to try and target its customer acquisition onto the most profitable types.

Results like these are not confined to particular countries or industry sectors. Another study, this time of a European commercial cleaning company, found that just 1% of its customers accounted for 50% of revenues and 49% of profits. The top 5% of customers brought in 74% of profits.

One of the consequences of introducing KAM practices to an organization is that the proportion of business coming from the company's key accounts typically increases. This tends to increase the supplier's dependency on fewer, larger customers. Although this can create huge value, it also carries risks. The loss of a very large customer could have a devastating effect on the company. Regular monitoring of the total profitability of key accounts as a percentage of the company's total profits can help alert the company to any problems of supplier dependence. The issue of risk in key account relationships will be discussed in the next chapter.

> When KAM is introduced, the proportion of business coming from the company's key accounts typically increases. This increases the supplier's dependency on its key customers.

The limitations of customer profitability analysis

Although customer profitability analysis is a useful tool for key account managers, it has one important limitation that key account managers need to be aware of. The limitation is whether the period under consideration is representative of the relationship as a whole. Although there are relatively few published accounts of the actual calculation of customer profitability, one such account clearly demonstrates that customer profitability can alter dramatically from one period to the next. Wilson (1996) discusses the example of a European printing equipment company that carried out a customer profitability analysis. In 1980 the largest 10% of customers accounted for 15% of total profits. When the analysis was repeated in 1992, the largest 10% of customers accounted for *minus* 3% of profits. In this example, a single-period customer profitability analysis could give a misleading view of the value of the relationship.

At the other end of the scale, single-period customer profitability analysis typically reveals a clutch of small, unprofitable customers. Such analyses sometimes persuade companies into thinking that they could improve their performance by cutting costs to these unprofitable customers or even by getting rid of them altogether. So they can, in the short term. The problem is that such actions may damage the organization in the longer term. Small unprofitable customers might be the large, profitable customers of the future. Or they might include a medium or even a large customer that has ordered very little over the past year. The appropriate response might be to try and find out what the problem is and fix it, rather than to reduce or withdraw service levels.

> Finding unprofitable customers through a single-period customer profitability analysis does *not* imply that those customers should be dropped. Instead, the company should consider how it can better manage its customer relationships.

Single-period customer profitability analysis has limited usefulness in KAM decision-making. KAM is concerned with long-term relationship development and management. In KAM relationships, customer profitability analysis may be used to establish the principle of measuring the value of customers and to test the calculation process. For developing key account strategies and managing the relationship, however, key account managers are more likely to be interested in future potential. The measure used to measure the future value of the relationship is customer lifetime value.

■ Customer lifetime value

> We are defining customer lifetime value here as the *remaining* lifetime in the relationship (i.e. the future), not including any past relationship the customer may have had with the company.

Customer lifetime value is the prediction of the net present value (NPV) of the customer over the remaining relationship lifetime; in other words, customer lifetime value is a forward-looking measure. This contrasts with customer profitability, which looks backwards in time to what happened in a previous period.

The calculation of customer lifetime value should be done at individual customer level for each of an organization's key accounts, but can be calculated segment by segment for smaller customers. The calculation is a four-step process.

The four-step method for calculating customer lifetime value

1 Forecast the length of the relationship (relationship lifetime).
2 Forecast the customer revenues, period by period.
3 Forecast the customer costs, period by period.
4 Adjust for the time value of money.

Forecasting relationship lifetime

The relationship lifetime is the probable remaining duration of the relationship. Where the relationship is contractual and the contract has to be renewed year by year, forecasting relationship lifetime can be difficult. In other situations it can be rather easier. Some key account managers can draw upon analysis of the existing relationship lifetimes or on their previous experience with certain types of customer to help them forecast what the remaining relationship lifetime will be.

When determining the figure you will use for relationship lifetime, it is important to recognize that there are practical limits to how far ahead a key account manager can forecast the revenues and costs associated with each customer. In most industries, the rule of thumb is that 4–5 years is as far forward as the key account managers can project a relationship. Where there is a good chance that the relationship will last much longer, there are techniques that accountants use to calculate the terminal value after the forecast period. You are advised to consult your Finance Director if the relationship you are considering is likely to continue further into the future than you can reasonably forecast.

At this point, the framework for the customer lifetime value calculation is shown in Table 5.7.

Table 5.7 Setting up the customer lifetime value calculation

Relationship lifetime	Year 1*	Year 2	Year 3	Year 4

*For clarity, by "Year 1" we mean the current trading year.

Forecasting customer revenues

The next step in calculating customer lifetime value is to forecast the revenues that will be received from the customer in each of the future years. Strictly, the key account manager should identify exactly when the revenues would be raised (i.e. how much in each month of the year in each future year), but we are aiming at a straightforward approach so we will make a simplifying assumption that all the revenues will be received in a lump sum at the end of each year.

When forecasting customer revenues, the skill of the key account manager is to use their deep understanding of that customer's business to forecast what products and/or services the customer will buy. This will be affected by a number of factors, such as:

- Changes in the economic and regulatory environment
- Growth in the key account's market
- The key account's main target customers or segments
- Changes in fashion or preferences
- Technological developments in the key account's markets
- Competitive pressures on the key account
- Institutional factors such as industry structure or the ownership of/independence of the key account
- The key account's own strategic objectives
- The product/service offerings of the supplier
- The product/service offerings of competing suppliers

Where the key account is an existing customer, there may be data on historic sales which can be useful in forecasting, particularly if trends are seen to be emerging over a number of years. It may give greater accuracy if product volumes and prices are forecast separately.

The format for the calculation is as shown in Tables 5.1 and 5.2, although the numbers are forecast rather than actual. It may be helpful to carry out the forecasting as a team exercise, so that other people who know the key account can contribute their expertise.

Some companies also keep a record of their revenue forecasts, broken down as shown in Table 5.1, so that they can compare this with the actual outturn at the end of each year. This simple technique helps key account managers to improve their forecasting accuracy.

Once the revenue forecasts have been agreed, they can be added to the customer lifetime value calculation framework (Table 5.8). This can be done product by product, as shown, or by product category, or simply as a total. If the simple total is shown, the expected product purchases should be shown elsewhere in the plan.

Table 5.8 Setting up the customer lifetime value calculation

Relationship lifetime	Year 1 (£)	Year 2 (£)	Year 3 (£)	Year 4 (£)
Revenues				
Product A	100,000	120,000	130,000	150,000
Product B	50,000	50,000	60,000	70,000
Total customer revenues	*150,000*	*170,000*	*190,000*	*220,000*

It may be useful at this point to remember that the forecast revenues should be based on *realized* amounts, not invoiced amounts, so future discounts, etc. need to be factored in.

The third stage in calculating customer lifetime value is to forecast costs.

Forecasting customer costs

As with customer profitability analysis, there are three types of customer cost that have to be forecast to calculate customer lifetime value:

● Direct product costs
● Costs to serve
● Customer-specific overhead costs (if any)

Forecasting direct product costs

The key account manager may need help from Operations or Finance to forecast product costs. A practical way to forecast direct product costs is to adjust current costs by some agreed inflation factor each year. So, if the cost of providing a particular product or service was €100 last year and Operations or Finance advise that production costs are likely to rise by 10% per annum for the next 4 years, the direct product cost per unit produced will be €110 this year, €121 (€110 × 1.1) in year 2, €133.10 (€121 × 1.1) in year 3, and €145.41 (€133.1 × 1.1) in year 4.

It is important to note that the cost of manufacturing a product or providing a service can vary quite considerably depending on the number of units manufactured or provided. It is a good idea for the key account manager to share the customer purchase forecasts used to forecast customer revenues with Operations, as this information may affect their estimate of costs.

> Key account managers should share their customer purchase forecasts with Operations, as this information may affect the latter's estimate of costs.

Forecasting costs to serve

Costs to serve can be forecast using the methods described in Table 5.5, but this time *forecasting* the number of standard operations (such as invoices, letters sent, etc.) and multiplying these by the standard cost (which may need to be adjusted for inflation).

When the key account manager is forecasting sales, KAM, and other activity costs, any changes in the composition of the KAM team, or in the way that the key account will be managed, need to be taken into account. Even if there are no other changes (e.g. where the account is managed by a single key account manager who is likely to continue to look after the same account for the foreseeable future), salary rises should be taken into account.

Forecasting customer-specific overheads

Forecasting customer-specific overheads is another activity for which key account managers should consult internally. Will there be any changes in the dedicated customer space? Will the dedicated customer area or other costs be affected by the key account manager's forecasts of the products or services that the customer will be buying in future? If new products or services are to be introduced or older products or services phased out, will that affect customer-specific overheads? Sometimes the best that can be done is to adjust the existing customer overhead costs by some agreed percentage.

Once all these questions have been discussed, the key account manager can enter the costs into the customer lifetime value calculation framework. This allows the year by year future customer profits (total customer revenues less total customer costs) to be worked out (Table 5.9).

Table 5.9 Adding forecast costs to the customer lifetime value calculation

Relationship lifetime	Year 1 (€)	Year 2 (€)	Year 3 (€)	Year 4 (€)
Revenues				
Product A	100,000	120,000	130,000	150,000
Product B	50,000	50,000	60,000	70,000
Total customer revenues	*150,000*	*170,000*	*190,000*	*220,000*
Product costs	55,000	58,000	61,000	64,000
Costs to serve	15,000	20,000	25,000	28,000
Customer-specific overheads	–	5000*	5000*	5000*
Total customer costs	*70,000*	*83,000*	*91,000*	*97,000*
Year by year profit	*80,000*	*87,000*	*99,000*	*123,000*

* Customer-specific overheads relate to introduction of new service from year 2 onwards.

However, the profit numbers shown in Table 5.9 are expressed in notional future period amounts. Revenues are predicted future purchases at expected future prices, and costs are predicted future costs. To arrive at the value of this customer in *today's money*, the time value of money is applied.

The time value of money

A bird in the hand is worth two in the bush.

> Customer lifetime value is the NPV of a customer's future profits or cash flows.

The promise of money in the future is less attractive than actual money now. Factors such as inflation erode value over time, and there is always some risk that the future profits will not be realized. This is a problem where a manager wants to compare two activities with different profit profiles. Take the example of a key account manager who has two clients. Both are forecast to bring in €100,000 of profits, but customer A will in fact bring in €90,000 next year and €10,000 the year after. Customer B will bring in just €20,000 next year but €80,000 the year after. In this example, although both customers are going to bring in the same profit, they do not have the same value. Customer A is more valuable than customer B, because the profits from customer A are delivered sooner. The tool that accountants use to compare these sorts of situations and values is called the time value of money. The value today of a stream of future profits or cash flow is known as its NPV. Customer lifetime value is the NPV of a stream of value from a customer.

To calculate the NPV of a customer, the key account manager has to find out what the time value of money is to his/her company. Most companies have a discount rate (sometimes called a hurdle rate) which they use to calculate NPV. The discount rate is the rate that the company has nominated to represent the time value of money. Some listed companies, however, use their weighted average cost of capital (WACC), to calculate NPV. The WACC reflects the market cost of equity funding to the company, the market cost of debt, and the proportions of equity and of debt that the company uses for funding. Thus, the WACC is influenced by the view taken by external lenders (the bank and shareholders) of the risk of the company.

How WACC is calculated

Cost of debt ⨯ Proportion of debt	+	Cost of equity ⨯ Proportion of equity
	= WACC	

The discount rate or WACC will usually be provided to the key account manager as a percentage. To calculate customer lifetime value, this percentage can be turned into a discount factor, which is then multiplied by the notional value of the customer.

Calculating the NPV of a customer

The best way to illustrate the difficult concept of the time value of money is through an example. This example illustrates the simplest case, already described, in which the customer makes a single payment at the end of each year, so all the revenues come in at the end of the year.

To illustrate the principle of calculating customer lifetime value, we will assume that the discount rate that the key account manager's company uses is 5% per annum. The year by year profit is:

	Year 1	Year 2	Year 3	Year 4
Year by year profit	80,000	87,000	99,000	123,000

The formula for calculating the NPV of each profit number is:

$$\frac{1}{(1+i)^t}$$

Where i is the discount rate and t is the time period. The equation can be explained in words as:

$$\frac{1}{(1+\text{discount rate})^{\text{time period}}}$$

It is important to express the discount rate correctly, as a decimal. The calculation in this example is *not* $(1 + 5\%)$ but $(1 + 0.05)$, or 1.05. This figure is then raised to the power of the time period. So, in this example, the year by year equation is:

	Year 1	Year 2	Year 3	Year 4
Equation	$\frac{1}{(1+0.05)^1}$	$\frac{1}{(1+0.05)^2}$	$\frac{1}{(1+0.05)^3}$	$\frac{1}{(1+0.05)^4}$

Solving these equations, the discount factor for each year is:

	Year 1	Year 2	Year 3	Year 4
Discount factor	0.952	0.907	0.864	0.823

The present value is the future profit multiplied by the discount factor, as shown in Table 5.10.

Table 5.10 Completing the customer lifetime value calculation

Relationship lifetime	Year 1 (€)	Year 2 (€)	Year 3 (€)	Year 4 (€)
Revenues				
Product A	100,000	120,000	130,000	150,000
Product B	50,000	50,000	60,000	70,000
Total customer revenues	*150,000*	*170,000*	*190,000*	*220,000*
Product costs	55,000	58,000	61,000	64,000
Costs to serve	15,000	20,000	25,000	28,000
Customer-specific overheads	–	5000	5000	5000

Table 5.10 (Continued)				
Relationship lifetime	Year 1 (€)	Year 2 (€)	Year 3 (€)	Year 4 (€)
Total customer costs	70,000	83,000	91,000	97,000
Year by year profit	80,000	87,000	99,000	123,000
Total notional value				€389,000
Discount factor*	0.952	0.907	0.864	0.823
Present value of future profits	76,160	78,909	85,536	101,229
Customer lifetime value				€341,834

*Based on a discount rate of 5%.

As Table 5.10 shows, although the total notional value of this key account is €389,000, the true value of the customer in today's money is €341,834.

A note about the calculation of customer lifetime value

The process for calculating the discount factor illustrated here is the standard format, although this standard format is in fact a simplification of a complex problem. The simplification is that the customer receipts have been treated as though they all come in as a lump sum at the end of the year.

The effect of this simplification is that it slightly *understates* the true lifetime value, since some of the revenues arrive earlier than the end of the year. The understatement is small at low discount rates. If you use the same calculation method for all customers, and if they have similar cash flow patterns, you will still be able to compare their lifetime values using this method.

There is a slightly more complex form of the calculation which gives a more accurate result, if needed. It is even possible to adjust the NPV for the actual day on which the receipt is made, if a very high degree of accuracy is needed. However, for most practical purposes, the method we have demonstrated gives completely acceptable results.

■ Using customer lifetime value in KAM planning

Customer lifetime value is an essential tool in KAM planning, as it indicates what potential there is in the customer relationship. This, in turn, helps the key account manager decide what strategies to adopt when managing the key account.

Changes in lifetime value give the key account manager vital information about the financial impact of changes in customer management strategy.

It is important to note that customer lifetime value is a forecast and, like any forecast, it is vulnerable to unexpected changes in the customer's circumstances. It can also be affected by the actions of the supplier company. Although these factors are a problem in any kind of forecasting, a key account manager can turn this apparent disadvantage into an advantage. There does not have to be one single figure for customer lifetime value; the lifetime value could alter, depending on assumptions about potential and about the strategies the supplier decides to adopt. Customer lifetime value is a measure of the customer's potential, and the potential may change depending on changes in strategy. Changes in lifetime value give the key account manager vital information about the likely payback to changes in customer management strategy. Multiple scenarios can be created, showing the expected value of the key account based on current strategies (the "base case"), and what happens to that value if the customer is managed differently, remembering that both revenues and costs may change. The most interesting scenarios may be outlined in the KAM plan.

Customer lifetime value calculations for a portfolio of several key accounts can be used to support marketing portfolio management. Where customer lifetime value calculations have been made for several key accounts, the key account manager can calculate the best probable use of his/her time by considering the way that the lifetime value of several customers might change if more effort was put into some and less effort into others. The lifetime value of some key accounts might go down, but this could be offset by greater increases in the lifetime value of other key accounts.

Using customer lifetime value as a portfolio management tool helps to link marketing to shareholder value.

Using customer lifetime value as a portfolio management tool helps to link marketing to shareholder value. Shareholder value is a measure of business performance that takes risk into account. Too often, marketing is viewed by companies as a cost, not as an investment. Calculating customer lifetime value helps key account managers to make the case that their activities contribute to value creation. It may also reveal that certain activities do not contribute to shareholder value creation, or even destroy it. One example is how companies treat customers with a negative lifetime value.

What do you do about loss-making key accounts?

It is not uncommon that companies who begin to measure the value of their customers find out that some are unprofitable. Sometimes the unprofitable customers can be key accounts, as in the Kanthal example earlier in this chapter. Very big customers combine the muscle to demand higher service levels with the power to demand lower prices. Sometimes, this can lead to situations in which a supplier finds that it is not making money from a key account relationship. Losses in a single year are one matter and may be related to special circumstances; more serious is the case in which a supplier calculates the customer lifetime value of its key account and discovers that it has no prospect of making money from the relationship in the foreseeable future. The relationship is destroying shareholder value.

Where a key account has negative customer lifetime value, the key account manager must develop plans to address the problem. One set of actions might be related to reducing costs, perhaps encouraging the customer to use Internet procurement or reducing visit frequencies. If the problem lies in production costs, the customer might be asked to increase their minimum order quantity or reduce delivery complexity.

Another set of actions might address revenues. Perhaps the customer could be encouraged to buy more products, or to change the product mix so that revenues rise. Or, it might be possible to increase prices (or reduce discounts and rebates), which will also have the effect of increasing revenues. Some key account managers also use price unbundling in these situations, unpicking the package of goods and services that the customer receives and making sure they only receive services that they are prepared to pay for. Unbundling may affect both revenues and costs.

Where customer lifetime value analysis reveals that a key account is persistently losing money for the supplier, an important element in planning and managing the situation is for the key account manager to discuss it with the customer. The key account may value the relationship but be completely unaware that the supplier is not making money from it. Many key accounts are willing to negotiate about terms and service levels, and some suppliers will even have "open book" arrangements with key accounts that they are closest to, that enable them to earn an agreed return on the relationship.

> The key account may value the relationship but be completely unaware that the supplier is not making money from it.

In some cases the key account is intransigent and negotiations to reduce costs and/or increase revenues fail. This can be a sign that the key account is not particularly interested in a relationship with the supplier, perhaps because the supplier is of little strategic importance (although it may be quite the reverse on the supplier's side). Other times, a key account may be culturally unused or unwilling to engage in give-and-take negotiations. In this case, the supplier has two decisions to make: does the relationship create value for it in other ways, and does this relationship value justify going on with the relationship.

Other sources of value from relationships

The value of a key account is not measured only in terms of its profitability or customer lifetime value. Customers, particularly, of strategic importance – that is, key accounts – create value for organizations in other ways. The best key account managers will consider other sources of value from key account relationships and will plan to obtain as much additional value as possible.

Contribution is one source of value from a key account. The argument here is that the large volume associated with a key account's business helps keep the supplier's unit costs down. Large volumes may bring economies of scale in supplier procurement and production, and experience curve effects which contribute to lower unit costs as the supplier learns by doing. Key account managers sometimes argue that contribution is a justification for retaining a key account with negative lifetime value.

The problem with the contribution argument is that, at the end of the day, this is an unprofitable customer. The cost of retaining the customer needs to be weighed up against the cost contribution it brings. In addition, the unprofitable relationship is being subsidized by other, profitable relationships. Supplying large but unprofitable volumes to a key account could lock the supplier into a particular relationship and way of doing business. Because competitors are not locked into these unprofitable relationships, they are free to develop newer and more efficient processes. If they succeed, they will be able to pick off the more attractive customers by offering them better deals than the existing supplier. The stark reality is that profitable customers subsidize a supplier's relationships with its unprofitable customers, and that cannot be in the best interests of the profitable customers. If there is no prospect of turning a costly relationship into positive lifetime value, the key account manager should at least consider whether his/her time would be better spent on other customers, as in the case of the bathroom equipment manufacturer:

> **Profitable customers subsidize a supplier's relationships with its unprofitable customers.**

Saying goodbye to a costly customer

B&Q is the UK's largest DIY and building products retailer, and a tough negotiator with its many suppliers. One supplier, a medium-sized manufacturer of bathroom fittings, calculated that B&Q was by far its biggest customer, accounting for 20% of its total turnover. The problem was that the B&Q relationship was unprofitable and had a negative lifetime value. The supplier tried to negotiate with B&Q but was not able to resolve the issue. After considerable debate between the KAM team and the senior managers, the company decided to cease supplying B&Q. By a stupendous effort, it took the team just 6 months to replace the 20% of turnover. They acquired new customers and extended the relationships they already had. All of the replacement business was profitable, and the supplier's overall financial results improved.

It is a brave and unusual decision to stop dealing with a key account, but it can sometimes be the right thing to do if all other avenues have been explored unsuccessfully.

Referrals and references, by contrast with the contribution argument, can be excellent sources of value from key accounts. Referrals are positive recommendations by the customer, and references are when the key account gives permission for its name or other details to be used in the supplier's promotional materials. This permission can take the form of a customer name on a supplier's brochure, a case study, site visits, or a web link. Referrals and references act as "door openers", making it easier, faster, and cheaper for the supplier to gain new customers.

The KAM plan should consider whether there are possible referrals and/or references that the customer could give. However, two factors need to be taken into account: the value of the referral or reference, and the timing of the request from the key account manager for a referral or reference.

The value of a referral or reference will depend, at least in part, on the strength of the key account's brand. The customer's brand values should also be taken into account. Not all key accounts have strong brands, or attractive brand values with which the supplier wants to associate itself. In addition, some researchers have suggested that referrals tend to attract customers that are similar in profile to the referrer. If so, the characteristics that make a customer unprofitable might also be present in the new customers referred by an unprofitable customer. Brand strength, brand values, profit profile, as well as willingness to give referrals or references, should all be considered before asking a key account for a referral or reference.

> The KAM plan should consider and plan for all sources of value from key customers, such as referrals and/or references that the customer could give, learning, and shared innovation.

If the key account manager does decide to approach a key account to ask for a referral or reference, he/she will need to make a second decision about when it is right to ask – at what stage in the relationship is a key account most likely to refer? Early research on this topic suggested that the value of referrals increased over the lifetime of the relationship, although more recent research has suggested that referrals should be sought in the first few months of a relationship, in the honeymoon period before anything has gone wrong to mar the customer's positive view of the supplier.

Innovation and learning are also potential sources of value from a key account relationship. Innovation and learning covers a range of activities that can improve the efficiency or increase the value of a supplier's business, from shared new product development to process improvement and benchmarking. In some KAM relationships, the key account is involved at a very early stage in new product development, working with the supplier even at the concept stage. The KAM plan should describe any innovation and/or learning opportunities that the key account manager has identified, who should be involved, and how much investment might be required. Some innovation and learning opportunities require investment from both parties, supplier and customer, and this needs to be taken into account.

■ KAM planning and shareholder value

A well-planned KAM relationship should give the supplier substantial financial benefits (volume, revenues, and most of all customer lifetime value) but may also bring with it other sources of value through relationship benefits. In fact, there can be cases where the relationship benefits are so great that the supplier considers the customer to be a key account, even where the customer has negative lifetime value. Once a key account manager has information about the financial and relationship value of his/her key accounts, the selection and deselection of key accounts becomes more sophisticated (Figure 5.1).

Information about financial attractiveness and other sources of value from a key account is fundamental to the development of a KAM plan that sets out how the relationship is to be managed. Without this information, the key account manager cannot be certain that he/she is creating shareholder value. On a practical level, information about the value generated

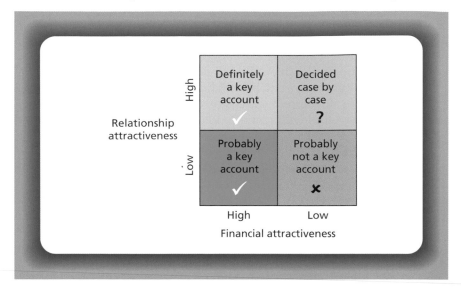

Figure 5.1
Using value criteria to identify key accounts.

by the key account relationship helps the key account manager to negotiate and manage more effectively.

Shareholder value is a way of measuring business performance that is widely used by investors and managers. Many books and articles have been written on the topic of shareholder value, and there are increasing calls for marketing to become more accountable for its contribution to shareholder value creation. Although it is outside the scope of this book to examine the calculation of shareholder value in great detail, key account managers need to be aware that their role is more and more concerned with the delivery of positive customer lifetime value and other sources of value.

One other aspect of shareholder value thinking that is important and useful for key account managers is the notion of risk. Many accountants now believe that the treatment of risk in conventional profit calculations is inadequate, since debt costs (interest charges), but not equity costs, are taken into account. This may lead businesses inadvertently to adopt discount rates that are too low because they do not reflect the real risk. We have already seen how WACC can be used to give a more accurate picture of the risk of the business as a whole. In the next chapter, we will examine the problem of risk in KAM relationships and introduce some tools for risk management of key accounts.

Increasingly, the role of the key account manager is to manage the lifetime value of his/her key accounts. This has an impact on the overall value of the company.

References

Cooper, R. and Kaplan, R.C. (1991). Profit Priorities from ABC. *Harvard Business Review*, 69(3), 130–134, May–June.
Wilson, C. (1996). "Profitable Customers," Kogan Page, London.

CHAPTER 6

Assessing the riskiness of key accounts

The lifetime value of a key account, which was discussed in the preceding chapter, must be tempered by consideration of the risk of the customer. Investing in a key account management (KAM) relationship is expensive, and when contemplating any type of investment, both risk and returns must be considered. High returns from investing in a KAM relationship are desirable, but not if the returns are outweighed by the risks.

Increasingly, key account managers are realizing that there are risks in KAM. Moreover, the risk differs between different key accounts. This chapter introduces the notion of the differing riskiness of key accounts and outlines three methods for assessing risk. Conventional wisdom about the measurement of risk is challenged and found wanting. Traditionally, companies measure risk in their business-to-business relationships in terms of the financial risk of their customers, using credit scoring to evaluate the risk that the customer will default on payment or even go bankrupt. However, measuring the risk of customer default is irrelevant to most key account managers. Instead, key account managers need to measure and manage relationship risk. This concept is explained and the notion of the relationship risk scorecard is introduced, together with guidance on how a key account manager can develop a relationship risk scorecard for themselves. This builds to an advanced technique, using the risk analysis to adjust customer lifetime value calculations, in order to assess whether the key account programme in total creates or destroys shareholder value.

■ Fast track

- As we have seen, introducing KAM tends to increase the proportion of a supplier's business that comes from its key accounts. This increases supplier dependency risk. The loss of an important customer can have a very serious effect on the supplier's performance. For this reason, part of the role of the key account manager is to monitor and manage customer relationship risk.
- The risk in a key account relationship is not usually the risk that the customer will default, although it is this risk that is measured by conventional credit risk measurement tools. So, the key account manager needs a different tool to evaluate risk. We call this the relationship risk scorecard.
- The main risks in a key account relationship are defection (total loss of the customer) or migration (partial loss of the customer's business). Other risks include volatile purchasing patterns, slow payment, and negative word of mouth.
- The relationship risk scorecard is put together by understanding the risk factors that affect KAM relationships in the customer portfolio and then collecting data about the actual risk against each factor for each key account.
- The risk of the customer should be taken into account when its lifetime value is considered. This can be done using the "traffic lights"

approach or by probability weighting the forecasts of customer life-time value. The relationship risk scorecard can be used to give a more objective view of the risk of the customer.

● The strategies that the key account manager develops to manage the key account may also have an impact on its risk. Therefore, risk mitigation should be taken into consideration when developing key account strategies.

■ Introduction

Successful KAM involves risk to the supplier. The supplier has to invest in the KAM relationship, appointing key account managers and sometimes making changes to the way the company works or is structured. As a successful KAM relationship develops, the supplier can expect to obtain more business from its key account (a higher share of spend). In turn, the higher share of spend makes the key account more important to the supplier, so there is an issue of supplier dependence on a few key customers. Loss of such a big customer is a major risk, as are fluctuations in business which can cause problems of over- or under-capacity.

The bigger the customer, the greater the risk. Yet most key account managers do not know how to evaluate the risk of their key accounts, or they use risk evaluation tools that are inappropriate for KAM relationships. The conventional approach to business-to-business risk evaluation is to use some form of credit scoring or credit rating. Credit scoring is usually provided by an external agency such as Experian, Standard & Poor's, Moodys, or Dun and Bradstreet. A credit score is a valuable tool in relationship management, as it examines the financial standing of a customer and helps the supplier set credit limits. The purpose of the credit limit is to limit the exposure of the supplier to the risk that the customer will default on payment. Normally, the supplier will supply goods on credit (i.e. before payment). As the credit limit is approached, the customer will be asked to pay off some outstanding invoices before they can be given more credit; or they may only be able to obtain goods for cash. Credit limits ensure that a supplier will not be brought down by the bankruptcy of a customer.

One issue with credit scoring in a KAM relationship context is that the credit scoring takes place at the outset. If the relationship endures for some years, the credit scoring gets out of date. This can mean that the credit limits are set too low, constricting business growth between the two companies. Regular review of the creditworthiness of the customer is needed to keep pace with changes in their business and financial situation.

A more serious drawback of credit scoring in a KAM context is that credit scoring is designed to measure the risk of default or business failure. However, in many KAM relationships, this is a low risk. Many key accounts are major corporations with international or global reach. Of course, such major companies do go bust from time to time, but the headlines that attend such events indicate how comparatively rare they are.

The concentration of business with a few key accounts can increase the risk of supplier dependency.

Credit scoring only measures the risk of default. It does not measure the risk that the relationship sours and the customer decides to take its business elsewhere.

The vast majority of business failures are amongst very small or micro enterprises that would never be big or important enough to be a key account. Moreover, the very closeness of the KAM relationship provides additional security; the level of analysis and planning that goes into a key account relationship gives key account managers a real insight into the situation of their key accounts.

Therefore, key account managers need a different insight into risk, one that is not given them by looking at the credit rating of their key accounts. They need to understand exactly what the risks to the supplier are in KAM relationships and how they can minimize these risks.

Supplier risk in a KAM relationship

Setting aside the (rare) risk of a key account going bankrupt, a series of interviews and conversations with key account managers and key account directors over a number of years has revealed that they are concerned about a relatively small number of risks:

● Defection or migration
● Volatile purchasing patterns
● Slow payment
● Negative word of mouth

They also mention litigation and fraud as minor risks, along with the risk of default. The main risk that key account managers are concerned about, by a considerable margin, is the risk of customer defection (total loss of the key account to a competitor) or migration (loss of part of the key account's business, measured as a falling share of spend).

Defection or migration

This is the real risk in a KAM relationship. Defection is the downside of supplier dependence. When a supplier engages in a successful KAM relationship, the risk is that more business comes from fewer customers. The loss of a big important customer can hit the firm very hard. Migration (partial loss of a customer) is also very damaging but can be harder to spot. However, it is an important signal of a deteriorating relationship. The risk of defection or migration is why key account managers should always measure share of spend as well as absolute levels of volume, revenue, and profit from their key accounts. Migrating customers are essentially customers who are defecting, but slowly. They still appear on the list of customers year after year, so they count as retained. It is even possible that the supplier's business with them is steady or even growing slightly, but more business is going to the supplier's competition than is being won by the supplier. Measuring share of spend will highlight this gradual deterioration and give the key account manager a chance to do something about it. The risk mitigation strategy is to understand and measure the factors causing defection or migration. A tool to do this will be introduced later in this chapter.

> The real risk in a KAM relationship is defection or migration, the total or partial loss of the key account.

Volatile purchasing patterns

Volatile purchasing patterns cause difficulties for suppliers. Some months, large orders come in and there are capacity problems in meeting the deadline. Then the supplier may have to bear the costs of overtime, additional shifts, or temporary workers, and perhaps pay more for emergency deliveries of raw materials. Other months, there are little or no orders coming in, workers are underemployed and machines stand idle. If a customer has volatile purchasing patterns, suppliers are at greater risk *both* of being overstocked and of running out of stock. The only mitigation strategy for volatility is working more closely with the customer to try and smooth out the orders and manage demand.

Slow payment

Slow payment is the bane of most suppliers' lives. It can be a reflection of the power imbalance between a small supplier and a large customer. The small supplier might set 30-day payment terms but lack the power to enforce the terms (and, of course, the will to enforce, if the customer is important enough for the supplier not to want to offend them). Then the customer takes 120 days to pay, and the supplier finds himself with cash flow problems. What is the supplier to do? There are three general risk mitigation strategies used by key account managers in these circumstances. The first is to reward prompt payment, perhaps through the pricing mechanism with a discount. This strategy has mixed results, as "baddie" customers have been known to take the discount and still pay late. The second strategy is to discuss the problem with the customer. This strategy has a better chance of success, as long as the relationship is important to the customer. The third strategy used by key account managers to tackle slow payment is to find out what is causing the problem and try to deal with the root cause, as in the case of a leading European beer producer.

Mini Case

A major European brewery sold a wide range of products to distributors. Orders were huge, and deliveries to the distributors were complex. From the distributors' point of view, receiving the complete order was very important and, if even one item was missing, they would delay paying the whole invoice. Once the brewery had realized that this was the case, they put extra effort into ensuring that deliveries to distributors were as accurate and complete as possible. The results were that payment speeded up and cash flow improved.

Negative word of mouth

Negative word of mouth is the flip side of positive recommendation but has the added downside that bad news travels faster than good. Some organizations have even tried measuring the impact of negative word of mouth in terms of lost future sales to that customer, plus lost sales to other customers who decide not to buy because of the negative word of mouth. Negative word of mouth is unusual in KAM relationships, which tend to be close collaborations. However, if problems do arise, the key account manager should aim to deal with them as quickly as possible, as negative word of mouth is more likely to arise when a customer perceives that their complaint is not being dealt with. Progress on chasing or resolving a complaint should be communicated frequently to the customer, as this will give them some confidence that matters are being attended to and will help reduce the risk of negative word of mouth. A follow-up meeting is advisable to ensure that the customer is satisfied. Some suppliers have key account directors or senior managers whose role is not only to visit the customer, perhaps only once a year, but to act as a conduit for complaints about the conduct of the relationship that could not be voiced directly to the key account manager.

All four types of supplier risk in a customer relationship (defection/migration, volatile purchasing patterns, slow payment, and negative word of mouth) can be reduced by careful management. As we have seen, however, the risk that key account managers are most concerned about is losing a key account. The other risks that suppliers bear in a KAM relationship (volatility, slow payment, and negative word of mouth) do not of themselves threaten the relationship. Defection signals the end of the relationship and so the risk of defection will be termed the "relationship risk". There is a tool that key account managers can use to help them evaluate and manage relationship risk. This tool is the relationship risk scorecard.

■ The relationship risk scorecard

The relationship risk scorecard is a way of assessing how risky a supplier's relationship with a key account is, where risk is defined purely as the risk of defection. It consists of a series of factors that tend to be associated with customer defection or retention, together with the scores for each key account against each factor.

> The risk of defection (total loss of the customer) or migration (partial loss) can be evaluated using a relationship risk scorecard.

The relationship risk scorecard works particularly well when a portfolio of several key accounts is studied, as the key account managers can then see the relative riskiness of their key accounts and develop strategies for reducing the risk. The relationship risk scorecard can act as an "early warning system" of problems in a KAM relationship.

The process for developing a relationship risk scorecard is set out in Table 6.1.

Each of these six steps will now be considered in more detail.

Step 1: Identify relationship risk factors

The first step is to find out what factors cause customers to defect. Most companies have little information about this and it is, therefore, useful to

Table 6.1 Process for developing a relationship risk scorecard

Step	Description	How	Who is involved
1	Identify relationship risk factors	Interviews with people in customer-facing roles, research into why customers were lost, company documentation	Key account managers, key account directors, customer service, senior managers.
2	Assemble scorecard framework	Discussion, review of step 1 data	Researcher, key account managers, senior managers
3	Analyse key account portfolio	Company records, survey key account managers	Key account managers of each key account in the portfolio
4	Produce completed scorecard	Compile data anonymously, if necessary	Researcher
5	Review overall KAM portfolio risk	Discussion, review of scorecard data	Senior managers, key account directors
6	Develop individual key account risk management strategies	Plans	Key account managers

ask questions about what factors cause customers to be retained. The retention/defection factors can be identified through interviews with key account managers and key account directors and a review of company documentation relating to customer retention, customer losses, complaints, etc., plus any previous company research the supplier may have carried out. Where there are good information technology (IT) systems and historic data, it may be possible to track defecting and retained customers and compare their characteristics and behaviours. This comparison may give additional useful information about relationship risk factors.

The process of identifying relationship risk factors may turn up a considerable number of factors. One way to focus the scorecard is to look for those factors that are mentioned frequently, as these are likely to be more important. Other factors will be things that the supplier cannot influence through relationship management, such as the risk that a key account is taken over. This might be a risk to the relationship and therefore of interest, but is not useful for KAM planning purposes as there is nothing that the key account manager can do to influence the outcome. The KAM team needs to decide whether they will include or exclude such factors.

> The relationship risk scorecard will usually focus on the risks to the relationship that the key account manager can influence. Other risks, such as the risk of takeover, which the supplier cannot influence, may be noted in the plan.

Some risk factors that are identified in Step 1 relate to the customer's perception of value rather than the relationship. Price, not having the right product, delivery problems, etc. are factors that should almost certainly be excluded from the relationship risk analysis. These factors are important, but they form part of the supplier's value proposition and should be dealt with elsewhere.

A list of relationship risk factors used to evaluate relationship risk is shown in Table 6.2.

Table 6.2 Relationship risk factors

Relationship risk factor
1 Customer has relationship with other business units at supplier
2 Customer buys across the product range
3 Long-standing relationship
4 Supplier has relationship with intermediary/influencer
5 Supplier has good relationship with key account
6 Supplier has multiple contacts at customer (depth of relationship)
7 Customer has multiple contacts at supplier (depth of relationship)
8 Supplier understands customer's business
9 Supplier understands customer's industry

At this point, nine relationship risk factors have been identified, but they are not expressed in a way that can be measured. The next step is to assemble a measurable and structured scorecard framework from the risk factors that have been identified.

Step 2: Assemble scorecard framework

To apply the scorecard, the factor measurement needs to be specified. Usually, this involves restating each factor in a way that makes the measurement clear. It is also helpful if the factors are grouped into broader categories. This allows the scorecard framework to be set up (Table 6.3).

Table 6.3 Relationship risk scorecard framework

Relationship risk factor	Score for this key account
Overall relationship with the supplier company	
1 Number of relationships key account has with other business units	
2 Number of products key account buys	
3 Duration of relationship in years	
Relationship with the key account	
4 Quality of our relationship with intermediary/influencer (scale 1–5)	
5 Quality of our relationship with key account (scale 1–5)	
6 Number of contacts at customer	
7 Number of contacts customer has with us	
Understanding of key account	
8 How well we understand customer's business (scale 1–5)	
9 How well we understand customer's industry (scale 1–5)	

Table 6.3 shows a relationship risk scorecard framework in which the relationship risk factors that have been identified are grouped into three broad categories: overall relationship with the supplier company, the specific relationship of this business unit with the key account, and the depth of understanding of the key account that the supplier has. Other categories are also possible; the example here is based on an actual example of a relationship risk scorecard.

Each factor has been restated to make it measurable. As far as possible, the factors should measure actual values. This will help to make the scorecard more objective. For some factors, however, there is no obvious objective measure. This is the case in Table 6.3 with factors 4, 5, 8, and 9. In these cases, a scale of 1–5 is to be used.

One additional aspect to consider is whether any factors are particularly important and whether an importance weighting should be added to the scorecard. If this is the first time that relationship risk is being evaluated, it may be best to leave the factors unweighted. Tracking the scorecard over time should reveal whether certain factors outweigh others.

The final column of the framework is where the key account manager or researcher records the actual values, key account by key account, in Step 3.

> To create a scorecard, factors and measures need to be identified. Remember, "what gets measured, gets managed".

Step 3: Analyze the key account portfolio for risk

Now that the relationship risk scorecard framework has been set up, the next step is to populate it with data for each key account. Where the factors have objective measures, such as the number of products bought or the number of contacts, the information can be gathered from the company's information systems. Where the factor is about the quality of the relationship or some other subjective measure, the key account manager will have to give their opinion. It is strongly advised that this process is made anonymous in some way, as the quality of the information gathered will be better. It is difficult for a key account manager to give himself/herself a low score on understanding either the customer's business or the customer's industry if they have to give the information openly in front of others or to their line manager.

Step 4: Produce completed scorecard

One scorecard framework should be completed for each key account. These are then consolidated to produce a completed scorecard (Table 6.4). The scorecard shows the relationship risk factor and the best and worst scores are recorded in the overall key account portfolio. The data shown in Table 6.4 are based on an actual relationship risk scorecard.

In this case, the completed relationship risk scorecard shows that there are some considerable variations between best and worst cases in the portfolio. Take, for example, factor 2, the number of products the key account buys. In this portfolio, the lowest number of products bought by any key account is 3 and the highest number is 10. It is widely accepted

Table 6.4 Completed relationship risk scorecard

Relationship risk factor	Worst case	Best case	This key account
Overall relationship with the supplier company			
1 Number of relationships key account has with other business units	0	3	0
2 Number of products key account buys	3	10	5
3 Duration of relationship in years	0.5	16	3
Relationship with the key account			
4 Quality of our relationship with intermediary/ influencer (scale 1–5)	1	5	3
5 Quality of our relationship with key account (scale 1–5)	1	5	4
6 Number of contacts at customer	2	8	3
7 Number of contacts customer has with us	3	10	3
Understanding of key account			
8 How well we understand customer's business (scale 1–5)	1	5	1
9 How well we understand customer's industry (scale 1–5)	1	5	1

that the purchase of multiple products from a supplier is associated with customer retention, so 3 products is riskier and represents the worst case in this portfolio. Similarly, factor 6 is the number of contacts that the supplier has at the customer. This ranges between 2 (relatively few, possibly high risk) and 8 (the best case).

The version of the scorecard shown in Table 6.4 also contains individual feedback to the key account manager. The final column shows how the score for one key account compares to the rest of the portfolio. In this case, although the account buys a moderate number of products and there is a reasonable relationship, the key account manager does not seem to know much about the customer or its industry (factors 8 and 9), which could be risky for this relationship.

Step 5: Review overall KAM portfolio risk

Although the relationship risk scorecard shows the best and worst cases for this particular KAM portfolio, there is no guarantee that the best case is the optimal case. Take, for example, factors 1 and 2, the number of relationships with other business units and the number of products purchased. In the relationship risk scorecard, the best cases are 3 and 10. But what if this is a supplier with 25 business units and a broad product range? Even the best case may not be particularly good. By reviewing the overall relationship risk scorecard, the KAM team might consider setting targets for the optimal value that are higher than the current best case.

It is important to note that the current measures on the relationship risk scorecard may not be the best possible outcomes. For example, the optimal number of contacts that a key account has with the supplier may be lower than the current lowest case, or higher than the current best case.

A slightly different issue is the possible risk management decision to be made around factors 6 and 7, the number of contacts at the customer and the number of contacts that the customer has at the company. Here, the best cases are 8 and 10 contacts, respectively. Although having more than one contact is known to reduce the risk of a KAM relationship (the relationship may be under threat if the sole contact on either side moves jobs or retires), it is not clear whether eight contacts at the customer might not be too many. Conversely, a key account who has 10 contacts at the supplier may indicate a lack of control in the relationship. The KAM team wants to review these numbers and considers whether they are appropriate, or whether a smaller number of contacts might result in better management of the relationship.

The KAM team should also use the relationship risk scorecard to identify areas of excessive risk within the key account portfolio. In the case shown, there are minimum scores on factors 4, 5, 8, and 9. These minimum scores do not all relate to the same KAM relationship; in other words, it isn't a question of one single very risky relationship that is skewing the results here. The portfolio scores indicate that there are some problems with relationships and with understanding the customer. However, there are other relationships in which the key account manager has scored a maximum 5 out of 5 on the same factors. It seems that there might be areas of good practice in this team, and there might be ways that the good practice could be passed on to the key account managers who are less good at managing relationships and developing a deep understanding of the customer.

Reviewing the overall KAM portfolio risk may reveal some key account relationships that are highly risky (i.e. they tend to have low scores against most or all of the factors). The presence of very risky key accounts is not surprising, but the KAM team needs a plan to deal with that risk. As well as individual key account risk management strategies to reduce the risk of defection (Step 6), the team might decide that they should spend more time on new customer acquisition, to replace key accounts that are likely to defect. In this way, the relationship risk scorecard can help inform debates about the balance of how key account managers divide their time between customer acquisition and customer retention.

Step 6: Develop individual key account risk management strategies

Many KAM strategies are designed to increase revenues and/or reduce costs. Examples include product upselling (increases revenues) or standardization of packaging or delivery (reduces costs).

Some strategies, however, reduce risk. An example might be developing better customer information or improved planning, or investing in shared processes or electronic data interchange (EDI), or developing new contacts. These strategies involve some investment of time, effort, and money on the part of the supplier, but they do not immediately deliver financial benefits. However, they could reduce the relationship risk of a key account considerably.

When developing strategies, consider the risk-reducing, as well as the revenue-enhancing, aspects.

Other strategies may have the dual benefit of increasing financial returns from a key account relationship and, at the same time, reducing risk. Cross-selling additional products and facilitating the development of relationships between the key account and different supplier business units are both examples of strategies that are likely to increase the financial value of the customer and also reduce the risk of defection.

Step 6 of the relationship risk scorecard is for the key account manager to review the scores for each key account that he/she manages, against the best and worst cases in the supplier's KAM portfolio (and the optimal case, if this differs from the best case), and decide on any risk management strategies that he/she should adopt.

In the example shown in Table 6.4, the scores for one key account are shown in the final column. This key account buys a moderate number of products (factor 2), has a reasonable relationship duration (factor 3), the relationship quality is good (factors 4 and 5), and there are several contacts (factors 6 and 7). However, the key account has no relationships with the other business units of this supplier (factor 1) and the key account manager's understanding of the key account and its industry is poor (factors 8 and 9). The relationship risk scorecard should lead the key account manager to make plans to learn more about the customer and his industry. Better knowledge and a deeper understanding of the key account might enable the key account manager to identify areas of opportunity for other parts of the supplier's business.

■ The impact of risk on the value of the customer

In the previous chapter, we looked at the time value of money and how we need to use a discount rate or a weighted average cost of capital (WACC) to calculate the net present value of a customer.

However, the discount rate or WACC represents the risk of the business unit (discount rate) or company (WACC). The higher the risk, the higher the discount rate or WACC and the lower the net present value.

As key account managers begin to think about the risk of their key accounts and to develop relationship risk scorecards, they quickly become aware that there are considerable differences in risk between different relationships. Using a single, company-wide WACC to calculate the lifetime value of key accounts does not reflect the risk of each individual key account relationship.

> Using a single, company-wide WACC to calculate the lifetime value of key accounts does not reflect the risk of each individual key account relationship.

Since the principle risk in KAM is the risk of defection, of losing the key account, the logical conclusion is that the risk of defection could affect the lifetime value of a key account since, if it is high risk, there is a danger that future profits may not be achieved.

Consider two key accounts, each with a customer lifetime value of £100,000. One has a low risk of defection; the £100,000 is likely to be received. The other has a high risk of defection; in this case, the £100,000 is much less certain. However, looking only at the customer lifetime value would not tell the key account manager that there was any difference between the two. In customer lifetime value terms, both key accounts are worth £100,000. The question is how the higher risk of the first key account, revealed through the relationship risk scorecard analysis, can be reflected in the customer lifetime value.

Three methods of risk adjustment can be considered: a simple "traffic light" risk rating, adjusting the discount rate, and probability weighting the lifetime value.

Risk rating customer lifetime value calculations

A quick and relatively straightforward, although subjective, technique for incorporating risk into the calculation of customer lifetime value is to use a simple "traffic lights" approach. This consists of reviewing each key account against the relationship risk scorecard and setting parameters that describe green (low risk), amber (medium risk), and red (high risk).

For example, we have been considering a relationship risk scorecard containing nine risk factors. Depending on the actual values in the KAM portfolio, the traffic light definitions might be as shown in Table 6.5.

Table 6.5 Defining the traffic lights

Traffic light	Definition	Symbol
Green – low risk	Fewer than three minimum scores against the nine risk factors	◯
Amber – medium risk	Between three and six minimum scores against the nine risk factors	◯
Red – high risk	More than six minimum scores against the nine risk factors	●

The traffic lights would then appear against the customer lifetime value for each key account in the portfolio. Where the traffic light is red, this indicates that the customer lifetime value forecast is less certain because the risk is high. Where it is amber, the forecast is made with moderate certainty. Where the traffic light is green, the customer lifetime value forecast is made with confidence as the relationship risk is low. A key account portfolio consisting of 10 key accounts might be represented as in Table 6.6.

Although the traffic lights system has the advantages of being quick and easy to apply and to understand, the consequences for KAM planning are less clear. In the KAM portfolio shown in Table 6.6, it is clear that customer A must be a priority, with a low-risk customer lifetime value of €2.3 m. But how should the key account manager prioritize and manage the relationships with customers C, D, and E? Is a high-risk relationship

Table 6.6 Customer lifetime value using traffic lights

Customer	Lifetime value	Risk	Cutomer	Lifetime value	Risk
A	€2.3 m	⚪	F	€900 k	⚫
B	€2.1 m	⚫	G	€800 k	⚪
C	€1.8 m	⚫	H	€750 k	⚪
D	€1.5 m	⚪	I	€350 k	⚪
E	€1.2 m	⚪	J	€200 k	⚪

worth €1.8 m a lower or higher priority than a moderate risk relationship worth €1.5 m or a low-risk relationship worth €1.2 m?

Traffic light systems are useful to alert key account managers and key account directors of potential issues in KAM relationships and they are used in KAM plans to indicate relationship quality and financial status of the key account.

However, the appropriate strategies and priorities to adopt in managing a portfolio of key accounts can be unclear where key accounts are close in value but have different risk profiles (consider customers F and G in Table 6.6). For this reason, some key account managers prefer to adjust the customer lifetime value for risk. They adjust the discount rate or probability weight the customer lifetime value. Both methods will now be discussed.

Adjusting the discount rate

One obvious method of reflecting risk in the customer lifetime value calculation is to adjust the discount rate or WACC that is used. So, instead of a single discount rate or WACC that is used to calculate the lifetime value of each key account, higher discount rates would be used to calculate the customer lifetime value of riskier customers and lower discount rates would be used to calculate the customer lifetime value of less risky customers.

Table 6.7 takes the customer lifetime value calculation from the previous chapter and shows what happens to the lifetime value of this key account when the discount rate doubles from 5% to 10%.

The customer lifetime value using a discount rate of 10% is €302, 940, which is 11% less than the customer lifetime value of €341,834 based on a 5% discount rate.

The worked example in Table 6.7 illustrates a drawback with the discount rate adjustment method: even if the discount rate doubles, the impact on the customer lifetime value is relatively slight. The reason for this is that the time horizon over which key account managers can forecast

> The risk of a key account can be incorporated into its lifetime value by adjusting the discount rate used to calculate that customer's lifetime value.

Table 6.7 Customer lifetime value using risk-adjusted discount rates

Relationship lifetime	Year 1 (€)	Year 2 (€)	Year 3 (€)	Year 4 (€)
Year by year profit	80,000	87,000	99,000	123,000
Total notional value				389,000
Discount factor at 5%	0.952	0.907	0.864	0.823
Present value of future profits	76,160	78,909	85,536	101,229
Customer lifetime value				*341,834*
Discount factor at 10%	0.909	0.826	0.751	0.683
Present value of future profits	72,720	71,862	74,349	84,009
Customer lifetime value				*302,940*

customer lifetime value with any degree of confidence is relatively short. If the customer lifetime value horizon was much longer – 10 years or more – the impact on the customer lifetime value of changing the discount rate would be much greater as the time value of money decreases the more distant the time in which it will be earned.

A solution to this difficulty with the adjusted discount rate method would be to make very large changes to the discount rate. In the worked example in Table 6.7, the discount rate changes from 5% to 10%. If it had changed from 5% to 20% or 30%, the impact on customer lifetime value would have been far greater. However, quadrupling the discount rate raises another difficulty, which is how such decisions can be made. Quadrupling the discount rate would suggest that the key account whose lifetime value is to be adjusted is four times riskier than the standard investments that the company makes, which seems implausible.

Because changing the discount rate on a short-term forecast such as those used to calculate customer lifetime value has little impact, and decisions to change the discount rate can seem somewhat arbitrary, an alternative method of adjusting customer lifetime value calculations to take account of risk can be considered. The alternative is to weight the customer lifetime value forecast by the probability that it will be achieved.

Probability-weighted customer lifetime value

An interesting technique for incorporating the relationship risk of a key account into the calculation of that key account's customer lifetime value is to ask the question, "what is the probability that these future profits will be achieved?"

The answer to this question, expressed as a percentage, can be used to weight the stream of future profits that have been forecast as part of the customer lifetime value calculation. This has a considerable impact on the perceived lifetime value of the customer, as demonstrated in Tables 6.8–6.10.

The impact of probability weighting on both revenues and costs must be considered. The first step is to apply a probability weighting to forecast customer revenues.

Probability-weighted customer revenues

This section illustrates the impact that applying a probability weighting can have on perceived customer revenues. The probability weighting shown in Table 6.8 could be estimated outright by the key account manager or the relationship risk scorecard could be used to develop probability weightings. Where the weighting comes from will be discussed later in this chapter. For now, the application of probability weighting to the customer lifetime value calculation will be demonstrated.

> Adjusting the discount rate tends to have relatively little impact on customer lifetime value, unless the lifetime value of the relationship is particularly long. For this reason, considering the probability of future revenues or cash flow may be the preferred method of incorporating the risk of the key account into the lifetime value calculation.

Table 6.8 Probability-weighted customer revenues				
Relationship lifetime	**Year 1 (€)**	**Year 2 (€)**	**Year 3 (€)**	**Year 4 (€)**
Revenues Product A	100,000	120,000	130,000	150,000
Probability	100%	100%	80%	80%
Probability-weighted revenues, Product A	100,000	120,000	104,000	120,000
Product B	50,000	50,000	60,000	70,000
Probability	50%	50%	50%	50%
Probability-weighted revenues, Product B	25,000	25,000	30,000	35,000
Unweighted customer revenues	150,000	170,000	190,000	220,000
Total notional revenues (unweighted)				*730,000*
Probability weighted customer revenues	125,000	145,000	134,000	155,000
Total notional revenues (probability weighted)				*559,000*

Table 6.8 shows that the key account manager has a very high degree of certainty that the key account will buy product A in years 1 and 2, so this is scored 100%. This might, for example, be a 2-year contractual relationship, so the revenues are virtually certain. In years 3 and 4, however, the certainty reduces somewhat, although it is still high at 80%. The key account manager expects to sell €130,000 worth of product A to this key account in year 3, but with 80% certainty, so the risk-adjusted value of those sales is €130,000 × 80%, or €104,000.

The sales of product B are much less certain. In fact, the key account manager estimates that the likelihood of achieving this level of sales is only 50/50 in each of the 4 years for which forecasts are available. So, the revenues for product B are multiplied by 50% in each year to give the probability-weighted revenues for product B.

The impact of probability weighting the revenue forecasts is considerable, far greater than doubling the discount rate. The total notional revenues from the key account (before adjusting for the time value of money) are €730,000, but the probability-weighted revenues are €559,000, a difference of more than 23%.

However, there is another step to go, before the probability-weighted customer lifetime value can be calculated. First, the key account manager needs to consider what might happen to costs.

Probability-weighted customer costs

In the customer lifetime value calculation we looked at in the previous chapter, three types of costs were identified: product costs, costs to serve, and customer-specific overheads (Table 6.9).

Table 6.9 Impact of probability weighting on costs

Relationship lifetime	Year 1 (€)	Year 2 (€)	Year 3 (€)	Year 4 (€)
Product costs	55,000	58,000	61,000	64,000
Probability-weighted costs	50,000	50,000	55,000	55,000
Costs to serve	15,000	20,000	25,000	28,000
Customer-specific overheads	–	5000	5000	5000
Total unweighted customer costs	*70,000*	*83,000*	*91,000*	*97,000*
				341,000
Probability-weighted customer costs	*65,000*	*75,000*	*85,000*	*88,000*
				313,000

In the example shown in Table 6.9, the key account manager considers that product costs may be somewhat lower than forecast, although they will not fall as much as revenues because of the loss of economies of scale. Costs to serve will remain the same, because the key account manager is assuming that there will be just as many visits and customer issues to resolve, even if the key account only buys product A. The expenditure on customer-specific overheads will still be incurred in respect of this key account, because the key account manager expects that his company will still go ahead and invest in customer-specific stock.

As a general rule, costs will not fall as much as revenues because of economies of scale and efficiency effects. The costs of making one sale in a year may be just the same as the costs of making 20 sales. Costs to serve might even go up, if the company decided to increase its efforts to win more business if sales to this key account are disappointing. In this example, there is a reduction in product costs and this translates into a fall in total notional costs from €341,000 to €313,000.

> As a general rule, when adjusting customer lifetime value for risk, costs will not fall as much as revenues because of economies of scale and efficiency effects.

Calculating probability-adjusted customer lifetime value

The effect on customer lifetime value of including a probability weighting can be substantial, as shown in Table 6.10.

Table 6.10 Calculation of probability-weighted customer lifetime value

Relationship lifetime	Year 1 (€)	Year 2 (€)	Year 3 (€)	Year 4 (€)
Unadjusted customer revenues	150,000	170,000	190,000	220,000
Unadjusted customer costs	70,000	83,000	91,000	97,000
Year by year unadjusted profit	80,000	87,000	99,000	123,000
Discount factor*	0.952	0.907	0.864	0.823
Present value of future profits	76,160	78,909	85,536	101,229
Unadjusted customer lifetime value				*341,834*
Probability-weighted customer revenues	125,000	145,000	134,000	155,000
Probability-weighted customer costs	65,000	75,000	85,000	88,000
Year by year probability-weighted profit	60,000	70,000	49,000	67,000
Discount factor*	0.952	0.907	0.864	0.823
Present value of future profits	57,120	63,490	42,336	55,141
Probability-weighted customer lifetime value				*237,127*

* Based on a discount rate of 5%.

In the first part of the table, a summary of the unadjusted customer life-time value is shown. Then, the second part of the table (shaded) summarizes the probability-weighted revenues and costs and shows the probability-weighted profit. Year by year probability-weighted profit is lower than the unadjusted profit, and dips in year 3 when the probability of the revenues from product A falls to 80% from 100%.

It is important to remember that the adjustment being made here is for relationship risk, not for the time value of money. Therefore, the adjusted year by year profits still need to be discounted back to present-day values using the 5% discount rate.

The effect of making some straightforward probability adjustments within reasonable probability parameters is a considerable reduction in customer lifetime value from €341,834 to €237,127, a difference of 31%. Customer lifetime value calculations, even if the forecast lifetime is relatively short, are more responsive to changes in probability than to changes in the discount rate. In addition, getting key account managers to think about the probabilities of their forecasts is an interesting and useful exercise in itself and will certainly spark some spirited debate within the KAM team about the likely probabilities.

Adjusting the customer lifetime value by forecast probability of achieving future profits is an unambiguous method for incorporating the relationship risk of a KAM relationship into the value of the customer. As noted above, the probabilities can be ascribed directly by the key account manager for each key account that he/she manages. However, simply setting a probability could be seen to be subjective. There could also be issues of comparison across key accounts; one key account manager might deem the profits from a low risk account to be 90% certain; another manager might think his/her account was equally certain but ascribes 70%. Even if the KAM team defines a scale of probabilities, saying what constitutes 90% probability, what constitutes 80%, 70%, and so on, differences in interpretation could still arise.

Interpretation problems in assigning probabilities can be avoided by adapting the relationship risk scorecard so that the responses to the scorecard are used to generate the probability. This method will be discussed in the following section.

> If the key account manager assigns probabilities, these could be subjective. The relationship risk scorecard could be used to increase the objectivity of the risk probability.

■ Probability and the relationship risk scorecard

The relationship risk scorecard can be set up to generate the probability weighting that should be applied to each key account. To do this, the KAM team or its advisors need to define what probability of retention is associated with which scores.

To show how this is done, we will return to the completed relationship risk scorecard set out in Table 6.4. This time, using the best and worst cases in the KAM portfolio, probability weightings have been ascribed to various scores (Table 6.11). These probabilities are for illustration purposes, but are based on an actual example.

The probability weighting may not be a simple linear scale, but should, instead, reflect the supplier's previous experience and its views about what influences customer retention, supported by academic research.

Table 6.11 Using the scorecard to identify probabilities

Relationship risk factor	Worst case	Best case	Probability weighting
Overall relationship with the supplier company			
1 Number of relationships key account has with other business units	0	3	1 or fewer = 60% 2 = 80% 3 = 90% >3 = 100%
2 Number of products key account buys	3	10	Fewer than 4 = 60% 5–6 = 80% 7 or more = 100%
3 Duration of relationship in years	0.5	16	1 or less = 30% Between 1 and 3 = 50% 3+ to 5 = 80% More than 5 = 100%
Relationship with the key account			
4 Quality of our relationship with intermediary/influencer (scale 1–5)	1	5	1 = 30%; 2 = 40%; 3 = 50%; 4 = 70%; 5 = 100%
5 Quality of our relationship with key account (scale 1–5)	1	5	1 = 30%; 2 = 40%; 3 = 50%; 4 = 70%; 5 = 100%
6 Number of contacts at customer	2	8	2 or fewer = 30% 3–6 = 80% More than 6 = 90%
7 Number of contacts customer has with us	3	10	2 or fewer = 30% 3–6 = 80% More than 6 = 90%
Understanding of key account			
8 How well we understand customer's business (scale 1–5)	1	5	1 = 30%; 2 = 40%; 3 = 50%; 4 = 70%; 5 = 100%
9 How well we understand customer's industry (scale 1–5)	1	5	1 = 30%; 2 = 40%; 3 = 50%; 4 = 70%; 5 = 100%

Take, for example, the probability weighting for factor 5, quality of relationship with the key account. A simple linear scale would suggest that score 1 = 20%, 2 = 40%, 3 = 60%, and so on. In fact, previous research has shown that customer satisfaction, which is a popular measure of relationship quality, is only loosely linked with customer retention and only when the satisfaction scores are very high. So, in Table 6.11, the probability weighting is skewed towards the top of the scale.

In this example, the company has also used its previous experience and its view of the optimal number of contacts to set the probability scale for factors 6 and 7, the number of contacts the key account manager has with the customer, and the number of contacts the customer has with the supplier. The scaling here reflects a company view that three to six contacts is the optimal number (probability 80%). Having fewer than three contacts is viewed as risky and attracts a profit achievability probability of just 30%. More than six contacts increase the probability slightly, but only by 10%.

> For very large and data-rich organizations with good CRM systems, it should be possible to track the scorecard over time and check that the probabilities reflect the realities of customer retention.

The probability weighting exercise can be done as a workshop in the first instance. It may be useful to involve managers from other areas, such as finance and customer service. For very large and data-rich organizations with good customer relationship management (CRM) systems, it should be possible to track the scorecard over time and check that the probabilities reflect the realities of customer retention.

Assigning a probability using the relationship risk scorecard

Assigning probabilities based on the relationship risk scorecard, rather than on the key account manager's opinion, means that probabilities are assigned based on the key account managers' responses to the questions about their accounts or on factual data gathered from the company's management information or CRM systems. This helps to make the probabilities less subjective and the assignment of the probabilities is consistent across all key accounts in the portfolio.

Another advantage of using the relationship risk scorecard to assign a probability to each key account is that the scorecard can easily be set up on a spreadsheet or KAM system so that the individual key account manager cannot see what the probabilities are. The probability is assigned based on his/her answers, and the key account manager may only see one figure, which is the overall assigned probability at the bottom of Table 6.12.

In the worked example shown in Table 6.12, the answer to factor 1, the number of relationships that the key account has with other business units of this supplier is 0. This comes into the category of "1 or fewer", so the probability is 60%. For factor 2, the response shows that this key account buys five products from the supplier, which puts it into the "5–8" category and it receives a probability of 80%. The two lowest probabilities are shown against factors 8 and 9, where the key account manager's knowledge of the customer's business and industry is only 1 out of 5, scoring 30% in each case.

Table 6.12 Using the scorecard to assign a probability weighting

Relationship risk factor	This key account	Probability weighting	Probability (%)
Overall relationship with the supplier company			
1 Number of relationships key account has with other business units	0	1 or fewer = 60% 2 = 80% 3 = 90% >3 = 100%	60
2 Number of products key account buys	5	Fewer than 4 = 60% 5–6 = 80% 7 or more = 100%	80
3 Duration of relationship in years	3	1 or less = 30% Between 1 and 3 = 50% 3+ to 5 = 80% More than 5 = 100%	50
Relationship with the key account			
4 Quality of our relationship with intermediary/influencer (scale 1–5)	3	1 = 30%; 2 = 40%; 3 = 50%; 4 = 70%; 5 = 100%	50
5 Quality of our relationship with key account (scale 1–5)	4	1 = 30%; 2 = 40%; 3 = 50%; 4 = 70%; 5 = 100%	70
6 Number of contacts at customer	3	2 or fewer = 30% 3–6 = 80% More than 6 = 90%	80
7 Number of contacts customer has with us	3	2 or fewer = 30% 3–6 = 80% More than 6 = 90%	80
Understanding of key account			
8 How well we understand customer's business (scale 1–5)	1	1 = 30%; 2 = 40%; 3 = 50%; 4 = 70%; 5 = 100%	30
9 How well we understand customer's industry (scale 1–5)	1	1 = 30%; 2 = 40%; 3 = 50%; 4 = 70%; 5 = 100%	30
		Assigned probability	58.8

The overall probability that will be assigned to the customer lifetime value of this key account is the average of the nine probabilities, which is 530/9 or 58.8%. Note that this is an unweighted scorecard in which each of the nine factors is treated as equally important. Thus, the assigned probability is a simple average of the nine. If the factors in the scorecard are given different importance weightings, the assigned probability would be based on the weighted average, not the simple average.

If the risk factors in the scorecard are given different importance weightings, the overall assigned probability should be based on the weighted average of each risk factor.

Using the assigned probability from the relationship risk scorecard

The assigned probability generated from the relationship risk scorecard can be used directly in the calculation of risk-adjusted customer lifetime value. Since the scorecard reflects relationship risk, which affects the achievement of customer revenues, the assigned probability is multiplied by the customer revenues in the way described earlier in this chapter.

The relationship risk scorecard generates a single probability based on the current situation and the current relationship with the key account. However, if the KAM plan contains strategies for reducing risk in future years, the scorecard could be rerun using the target data for number of products, number of relationships, etc. This would give a revised probability number that can be used to adjust the revenues of future years.

The probability from the relationship risk scorecard can also be used in conjunction with the "traffic lights" method described above. If a KAM team prefers to work with the traffic lights system to warn them of the risk of their key accounts, they could still use the relationship risk scorecard to calculate probabilities but then display these as a traffic light. So, for example, the traffic lights could be defined as:

Green	=	Low risk	=	Probability	80% and above
Amber	=	Medium risk	=	Probability	60–80%
Red	=	High risk	=	Probability	less than 60%

In the example given in Table 6.12, with an assigned probability of 58.8%, this key account would fall just into the red traffic lightband.

The real value of evaluating the relationship risk of a key account is the role this evaluation plays in the development of key account objectives, strategies, and tactics. Effective management of a key account depends on development of strategies that are appropriate to the value of the key account and its risk. How these strategies are developed is the subject of the next chapter.

CHAPTER 7

Developing key account objectives and strategies

The early stages of key account management (KAM) planning are concerned with analysis and developing a deep understanding of the customer. The later stages are about turning the plan into reality. To do this, the key account manager has to set out objectives and strategies for each key account.

Many KAM plans suffer from confusion between objectives, strategies, and tactics. This confusion can lead to lack of clarity between what the key account manager is trying to achieve with this key account (objectives) and how the account is to be managed, in broad terms (strategies). Or, the broad long-term strategy for dealing with a key account can be obscured by too great an emphasis on the short-term detailed planning (tactics and actions). Tactics and action plans will be dealt with in the following chapter.

In this chapter, we expand on the explanation of objectives, strategies, and tactics given in Chapter 4. Based on the analysis in earlier chapters, and using the extended Ansoff Matrix as a tool, key account managers are shown how to prepare specific objectives for their key account. Then, for each objective, strategies are set out. Finally, we demonstrate how to record key account objectives and strategies in the KAM plan.

■ Fast track

- Key account objectives set out the key account manager's specific targets for a key account. They should be measurable and time-based.
- Strategies say how, in broad terms, the objectives are to be achieved. For KAM plans, they are about the 7Ps (product, price, promotion, place, people, processes and perception of customer service/physical evidence).
- For every objective, there should be at least one strategy. Otherwise, the objective is unlikely to be realized.
- Objectives for the key account should ultimately be linked to the objectives of the firm, through a hierarchy of objectives.

■ Introduction

The real test of a key account plan is whether it delivers actionable strategies which are based on clear and well-formulated objectives. Only if the KAM plan has clear objectives, strategies, and tactics it is likely to deliver real results. At this vital point in the planning process, the key account manager is considering outcomes rather than inputs.

There are two main problems that typically arise in KAM plans at this point. The first is that the objectives and strategies are missing completely, and the plan leaps directly from analysis to tactics. The reason for this might be that the organization's mindset is inappropriately short term (after all, a key account relationship is a long-term investment); or the key account manager himself/herself may be too used to thinking in terms of the next transaction, rather than planning for longer-term success. Failing to think through and then document the key account strategies in the

> The real test of a key account plan is whether it delivers actionable strategies which are based on clear and well-formulated objectives.

KAM plan can mean that the key account manager misses some vital change in the key account's business circumstances, or fails to spot an important opportunity, because the focus is all on "business as usual" and doing more of the same thing.

A second problem that is found in KAM plans is that the analysis of the customer is done well and in detail, but that this somehow fails to inform the objectives and strategies. It is as though a gulf has opened up between the first half and the second half of the plan, between analysis and outcomes. Sometimes this comes about because the key account manager is not used to thinking strategically, or does not have the tools to do so.

This chapter sets out an integrated process for developing key account objectives and strategies. By following the guidelines in this chapter, a key account manager should be able to produce a consistent and thorough strategic key account plan.

■ The difference between objectives, strategies, and tactics

Often, problems with the strategy and implementation stages of KAM planning come about because a key account manager gets confused between objectives, strategies, and tactics. Therefore, we begin by setting out some clear definitions and indicate which tools should be used for developing each (Table 7.1). The tools that are used to develop objectives and strategies will be explained later in this chapter. Guidelines for implementing KAM plans through the development of tactics and action plans will be given in the next chapter.

Table 7.1 Objectives, strategies, and tactics

Planning activity	Definition and guidelines	Tools used to develop
Objectives	Say what is to be achieved. Must be measurable and time-based, as progress will be measured against these.	Extended Ansoff Matrix; Hierarchy of Objectives
Strategies	Say how, in broad terms, the objectives are to be achieved.	7 Ps
Tactics	Say how, in detail, each of the strategies will be achieved. Answer questions relating to who, what, when. Short term. Best if these are measurable and time-based.	Implementation plan

Objectives should be thought of as setting out some specific targets that the key account manager wants to achieve with or from that key account. Key account objectives are largely concerned with the products that the key account manager wants to sell and the divisions or departments of the customer that are to be sold to. They will therefore often be concerned with revenues, customer lifetime value, share of wallet, and relationship benefits. This explains why it is impossible to set effective objectives without having a good understanding of the value of the customer.

Strategies say how, in broad terms, each objective will be achieved. Thus, each objective must be linked to a strategy. A common mistake is to be too specific; strategies are the headlines setting out how the objectives are to be attained, not the detail. It should be possible to state a strategy in a few words or a brief description. The strategy should *not* discuss who will do what and when, as this is tactical. The purpose of keeping the strategy broad is to encourage the key account manager to think about the longer term without diving down into too much detail too soon.

> Objectives define the specific, measurable targets for the key account. Strategies say how, in broad terms, these targets are to be reached. Tactics set out how each strategy is to be implemented.

Tactics say how each strategy will be achieved. Therefore, there must be at least one tactic for each strategy, and often there will be several tactics per strategy. Tactics answer the questions "who will do what, when, how, how much, how long will it take…". A useful rule of thumb is to think of tactics as being small-scale objectives, each with its own measure and time frame. Tactics will be short term (i.e. usually within a year); they will have someone's name against them for delivery; and they may have some indication of resources required. Tactics, and how to draw up their accompanying action plans, are discussed in the following chapter.

■ How to develop key account objectives

Objectives setting is an important function of the key account manager. Key account managers sometimes use the mnemonic "SMART" (specific, measurable, achievable, relevant, and time-based) to help them to set effective objectives. The main thing that a key account manager needs to remember, however, is the "M" and the "T" of SMART. M is measurable, and T is time-based. So, a quick check for any key account objective that the key account manager sets is:

> "SMART" objectives are: Specific, Measurable, Achievable, Relevant, and Time-based.

- "What is the measure of progress/success?"
- "By when should this objective be achieved?"

An example might be a key account manager selling burger buns to a fast food retailer. There are several competing suppliers of burger buns and this supplier is currently number 2 with the key account for which the plan is being developed. The key account manager's goal is for her company to become the number 1 supplier of burger buns to this key account. To state this as an objective, she would need to think about success measurement – how would the supplier know when they had achieved it? One measure of success would be their share of customer spend on burger buns. Another might be whether the key account manager can persuade the key account to buy across the product range. So, the objectives in this key account manager's KAM plan might be:

1 To increase our share of customer spend on existing plain white burger buns from 25% to 35% by end of year 3; and
2 To get one order each for new low fat and high fibre burger bun products from existing customer divisions by end of year 2.

However, to become the number 1 supplier of burger buns to an international or global company, the supplier might have to do much more. So, additional objectives might be set:

3 To achieve €100,000 sales of white buns to German division by end of year 2;
4 To obtain first order for high fibre bun from Canadian division by end of planning period; and
5 To implement just in time (JIT) delivery of white buns across all US customer delivery depots by end of year 3.

Key account objectives are broadly based on the Ansoff Matrix (explained below), but can also be about efficiency improvements (process improvements or cost savings).

Objective number 5 is a slightly different kind of objective which recognizes that, in order to obtain lead supplier status, the supplier often has to carry out some process improvements. Process changes may be demanded by the key account, so that the supplier is in line with the way it likes to do business; some key accounts will help their suppliers with process improvements, sharing their knowledge and expertise and even, occasionally, sharing the cost.

Setting objectives using the extended Ansoff Matrix

A useful tool for helping key account managers to think through the specific marketing objectives that they will set for each key account is the extended Ansoff Matrix. The original Ansoff Matrix is named after Igor Ansoff, the respected corporate strategist. It examines the alternatives open to a company in terms of products (existing and new) and markets (existing and new). The original matrix had four boxes:

1 Existing products into existing markets (market penetration).
2 New products into new markets (new product development).
3 Existing products into new markets (market extension).
4 New products into new markets (diversification).

We have adapted the Ansoff Matrix for KAM planning so that it is *customer* markets that are considered, and extended it so that process and systems change is incorporated in the fifth box, labelled "Efficiency improvements" (Figure 7.1).

Selling more of a supplier's existing product into the customer business units with which the supplier already has a relationship is customer penetration (top left box in the extended Ansoff Matrix). This is a core objective

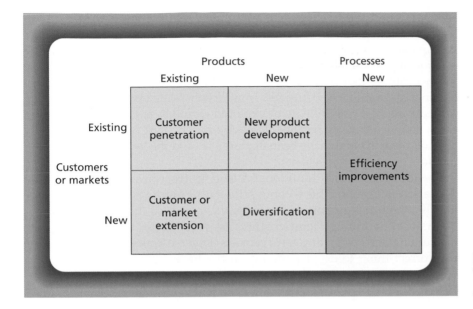

Figure 7.1
The extended
Ansoff Matrix.

in most KAM relationships, and it is usually a low-risk objective. The measure of success in customer penetration could be share of spend, which is an important metric used to measure the strength of a KAM relationship. Another measure of success could be volume sales on specific product lines.

Once the key account manager has set customer penetration objectives, the next area for consideration is new product development (upper middle box). It is important to remember that new product development does not necessarily imply groundbreaking innovation and new-to-the-world products. The vast majority of new product development involves minor modifications to existing products to tailor them in some way. Minor new product development would also include changes to packaging that a customer might need. Note here that, in a relationship-oriented situation such as KAM, the key account manager is well advised to consider new product development (usually, some form of product or packaging modification) *before* customer or market extension. In other words, where there is a strong existing KAM relationship, it is well worth considering whether any additional business can be won from an existing key account by modifying existing products, before the key account manager sets out to develop links with other parts of this key account or to acquire new customers.

The third area that the key account manager should consider when setting key account objectives is customer or market extension (bottom left box). This box is about customer acquisition, so it is likely to be a more time-consuming and risky option than customer penetration or new product development. Where the key account manager is tasked to acquire new business, there are some general guidelines that can be useful and which help to reduce the time, effort, and risk of the customer or market extension option. As with products, so with customers and markets: there are different degrees

Share of spend is an important metric used to measure the strength of a KAM relationship.

> If new business is required, the key account manager should start by developing relationships with other divisions or business units of existing key accounts, where possible using introductions from the existing relationship.

of newness. If new business is required, the key account manager should start by developing relationships with other divisions or business units of existing key accounts, where possible using introductions from the existing relationship. These other business units may be international regions of the key account, or they may be different product divisions. If there are no possibilities of obtaining new business from closely related parts of the same key account, the next possibility to be explored would be to chase business from firms known to the key account, if possible based on recommendation. Only after all these avenues have been explored should the key account manager aim for completely new clients.

The fourth box of the traditional Ansoff Matrix (lower middle in Figure 7.1) is diversification. This is about selling new products to new customers, and is a high-risk option. Companies try to reduce the risk by attaining diversification through joint ventures or acquisitions, but these are time consuming and costly long-term projects. Diversification can, of course, be the correct thing to do, depending on the business circumstances, but a wise key account manager will explore the less risky options first.

Connecting with less risk

An American company developed a substantial market position in the manufacture of high-specification, high-quality fireproof connectors which it sold internationally for use in the aviation and defence industries. Its traditional industries were under pressure and there were no options for customer penetration. Instead, the manufacturer adopted a high-risk strategy of diversification into consumer electronics. The move was unsuccessful: the company did not have the capability to manufacture the standard, fit-for-purpose connectors used in washing machines and televisions in the kind of volumes and at the low prices that its new customers required.

Following a change of management, the company returned to its traditional customers and sought new applications for existing and slightly modified products, picking up business in marine and submarine divisions of some of its key accounts. Soon, one key account asked the supplier whether it could develop connectors suitable for use in telecommunications. Today, the supplier offers an extensive range of connectors and has a strong presence in the telecommunications industry.

The extended version of the Ansoff Matrix has a fifth box, efficiency improvements. This box has been added to the Ansoff Matrix to reflect the importance of processes in the successful development of key account relationships. Process development can apply to existing and to new key accounts. The main areas of efficiency improvement that the key account manager should consider for inclusion in his/her KAM plan are cost reduction and process improvement.

Cost reduction is an important element in delivering successful KAM. Many supplier companies lose sight of the cost reduction imperative and are mortified to discover that, despite their introduction of KAM, customers still want annual price decreases! Relationship building with key customers will not completely insulate a supplier from the pressure to reduce costs. No key account will knowingly continue a relationship with a supplier simply for the sake of the relationship, if it can get an absolutely identical product and service elsewhere. What a KAM relationship does offer is a number of opportunities to achieve cost reductions. For example, international product (and sometimes price) harmonization reduces the cost of complexity. Closer relationships should make forecasting easier and reduce the risk of unpleasant surprises. Working together, suppliers and key accounts can reduce stock holdings at both parties, again reducing costs. As trust develops, the need for costly checking and inspection reduces. High prices and high stock holdings are devices that companies use to protect themselves against the risk of unforeseen events. One of the benefits of a KAM relationship is the reduction in this particular kind of risk, although it might need a conscious effort of corporate will (and some intensive discussions with the key account) to persuade both parties to change the way they work.

> Cost reduction is an important element in delivering successful KAM.

Process improvement is an interesting area for key account managers to explore. In particular, there can be opportunities to improve processes jointly with the key account. The major motor manufacturers, such as Toyota, famously train their suppliers to operate more efficiently. Some of the large insurance providers in the UK are developing links between their IT systems and those of the insurance brokers. These initiatives can help both sides to operate more efficiently, but are likely to involve some investment on the part of the supplier and possibly the key account as well.

> Process improvement initiatives can help both sides to operate more efficiently, but are likely to involve some investment on the part of the supplier and possibly the key account as well.

Another area of improvement that suppliers are increasingly exploring with their key accounts is involvement in the new product development process. Testing new products or services on key accounts has long been a feature of innovation in industries such as software (where it is known as beta testing) so that the bugs can be removed before the product goes on general release. Increasingly, however, key accounts are getting involved in the early stages of new product development so that they are able to influence the concept design. This gives the key account a much greater say in the look, feel, and functionality of the final product. The later the key account is involved in the new product development process, the less they can influence the final outcome. Earlier involvement in new product development can be a powerful assistance to the supplier. Figure 2.11 in Chapter 2 showed that an estimated 75% of total eventual manufacturing costs are determined by the very early concept and design stages. Getting it right early on can reduce both the chances of failure and the costs of redesign. However, the supplier needs to be careful that the new product does not become so tailored to one customer's individual needs that it is effectively unsellable elsewhere.

Some key account managers take the issue of collaborative new product development and introduction very seriously and plan carefully for it. One company identifies not just the key accounts, but the individuals within the key accounts, who it would like to work with on new product development:

Innovation in medical gases

There is considerable product development in the production of medical gases for purposes such as anaesthesia. Manufacturers are looking to increase the speed and effectiveness of the anaesthetic whilst reducing some of the side effects, which can range from nausea to more serious problems with breathing. A European provider of medical gases is a leader in this field. The secret of its success is, at least in part, the way that it tests and disseminates its new products.

The manufacturer has identified a number of leading teaching hospitals as its key accounts. However, persuading them to switch over to new products can be a slow business. Many surgeons, anaesthetists, and registrars prefer to continue using older products whose effects they understand thoroughly.

To enable the faster adoption of its new products, the medical gases provider has identified four key accounts (all of them teaching hospitals) which are willing to adopt new products. Not only that but, based on careful research by the key account managers, the supplier has identified some influential doctors and consultant anaesthetists within the four teaching hospitals who are early adopters. Now, when a new gas product is launched, these key individuals are approached. They have been selected based not just on their willingness to switch to a new product (although that is very important); they have also been selected for their status within the health industry and how influential they are amongst their colleagues.

Connecting objectives to strategies: the hierarchy of objectives

Senior managers sometimes describe running a big business as being like sailing a supertanker. Like the captain on the bridge, they give orders for a change of direction to the engine room, but it takes a very long time indeed before the supertanker changes direction. Sadly, in all too many cases, the supertanker – in this case, the supplier organization – does not change direction at all.

The hierarchy of objectives is a tool for ensuring that decisions taken higher up the organization are actually implemented by the people lower down. It is a useful tool for the key account manager for two reasons:

> The objectives in each key account plan should tie in to the overall objectives of the KAM team, which should in turn help deliver the organizational objectives.

1 It acts as a check that the objectives in the KAM plan are in line with the overall corporate objectives;
2 It helps connect objectives to strategies, improving the implementability of the key account plan.

The way that the hierarchy of objectives works is shown in Figure 7.2.

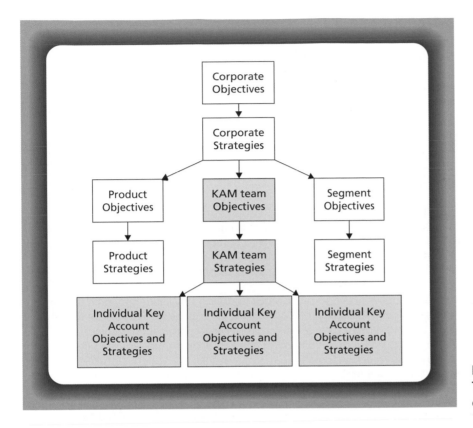

Figure 7.2
The hierarchy of objectives.

The corporate objectives and strategies, set by the main Board of the business, affect the decisions that are made about products, key accounts, and other customer segments. When agreeing their own objectives and strategies, the KAM team should be mindful of how their objectives and strategies will help deliver the corporate objectives and strategies. Similarly, the key account manager should be setting key account objectives and strategies that help deliver the overall KAM objectives for the organization. If this hierarchy of objectives is in place, the plan is considerably more likely to be delivered successfully.

The hierarchy of objectives also reminds key account managers that, when it comes to developing key account strategies, successful KAM is closely connected to other parts of the business such as the firm's product strategies. How key account strategies are developed will now be considered.

■ Developing key account strategies using the 7 Ps

Marketing objectives are attained through marketing strategies which, in a relationship-minded world such as that inhabited by the key account manager, is linked to the 7 Ps.

The 7 Ps are: product, price, promotion and place, people, processes, and perception of customer service/physical evidence.

The 7 Ps are an extension to the classic concept of the 4 Ps. The 4 Ps were product, price, promotion, and place. Increasingly, however, the drivers that key accounts look for in their partnership suppliers go beyond the 4 Ps and relate also to people, processes, and perception of customer service/physical evidence (Table 7.2).

Table 7.2 The 7 Ps of key account strategy

	Strategy	Definition in KAM context
1	Product	Product attributes, specification, and quality; product modification; new product development; product deletion; packaging.
2	Price	Overall pricing strategy, price levels and competitive pricing; discount and rebate strategy; relationship pricing.
3	Promotion	Branding, brand image, and values; advertising; promotions (trade and consumer); point-of-sale support.
4	Place	Availability; delivery and logistics; stock handling (VMI, category management, etc.); geographical scope of KAM agreement; provision of special delivery services (e.g. emergency delivery, temperature-controlled delivery).
5	People	Relationships; skills and credibility of the key account manager; ability to resolve issues; access to other parts of supplier as needed; cultural fit.
6	Processes	Ease of use of supplier's services, from order taking to delivery and complaint resolution; efficiency; transparency; harmonization; continuous improvement.
7	Perception of customer service	Physical evidence – paperwork accuracy and appearance; appearance of supplier facilities, offices, branches, factory, etc.; appearance of people and vehicles; usability of documentation, manuals, website, etc.; responsiveness to queries; general demeanour.

The 7 Ps can be considered as a checklist. The key account manager would not be expected to do something about everything on the checklist in Table 7.2, but he/she should use it to develop this vital element in the KAM plan. Each of the 7 Ps will now be considered in a KAM context.

Product strategies

Product strategies can relate to existing or new products. A key account product strategy could be about when a customer is to be offered a customized or a new product, or about how the key account manager will get a product modified. Product strategies may also set out how customers are to be transitioned from one product to another, an important issue in an ongoing key account relationship.

Product strategies for a key account may include new product introduction, product deletion, product modification, and packaging.

Product strategies in a KAM plan may also cover research or product trials. If the key account has requested special packaging or palletization, this would form part of the product strategy. The key account manager must discuss this part of the plan with the relevant product managers before committing the supplier to potentially expensive new product development.

Pricing strategies

Pricing strategies in a KAM plan usually set out any customer-specific deals or pricing structures, if relevant. Alternatively, the key account manager may set a commitment to reduce price, or to continue to price competitively (specifying who this is to be measured against).

Recent research has found that suppliers to key accounts try hard to implement value-based pricing (i.e. pricing based on the value to the customer of the product). Sometimes, this eagerness to deliver value for the customer leads the supplier to develop "value-added" elements that customers didn't want and refused to pay for. This could result in a customer being thought of, wrongly, as driven mainly or entirely by price.

Suppliers who do manage to implement value-based pricing do so using different approaches. Five approaches to value-based pricing are shown in Table 7.3, ranging from traditional premium fixed price to shared profits.

	Basis	Description	Perceived advantages	Perceived disadvantages
Table 7.3 Five approaches to value-based pricing in KAM				
1	Traditional premium fixed price.	Customer accepts premium pricing arguments. May include adjustments (e.g. for fluctuations) in raw materials costs.	Very profitable if achievable.	Increasingly difficult to sustain. May be seen as exploitative by customer.
2	Bundled solution pricing.	Standard product or service offering wrapped with value-added services and sold as a complete solution.	Value-added services often high margin even if underlying product is not. Cost opacity.	Customers increasingly exert pressure to unbundle.
3	Confirmed price reductions.	Annual reductions in supplier prices, either as a percentage or as a target price.	Very visible benefits to customer.	Supplier expected to make cost savings themselves.
4	Shared cost savings.	Supplier and customer working together to reduce costs. The savings are then shared.	Benefits of collaboration with supplier very visible to customer.	Can result in one-off savings but then new lower cost base becomes the norm; progressively more difficult to obtain benefits.
5	Shared profits.	Supplier invests in major project alongside the customer and shares the profits. Most common for larger, under-funded projects and in the public sector.	Benefits to both parties can be considerable.	Longer term and higher risk; also requires investment by both parties.

Source: Adapted from Woodburn et al. (2004).

Traditional premium pricing, although highly profitable for the supplier, is increasingly under pressure from customers. Bundled solution pricing is also under pressure because of its perceived opacity. Bundled prices is where the customer is sold a package of goods or services for a package price. Individual elements are not priced separately. Price bundling is done to encourage customers to take a complete package.

Customers can't always understand price bundling and may suspect that they are being overcharged. They prefer the third option in Table 7.3, confirmed price reductions, usually annual. The confirmed price reductions may even be set by the customer.

However, there are greater benefits to both parties if shared cost reductions or, even better, shared profits pricing can be implemented. Shared cost reductions are where both parties work to reduce costs in the supply chain. Examples might be to reduce stock levels or the frequency of checking (in a KAM relationship, duplication of goods out and goods in checking may be reduced). The benefits of these cost savings may be shared between the parties.

> The benefits to both parties are greater with shared cost reductions or, still better, shared profits pricing.

The shared profit route offers substantial rewards but does also require considerable commitment on both sides. This is where both sides invest in a joint project and then share the profits. Research has suggested that the profits in these collaborative projects are often shared more-or-less equally between both sides, even where the power imbalance is considerable. The shared profits route is particularly appealing in an interdependent or integrated KAM relationship, where there is already a high degree of trust and collaboration between the parties.

Promotion strategies

> Promotion strategies for a key account should be discussed with the marketing department, to ensure that the firm's other marketing activities do not undermine its key account relationships, and vice-versa.

Promotion strategies for a key account should be discussed with the marketing department, as promotion initiatives that are specific to a key account may clash with other promotion activities that the supplier is undertaking. This cuts both ways, as the following example shows. The key account manager can also learn what the marketing department is planning and ensure that it does not conflict with his/her KAM plans:

Red faces in financial services

When your company supplies financial services products direct to the public and also through intermediaries, as many suppliers do, it is important to let the left hand know what the right hand is doing. We are concealing the identities of all parties here, as this is such a humdinger.

A UK financial services provider had a strong key account relationship with a major high street retailer. Both are household names in the UK, and both are highly respected in their fields. The relationship went along happily for some months, managed by the financial services provider's new KAM team.

Meanwhile, a directive went out from above that the financial services company should look to develop its direct business, as this was more profitable and a growth area.

So, the marketing department designed a hard-hitting poster campaign that named the retailer and pointed out that consumers could buy financial services products cheaper by buying them direct. The posters were put up in bus shelters and underground stations in Central London, especially in locations close to the retailer's major outlets.

Not surprisingly, the supplier's relationship with the key account was badly damaged by this faux pas, and the key account manager had to take a lot of flak. Major learning point: integrated marketing communications and a broader view of how the company's promotion strategy could affect its KAM relationships are essential if a key account manager is to convince the customer that her firm is interested in partnership.

Place strategies

Place strategies can be powerful in delivering value in a KAM relationship. Place is about distribution and availability, so logistics are important here. There are considerable value-adding services that suppliers can offer to their key accounts, ranging from special delivery services through vendor managed inventory (VMI) or category management, where the supplier manages stock for the customer or even manages the entire category. Where the supplier agrees a Category Management deal with the customer, it is in a powerful position. Category Managers manage the goods and services of other suppliers on behalf of the key account. They may even manage the shelf space assigned to competing products. Probably the best option for both parties, however, is a CPFR relationship (Collaborative Planning, Forecasting, and Replenishment). In this system, the customer shares point-of-sales data with the supplier and both sides work together to improve sales forecasting and thereby optimize production scheduling and stock levels. A CPFR system should also give the supplier much longer warning of special promotions by the customer that might affect demand, and should also enable the supplier to discuss honestly and openly with the customer how to increase supply chain efficiencies and reduce costs.

"Place" in KAM can also be concerned with the geographical scope of the KAM agreement, and can add considerable value, especially if used in conjunction with other strategies such as product or price. For example, value can be added by the supplier by the provision of consistent products and/or services across geographical regions or through price harmonization. Key account managers are often wary of offering price harmonization because they perceive that this means a single price worldwide and will therefore lead to the supplier having to provide goods and

> There are considerable value-adding logistics and delivery services that suppliers can offer to their key accounts, including VMI or category management.

services at the lowest prevailing international price. In fact, suppliers who are good at price harmonization look at their cost base in all the countries in which they supply and create price bands according to cost base rather than geographical region. So, Bolivia could be in the same price band as Bulgaria, even though the two countries are geographically unrelated. Suppliers who do this preempt the demand for global pricing by offering their customers, not a single price world-wide, but a small number of price bands based on costs. Surprisingly, suppliers who operate these systems can find that the benefits of harmonization (mainly the benefits of reduced complexity) more than compensate for the lower prices they have to charge in some countries as a result of the harmonization. In other words, harmonization can be good for suppliers as well as for customers.

People strategies

People strategies are about the way in which the supplier manages the relationship. This can be about the KAM team, the individual key account manager, and the other people in the supplier team who might interface with the customer, such as administrators, operations people, and even company directors. The critical people issue is how to match the right key account manager to the right account, and having the correct skills. This is such an important set of topics that it deserves a full discussion and will be dealt with in a later chapter.

For the purposes of completing a KAM plan, the key account manager will want to consider the relationships between the supplier and the customer. Two useful and linked tools that key account managers use to analyse the relationship between the customer and the supplier are the decision-making unit (DMU) and contact mapping. Although this was discussed in Chapter 3, it is so important that this topic is expanded on here.

In business-to-business situations, decision-making is a longer and more complex process than in consumer markets and, crucially, involves more people. The DMU concept evolved to describe the different roles that are involved in making industrial purchasing decisions. For KAM planning purposes, the important thing is for the key account manager to recognize the existence of different roles in the decision-making process. There are six main roles: influencers and policy makers, specifiers, buyers, decision-makers, users, and gatekeepers. One person could have more than one role in the decision-making process (e.g. the buyer could also be the decision-maker) and each role could involve more than one person (there is likely to be more than one user). The importance of the DMU concept for key account managers is that:

● The key account manager must identify who is playing each DMU role at the customer. Doing this ensures that the key account manager has contact with all the important forces in the decision-making process. Neglecting this step could mean that the key account manager misses an important influence on the final purchase decision.
● The selling message to each role of the DMU should be tailored to address their specific concerns (Table 7.4).

Table 7.4 DMU members and their concerns

DMU role	Description	Main concerns/message
Influencers and policy makers	Influence overall policy. May include non-executive directors. Could be people outside the firm, such as journalists, professional advisors, consultants.	Status of the firm, and financial results.
Specifiers	Set out the technical specification that the supplier has to meet. This could be product quality or functionality, but could also cover service standards, supplier accreditation, etc. May even specify a particular product or supplier company.	Latest technology, something new and differentiated. Novelty and innovation appeals to specifiers.
Buyers	Tasked with getting the best possible deal. Often measured by amount of discount obtained. *Note*: some procurement managers are moving towards a strategic partnership view.	Price, and especially discounts and concessions. If interested in strategic procurement, may prefer to hear about total cost of ownership.
Decision-makers	Can be main board directors or senior managers. Consequently, are interested in personal as well as corporate status. Many directors move jobs every 2–3 years.	Financial results; prestige; innovation (but only if it carries a prestige angle). Will also be interested in what their competition is doing and how the key account manager's offer can give them an edge.
Users	Usually lower in the hierarchy than the preceding roles, there may be many of them and their opinions will carry weight. Interested in usability.	Does it function like the previous product? What are the additional benefits to them that will outweigh the hassle of having to learn how to use a new product? Will they get training?
Gatekeepers	The people who control access to the people the key account manager really wants to talk to! Secretaries, assistants, etc. Have "negative power" (the power to prevent things happening). Can be a useful source of information about the progress of the bid and about competitors. Can also have influence with the decision-makers.	Treat with respect. Gatekeepers often take a lot of flak and can respond well to a polite approach. They will gain kudos from finding solutions that will reduce the pressure on their boss.

Once the DMU members have been identified, the key account manager can move forward to contact mapping. In conjunction with the kind of detailed analyses from Figure 3.14 in Chapter 3, where the key account manager has worked out the kind of information required at which stage in the buying process, contact mapping can be very powerful. Contact mapping identifies the various contacts that the key account manager has with the customer, their importance in the decision-making process, and their attitude to the supplier. Combining contact mapping with the DMU analysis may reveal contacts that are important in the decision-making process, but where the supplier relationship is not good. Important decision-makers who have a poor relationship with the supplier are a clear threat to the key account manager making a sale. Contact mapping may also indicate that the key account manager is spending too much time with people who are of lower importance; it is a useful tool for ensuring that the key account manager spends time as productively as possible.

Contact mapping can be done using the customer's organization chart, or can be shown pictorially (Figure 7.3).

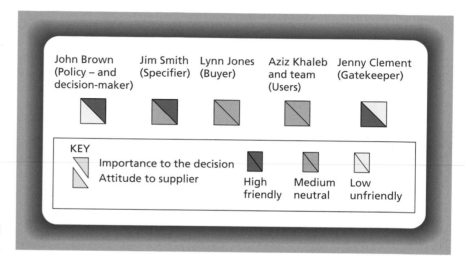

Figure 7.3
Contact mapping.

The contact mapping shown in Figure 7.3 reveals a relationship in which the main contacts at the customer are neutral or unfriendly to the supplier. There is a particular issue with the policy- and decision-maker, John Brown, who is important to the decision but is unfriendly towards the key account manager's company. The only strong supporter of this supplier is the gatekeeper, Jenny Clement, who has the lowest power. This analysis suggests that the key account manager needs to spend more time convincing the more important people in the decision-making process of the value of his company's offering.

Another version of a contact map is shown as Table 7.5.

Table 7.5 shows a fuller picture of contact from both sides. The members of the customer's DMU are shown, as before, on the horizontal axis. Members of the KAM team are shown on the vertical axis. Again, the scores indicate that the relationship with the policy- and decision-maker is weak, and this should be a particular concern for the key account director (KAD) and key account manager. However, the detailed analysis also shows that the relationship between the customer's specifier and the technical and operations people is good. This is useful information: the

Table 7.5 Detailed contact map

Customer contacts:	John Brown (Policy- and decision-maker)	Jim Smith (Specifier)	Lynn Jones (Buyer)	Aziz Khaleb and team (Users)	Jenny Clement (Gatekeeper)
Our KAM team					
Russell James (KAD)	1	1	3	3	2
Ann Lynton (KAM)	1	2	5	5	4
Sue Daley (Operations)	1	5	N/A	4	N/A
Dave Dee (Technical)	1	5	1	1	1

Warmth of relationship: 1 = very cool; 2 = cool; 3 = neutral; 4 = warm; 5 = very warm.

summary version of the contact map shown in Figure 7.3 suggests that the relationship with the specifier is only moderate but, in fact, it is very good with the people that the specifier needs to have contact with.

As this discussion shows, there are various formats that a key account manager can use for contact mapping in his/her key account plan. The important issue is to make sure that there is some form of contact plan in the KAM plan that addresses the main members of the DMU.

Process strategies

The process strategies that a supplier deploys are an important element in the smooth running of a KAM relationship. Research at Cranfield School of Management shows that key account managers spend up to 70% of their time based in their own businesses, rather than with customers, and much of what they spend their time doing is sorting out process issues that are getting in the way of the relationship.

No matter how good the personal relationships, and how likeable the supplier's people, a KAM relationship cannot be sustained if the supplier's processes are poor or are misaligned with those of the customer. Customers almost always monitor the performance of their suppliers using hard measures, which monitor factors such as percentage of deliveries that are on time, percentage order fill rate, overruns, etc. Even when the relationship moves to interdependent KAM, customers will still measure the hard performance factors (or expect the suppliers to monitor their own performance and report the results to them). By this stage, however, "soft" factors such as relationship quality, cultural alignment, values, responsiveness, and satisfaction will also form part of the customer's performance measurement of the supplier.

One frequent mistake that suppliers make is failing to take the hard performance factors seriously enough. Key account managers tend to respond quickly to adverse comments on key account surveys, but sometimes fail to recognize that the customer's grumbles can be the outward

Process strategies are an important element in KAM. Research shows that key account managers spend up to 70% of their time-based in their own businesses, often sorting out process issues that are getting in the way of the relationship.

The main process issues that key account managers encounter relate to ease of use and responsiveness.

manifestation of some deeper disappointment with service. A slow decline in hard factors like OTIF (On Time, In Full) delivery performance, can be overlooked by the key account manager simply because it is a gradual deterioration, or because it falls within the parameters of acceptable performance from the supplier's point of view. The customer, however, will notice and will eventually react, possibly migrating new business away from the supplier. "Acceptable" performance is unlikely to be good enough for a key account; these are customers that expect, and can get, preferential service levels from other suppliers.

The main process issues that key account managers may encounter relate to ease of use and responsiveness. Ease of use here relates, not to the physical product, but to the relationship with the supplier. Is the key account manager easy to contact, for example? Some suppliers use a single individual as the point of contact, usually the key account manager; others give their key accounts the direct line numbers of every member of the KAM team.

Ease of use also covers issues relating to who knows about the key account's business if the key account manager is not in the office. A key account has been told that it is important to the supplier and will expect to be treated as a priority customer by all the supplier's employees, not just by their own account manager. The supplier should have internal processes that indicate the status of the key account and enable everyone to track problems or resolve queries about orders, start dates, deliveries, previous purchases, etc. This requires the supplier to have a good knowledge management system that will carry this information. In addition, some companies use sales force automation or IT-based KAM systems to support their KAM relationships. One aspect of process management that is becoming more common is for key customers and suppliers to share process information, perhaps hosted on the supplier company's Extranet. The information shared in this way may include order placing and order tracking, but can also include contact information and even a shared strategic plan.

Responsiveness issues are about how flexible or rigid the supplier's processes are; a customer that has been told it is a key account will not take kindly to being told that "we can't do that" or "our systems won't accept that". Some suppliers resolve issues like these by creating specific written customer service policies that set out the service standards that are delivered to a key account as opposed to a major or standard account.

As well as the processes that support the management of key relationships, the key account manager should also be aware of the impact that the underlying operational processes can have on the KAM relationship. Key processes that can support KAM include online procurement, production or operational processes, automated warehousing, online invoicing, and open-book accounting. If there are persistent problems with key account orders, draw up a flowchart of each stage of the life of an order, following the order through from receipt of the order to final delivery and invoicing. This simple but powerful exercise can reveal areas of process weakness, particularly where an order passes from one department to another. Asking questions such as "what prompts this part of the process to happen" or "how is that initiated" can reveal some risk areas in the supplier's operational processes. This is illustrated by the tale of Arthur's diary:

Arthur's diary: a critical process weakness

Construction products are big-ticket items, and one of the biggest (in both senses of the word) is metal roofing and cladding. Metal roofing and cladding consists of very long lengths of steel, copper, or aluminium which are formed into corrugated strips and then have to be delivered to the building site. Roofing strips for large public buildings such as airports or power stations can be particularly tricky to handle as they can reach 30 m in length.

In fact, the difficulty of manufacturing the metal roofing strips is dwarfed by the logistical problems of delivering a 30 m load over long distances. Special pallets have to be made to support the strips; a specialist vehicle must be hired, that has a steerable bogie at the rear, because these abnormal loads cannot be taken round a normal traffic island with a front-steering lorry cab only; police forces have to be alerted to the passage of the load, which may require a police escort or road closures; and drivers need special training.

The logistical complexities mean that the transport arrangements have to begin before the strip is manufactured; often, indeed, before the order is finally confirmed. If the order falls through, all the logistics arrangements have to be unwound, or the manufacturer faces penalty payments.

How was all of this complexity managed? For one metal roofing manufacturer, it was Arthur's diary. Arthur was the logistics manager; an interview with Arthur during a process analysis project revealed that every scrap of logistics information was kept in his pocket diary. There was no back-up, and Arthur had no deputy. So, if Arthur had lost his diary or left the firm, there would have been chaos.

So far, the system had worked perfectly well. The roofing manufacturer had never missed a delivery. So why change things? In fact, a process analysis of the roofing company by an independent consultant revealed that Arthur's diary was the critical process weakness for this supplier, since successful completion of the most important customer orders depended crucially on it. Had anything gone wrong, the supplier's relationship with its key customers would have been irrevocably damaged. The consultant also commented that the company was frankly lucky not to have been the subject of any quality audits by a major customer to date as this process weakness could have cost them substantial orders if customers became aware that their vital order might easily be substantially delayed, delaying the construction project and making the customers liable for swingeing penalty payments.

Perception of customer service

Perception of customer service is an interesting strategic issue for key account managers. It relates to what is called the "physical evidence" of the product or service provided. As well as the absolute service levels, this may include the way that a product or service is presented. As such, it includes the appearance of the product or service, the vehicle or office in which it is delivered, the way the suppliers' people present themselves both in person and over the phone, and the accuracy, timeliness, and neatness of the paperwork.

Perception is particularly critical where there is no physical product. If the product is intangible, the customer will draw conclusions about its quality from the way that the supplier presents itself and its people. Some good examples of perception management and physical evidence can be found amongst the logistics service providers, who paint their containers and lorries in distinctive colours and set dress codes for their drivers and delivery personnel. These aspects of physical evidence positively influence the impressions that customers form about how good the firm is. Another example is GKN Chep, a global pallet pooling business. Chep pallets are blue, which readily distinguishes them from standard plain wood pallets, even in a mixed lorry load. The blue colour sends a strong and easily recognized message about the product.

Physical evidence can encompass many different strategic options, so this is not an exhaustive discussion, but some of the key issues that may appear in the KAM plan are briefly discussed below.

Paperwork, documentation, manuals, and website

Paperwork needs to be clear, well presented, and should follow a definite corporate style. Some companies have communications managers whose tasks include enforcing the corporate style. If the organization is big enough to have its own post room, the post room manager will be able to advise on whether the documentation passing through the post room is of good quality. Remember: the worst signal a company can send a customer is to get their name or title wrong ("you are a key account, but we don't even know who you are").

Other documentation will include important documents such as delivery notes, invoices, credit notes, and statements. Like general paperwork, these need to be clearly presented and accurate. Until a few years ago, procurement managers would summarize their measurement of delivery

Increasingly, customers measure supplier delivery performance in terms of OTIFNIE (On Time, In Full, No Invoice Errors).

quality as OTIF. Now, most would say delivery quality is measured in terms of OTIFNIE (On Time, In Full, *No Invoice Errors*). Quality perceptions will also be affected by the way the key account has asked to receive the paperwork. If the customer asks for the delivery note *with* the delivery, it is not satisfactory to send it separately through the post, even if that is the supplier's standard practice.

Manuals and websites share a common requirement, which is for navigability. A customer turns to a manual or to a website for one reason: to answer a question. Much effort and money has been wasted on designing feature-filled websites that take several minutes to download and then follow some internal logic of their own. The customer does not necessarily know what your internal jargon is! A good index is a very useful feature of a manual.

How to find things in an index …

We think this story is apocryphal, but it illustrates some of the puzzling ways that suppliers index products in their manuals.

The customer buys a car and, several months later, needs to change an indicator bulb. He can't see how to do this and so looks in the manual. First, he looks under I for Indicators; nothing. Then he checks out B for Bulb; still nothing. He even tries C for Change, but no joy. Finally, in sheer desperation, he reads the entire index from A onwards. At last he finds what he is looking for – under H, for How to change a light bulb!!

Websites, importantly, should be consistent with the corporate brand. Recent research has shown that inconsistency between the brand image of the website and the other promotional materials that the company issues is damaging to overall quality perceptions.

> Websites should be consistent with the corporate brand.

Supplier facilities, people, and vehicles

In addition to the impression created by documentation and websites, customers also make assumptions about the quality of the organization and its service based on the facilities they see, the way that people are dressed and present themselves, and the vehicles they drive.

Facilities include offices, branches, or retail premises, concessions, kiosks, and manufacturing or distribution units. If the facilities don't match the brand promise, don't let the customer visit them. Sure, the supplier will save money if the customer collects: but, if the facilities look run down and dirty, the customer will go away wondering about the quality of what they have been supplied.

Much KAM business takes place face to face with the client, so visual impressions are important. Some companies have dress policies to reflect their brand image; bankers don't usually come to appointments wearing

> Much KAM business takes place face to face with the client, so visual impressions are important.

shorts and Hawaiian shirts, for example. Similarly, telephone-based account managers usually reflect the corporate style. However, the style the supplier chooses to adopt should also reflect the customers' values: Coutts, the "rich people's" bank has dedicated teams and a website that reflects the needs and values of the customers, not the traditional banking style. Coutts adapts its style to address its different types of customer, from landowners to entrepreneurs, from family businesses to sports or rock stars (www.coutts.com).

Making physical evidence work for you: the case of Eddie Stobart

Eddie Stobart is the UK's largest independent haulage and distribution company. Astonishingly, it also has a 30,000 member fanclub. A link to the fanclub can be found on the company's main website: www.eddiestobart.co.uk.

The secret of the Eddie Stobart craze is in physical evidence. All Eddie Stobart drivers wear shirts and ties, challenging the traditional view of truck drivers as slobs in T-shirts. Most important, each Eddie Stobart truck has an individual girl's name painted across the front of the cab. This idiosyncratic feature started the spotting craze, where members of the fan club compete to "spot" as many different names as they can, rather like trainspotters. The fan club website hosts the "spotter's league", so participants can measure their performance against thousands of other Club members. There is a range of Eddie Stobart merchandise and clothing and even a juniors section with games and a fun truck character called Steady Eddie.

Once the key account manager has worked through the 7 Ps and considered possible strategies, the next step is to record these strategies against the objectives, ensuring that each objective is linked to a strategy.

■ Recording objectives and strategies in the KAM plan

The basic rule for successful KAM planning is that every objective should be connected to a strategy. However, it is not a simple one-to-one connection, as an objective could require more than one strategy and a strategy could deliver more than one objective. That said, there must be *at least one strategy* connected with every objective. If there is no strategy, the objective will not be delivered (or, if it is delivered, it will be by accident rather than design).

Earlier in this chapter, we considered five objectives for the key account manager selling burger buns to a major retailer. The strategies linked to each objective might look like those in Table 7.6.

Every objective should be connected to at least one strategy.

Table 7.6 Strategies linked to objectives

Objective	Strategies
1 To increase our share of customer spend on existing plain white burger bun from 25% to 35% by end of year 3	**1a.** *Price: quantity discounts* **1b.** Place: improve availability
2 To get one order each for new low fat and high fibre burger bun products from existing customer divisions by end of year 2	**2a.** *Promotion: sell health benefits*
3 To achieve €100,000 sales of white buns to German division by end of year 2	**3a.** Product: provide samples to product managers in Germany **3b.** Product: repackage in German-style packaging **3c.** *Price: quantity discounts*
4 To obtain first order for high fibre bun from Canadian division by end of planning period	**4a.** *Promotion: sell health benefits*
5 To implement JIT delivery of white buns across all US customer delivery depots by end of year 3	**5a.** Process: roll out JIT project nationwide

Some of the strategies are shown in *italics*; these are strategies that help the supplier to deliver more than one objective. If time or budgets are limited, these strategies should be considered as priorities. Of course, in a real plan, these strategies would be spelled out in more detail, as indicated in the appropriate sections in the KAM templates in Chapter13.

Only at this point, when all the serious strategic thinking has been done, should the key account manager turn his attention to tactics and short-term planning. This is the topic of the next chapter.

Reference

Woodburn, D., Holt, S. and McDonald, M. (2004). *Key customer profitability: Making money in strategic customer partnerships*. Report by the Cranfield Key Account Management Best Practice Club, Cranfield, January 2004.

CHAPTER 8

Tactics and action plans

The resource allocation and implementation phase of the planning process is very important in ensuring the success of the plan. Because they understand its importance, key account planners are sometimes too tempted to start with the short-term plan and then try to extrapolate to the strategic plan. *This is very dangerous and should be avoided at all costs.* In the longer term, it is vital to ensure that the key account manager has time to do the strategic thinking about the relationship, and that key steps such as the key account mission statement, goals, analysis, and SWOT (strengths, weaknesses, opportunities, and threats) are clear. If the strategic thinking and analysis are rushed or poorly developed, the relationship could be heading in the wrong direction.

Strategy is about doing the right things (effectiveness). Tactics are about doing things right (efficiency). If the strategy is bad, having a great tactical plan will actually make the damage worse. If the approach to the customer is inappropriate, the very worst thing you can do is to be efficient in making the customer the wrong offer!

So, if you have turned straight to this chapter and haven't yet worked through the first half of the book, we would strongly urge you to go back and put in the hard work of customer analysis and strategy development, before you read any further.

However, if you have completed your strategic thinking and are ready to implement your plan, please read on. In this chapter, tactics and action plans are developed using a straightforward template and some simple but important rules. Then, implementation problems are addressed using a force field analysis.

■ Fast track

- In most key account management relationships, the planning horizon will be 3–5 years, so the action plan will be for 1 year. Industry or individual circumstances may mean that this period is shorter or longer, but a 1-year action plan is typical.
- A common error is to have a 3–5 year strategic horizon, but only to create a 6-month action plan, or to develop a 1-year action plan in which all the actions are crammed into the first few months.
- A tactic is a task that has to be completed, in order for a strategy to be delivered. A second common error is to do the action planning at too low a level; a meeting is not a tactic.
- Every strategy must have at least one tactic attached to it; more usually, there will be a number of tactics for each strategy.
- Actions are the individual elements (the atoms) that make up each tactic. Actions can be grouped into their relevant tactics.
- Action plans may form a separate document from the strategic key account plan.
- Useful tools for action planning include: Gantt charts, colour coding to show progress, and Force Field analysis to identify barriers to and drivers for change.

■ Introduction

Implementation is the graveyard of strategy

Tactics set out what must happen for each strategy to be implemented. A tactic is a task or a group of actions that is attributed to a specific individual or team, is time based, and (as far as possible) is measurable. Thus, tactics are more detailed than strategies and they incorporate information about responsibilities and resources, which strategies do not. Objectives say what the supplier aims to achieve with the key account. Strategies say how (in broad terms) the objectives will be achieved, using the 7 Ps. Tactics say what will happen in detail – who will do what, by when, how long it will take, and how much time and/or money it will cost.

> If it is to be implemented, every strategy must have at least one tactic attached to it.

Every strategy identified by the key account manager must have at least one tactic attached to it, or it is unlikely to be carried out. Some strategies will have several related tactics. Tactics tend to be shorter term than strategies. In format, tactics have something in common with objectives, as they can be measurable and should have a time basis which indicates approximately when they are to be carried out.

The action plan breaks down each tactic into its component actions and presents these in the form of a Gantt chart. The action plan is the ultimate level of detail, as it sets out what individuals and teams should be doing over the next 12 months.

> The action plan enables the key account manager to see who is doing what, and when.

The advantage of an action plan is that it enables the key account manager to see who is committed to doing what, and when, and, of course, how much it will all cost. Presenting the information as a structured action plan will sometimes reveal problems: timetabling clashes, people who have had more than 100% of their time allocated, etc. The action plan also allows the key account manager to measure progress towards the completion of his/her strategies.

Plan implementation – tactics and action plans – is a project management task, and key account managers often find themselves acting as project managers for self-defined projects that have as their outcome a series of relationship objectives. With this in mind, key account managers can use the tools of project management and change management to achieve their objectives. Key account managers managing global accounts and large teams may even use project management software to help them keep track of the progress of the relationship and contract delivery.

Linking objectives, strategies, and tactics

1 Define a concise set of objectives for each key account, based on the extended Ansoff Matrix.
2 For each objective, identify one or more strategies that will deliver it.

3 Note any strategies that deliver more than one objective and prioritize these.
4 For each strategy, define one or more tactics. Each tactic should indicate who, when, and how much.
5 For each tactic, define the specific set of actions.
6 Develop the action plan and test for achievability: Will it cost too much? Have the named people or teams got the resources and time to carry out their tasks?

■ How to develop tactics

Each strategy *must* have at least one tactic associated with it. Otherwise, it will not translate into actions and will not be achieved. The secret of developing tactics is to look carefully at each strategy and ask, "What are the key tasks that will have to happen, for this strategy to be delivered?" In other words, if you had to brief somebody else to carry out a strategy, what would the key tasks be?

> Tactics answer the question, "What are the key tasks that will have to happen, for this strategy to be delivered?"

Sometimes it is difficult to see where the boundary lies between strategies, tactics, and actions. The key differences are the following:

● If it is about one of the 7 Ps, it is a strategy.
● If there is someone's name against it, it is a tactic.
● If it is about when things will happen within a short future period, it is a tactic.
● If it relates to something specific that the key account manager needs to ask another person or department to do, it is a tactic.
● If it is about resource, it is a tactic.
● If it cannot be broken down further into constituent parts, it is an action.
● If it relates to a specific event, it is an action.

In the previous chapter, five objectives were set by the key account manager for selling burger buns to a key account. This resulted in six strategies, two of which deliver more than one objective (Table 7.6). Table 8.1 shows how the key account manager defines a series of tactics based on each strategy. The format used in Table 8.1 is typical of that in a KAM plan, as it enables the key account director to review the main strategies and tactics without getting bogged down in the detail of action plans. The key account objectives have been already set out earlier in the KAM plan, but are included here for completeness. The objectives are identified here simply as O1 to O5 (see Table 8.1 for the full set of objectives). Linking the objectives, strategies, and tactics in the way shown in Table 8.1 enables the key account director to check that the KAM plan deals with each of the defined objectives.

Table 8.1 Summary of strategies and tactics for KAM plan

Objective	Strategies	Tactics	Who	When	Resource*
1 To increase our share of customer spend on existing plain white burger bun from 25% to 35% by end of year 3	**1a** *Price: quantity discounts*	Agree policy with KAD	KAM/KAD	February pricing meeting	L
	1b *Place: improve availability*	Update pricing manual	KAD	Late February	L
		24-hour delivery service	Logistics	By June	M
2 To get one order each for new low fat and high fibre burger bun products from existing customer divisions by end of year 2	**2a** *Promotion: sell health benefits*	Redesign presentation	KAM	February–March	L
		Meet customer's product managers for healthy eating products	KAM	Second half of year	L
3 To achieve €100,000 sales of white buns to German division by end of year 2	**3a** Product: provide samples to product managers in Germany	Develop relationship with German product managers	KAM	July trade fair	L
		Targeted samples	Tim in Marketing	November–December	L
	3b Product: repackage in German-style packaging	Design new packaging	Agency	April–May?	M
		Packaging approval	KAD/Board	July?	L
		Order packaging	Procurement	Autumn	M
		Publicity	PR/Marketing	Q4	M
	3c *Price: quantity discounts*	*As above*			
4 To obtain first order for high fibre bun from Canadian division by end of planning period	**4a** *Promotion: sell health benefits*	*As above*			
5 To implement JIT delivery of white buns across all US customer delivery depots by end of year 3	**5a** Process: roll out JIT project nationwide	Seek main Board approval	KAD/Board	July?	L
		Work with third-party logistics provider	KAD/KAM	September	M
		Work with operations and warehousing	KAD/KAM	September–October	H

Strategies in *italics* help to deliver more than one objective, so should normally be prioritized.
* Low, medium, or high resource requirements. This could be measured in terms of money or time.

As Table 8.1 illustrates, all five objectives are addressed, and each of six strategies has at least one tactic associated with it. Each tactic is assigned to an individual such as the key account manager (KAM) or key account director (KAD), or to a department or group such as Logistics or Procurement. Provisional timings are shown in the next-to-last column and some indication of resource requirements in the final column. This KAM plan requires a moderate to high commitment from both the key account manager and the key account director, which might be an issue if the key account director is also responsible for a number of other key account managers.

How to develop an action plan

Action plans, as we have seen, are about what the key account manager or team is going to do, and when they are going to do it, over the next 12 months. So, an action plan is a timetable for the achievement of a KAM plan. The action plan is a vital document for the key account manager as it tells him/her what he/she should be doing month by month if the objectives defined in the plan are going to be delivered. The key account manager should be referring to his/her action plan on a regular basis; this is an action document and should be treated as such. It is not the same as a strategic plan, which may only need updating once a year.

> An action plan is a timetable for the achievement of a KAM plan.

The action plan may be included in the KAM plan or, more often, can be a separate document. There are several reasons why the action plan may not be included in the KAM plan:

> The action plan may be a separate document from the strategic key account plan.

1   The action plan contains a great deal of detail. The action plan for a key account plan should detail a set of actions for every strategy.
2   The action plan is specific to the key account manager (or to the KAM team), so it has little relevance to senior managers who may read the key account plan.
3   The action plan may well be revised several times during the year.
4   Some key account managers and KAM teams find it helpful to develop action plans as spreadsheets or in other electronic formats, so that they can be shared by email or over an organization's intranet.

Breaking down tactics into component actions

The first step in defining an action plan is to review each strategy and its associated tactics and break down each tactic into its component actions. Each action is a task that is to be performed by a single individual or by a team or department. This section shows how the set of actions can be teased out of each tactic. It is useful if the key account manager records the strategy to which the tactics and actions relate.

One of the objectives defined for the burger bun supplier (O3) was to achieve €100,000 sales of white burger buns to the German division of the key account by the end of year 2. The key account manager identified a product strategy to deliver this objective, which was to repackage in "German style" packaging (Table 8.1).

Closer consideration of Table 8.1 makes it clear that the repackaging of the product should precede other strategies such as the provision of samples to Germany and price discounts. However, this supplier has a strong brand identity so the new packaging may take some time to produce. So, the key account manager assumes that the repackaging must take place by the end of year 1, so that the objective O3 can be achieved by the end of year 2.

Table 8.2 shows how tactics can be broken down into detailed actions that then form the basis for action planning. In Table 8.1, the key account manager had identified four tactics to deliver the product strategy of repackaging in "German-style" packaging. These tactics are reproduced in column A. Some of the tactics are sets of tasks that involve different individuals and departments, so these tactics have been broken down into their constituent actions (column B). Who will carry out each task is noted (column C), naming individuals where possible. Now that the actions have been defined in detail, it is possible for the key account manager to add when each action should be carried out (column D) and some indication of resource cost in terms of time cost and financial cost (columns E and F).

> Wherever possible, an individual's name (rather than a team or a department) should be shown against each action. This will increase the likelihood that someone will take responsibility for that action.

Some of the main points to note in Table 8.2 are that, where possible, an individual's name is shown as part of the tactic (column C). If a team or department is shown, it can be unclear whose responsibility it is to carry the action out. Some suggested timing is shown in column D; clearly, some events overlap. Time requirements are shown in column E; this allows the key account manager to ensure that he/she has not overloaded themselves or others and that the action plan is achievable. Finally, some indication of cost is shown (column F), even if this is only high, medium, or low cost. If most or all of the actions are shown as high financial cost, the key account manager would have to reassess the effectiveness and achievability of the strategy.

From actions to action plan

Some key account managers find it useful to present their tactics in the form of an action plan (Figure 8.1), perhaps on a spreadsheet.

The action plan shown in Figure 8.1 is in a Gantt chart format which uses shaded blocks for ongoing activities and crosses for one-off events or milestones such as meetings. The benefit of the Gantt chart format is that it allows the key account manager to see whether he/she has timetabled too many actions in one period. Sometimes, 12-month action plans turn out to have all their actions taking place in the first 6 months and then nothing for the second half of the year. In this case, the first three important actions have to be carried out by three different departments (KAM, Marketing, and Legal) in January or February. If the time allocation for these actions is unreasonable and one of these three actions is delayed, the timing of the whole action plan may be under threat.

Table 8.2 Breaking tactics down into actions

Product strategy: Repackage in German style packaging

A Tactic	B Actions	C Who	D When	E Time cost	F Financial cost* (H/M/L)
Design new packaging	Gather information internally about German packaging of other products	Key account manager	January–February	1 day	M
	Check market research on Germany	Marketing department	January–February	3–4 days	M
	Check legal guidelines for German packaging	Legal department	January	0.5 day	M
	Brief design agency	Tim from Marketing department	By end of March	0.5 day	L
	Review proposed designs	Tim/Head of Marketing/KAM team	End May	1 day	M
	Liaise with product manager	Key account manager	Early June	0.25 day	L
Packaging approval	Propose new packaging to Board	Key account director	July board meeting	0.5 day	L
Order packaging	Place pilot packaging orders	Keith from procurement	September	–	M
	Obtain sample for approval	Keith from procurement/ key account manager	September	0.25 day	L
	Full-scale packaging orders	Keith from procurement	September	–	H
Publicity	PR on launch	Sue from Corporate Communications	October–December	6 days	H

* H = High; M = Medium; L = Low.

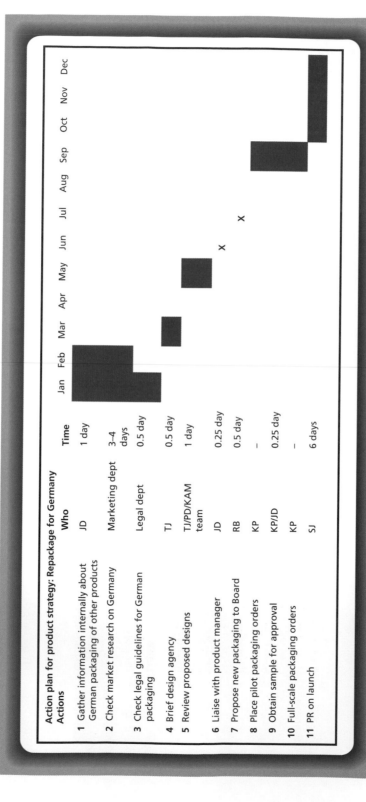

Figure 8.1
Action plan.

> **Tip: Planning with spreadsheets**
>
> To create an easy-to-read version of the tactics and action plan on a spreadsheet, group the actions under each tactic. Highlight the actions to be grouped and then select Group from the Data menu. Click on the minus sign in the left margin to conceal the actions; click on the plus sign to reveal them.

Colour coding can be used to indicate actions that are not yet begun (black), in progress (amber), late (red), and complete (green). Colour coding gives a visual sense of how the action plan is progressing.

For more complex relationships, some key account managers use project management software. This allows for further detail in planning and enables the key account manager to identify critical paths or dependencies. These are actions that must be completed in order for the next actions to take place (such as market research that must be completed in time to prepare an agency brief, or product samples that must arrive in time for a vital planning meeting). Project management software also calculates how much of a particular resource is needed, so it helps to overcome the problem of over-allocating the time of a particular individual or team.

■ Overcoming barriers to implementation

Sometimes, key account managers find that they have carried out a thorough planning exercise and developed specific objectives based on a deep understanding of the customer. This has led to clear strategies, defined tactics, and a feasible and affordable action plan. Yet, despite all this effort, they are struggling to implement the changes that they want. At this point it becomes clear to the key account manager that the issue is with the organization, not with the plan or the planning process.

There are many reasons why the implementation of plans is difficult. Some of them are listed below.

> **Barriers to implementing KAM plans**
>
> *Organization structure*: The company is organized into product or geographical silos, not around customers; or key account managers are not released from their line jobs in order to focus on their key accounts.
>
> *Hostile corporate culture*: The company does not fully believe in the benefits of planning; or there is competition rather than collaboration between different departments; or people are not rewarded for being customer focused.

Skill issues: The key account manager may not feel confident about his/her planning skills.

Status issues: The company may not recognize the importance of KAM, so the key account manager has no powers to implement.

Information issues: Key information may be missing, which reduces the key account manager's confidence in the plan and also reduces its credibility elsewhere in the organization.

Resource issues: The key account manager does not have enough time to plan. This can be linked to hostile corporate culture, as it suggests that the organization does not recognize the importance of planning as part of the KAM role.

Multiple formats: Various people are producing plans in multiple different and inconsistent formats. This makes the plans hard to read for senior managers, hard to consolidate into the corporate plan which supports high-level decisions, and causes confusion because of problems such as inconsistent terminology.

Fear: To put simply, most people do not like change, and implementing a KAM plan may require them to work differently. Fear of the unknown is a powerful barrier to change.

Many good plans remain unimplemented because the planner does not understand how to analyse and overcome the barriers to implementation. However, there is a simple but powerful tool that can help highlight problem areas and suggest ways that the barriers to implementation can be overcome. This tool is the Force Field analysis.

Analysing situations using a Force Field analysis

A force field analysis can be a useful brainstorming tool.

Force Field analysis, originally proposed by the American social psychologist Kurt Lewin, analyses situations in terms of drivers for change and barriers to change. This is an exercise that can be done either by the key account manager working alone, or as a brainstorming exercise by the KAM team.

Table 8.3 shows the result of a typical KAM brainstorming exercise, listing the barriers to implementation and the drivers for implementation and categorizing each force as strong, moderate, or weak.

From the list of barriers and drivers, the key account manager can create a force field analysis. The situation being analysed is represented by a horizontal line across the middle of the force field analysis. The barriers are shown in the upper half of the force field and the drivers are shown in the lower half.

Table 8.3 Barriers and drivers for the KAM plan

Barriers	Strength	Drivers	Strength*
No time to plan	W	Customer demanding KAM	S
MD is sceptical of benefits of KAM	S	KAD now appointed	M
Lack of information about key accounts	S	Competitors are already offering KAM to this customer	S
Key account managers measured on time out of office	W	Good relationships with key account	W
Lack of planning skills	M	Will to implement at key account manager level	M
		Process issues can be resolved through KAM	M
		Opportunity for collaborative innovation project	W

* S = Strong; M = Moderate; W = Weak.

Both barriers and drivers exert pressure (force) on the current situation. Each force is represented by an arrow. Strong barriers or drivers are strong forces and have long arrows. Moderate barriers or drivers exert moderate force and have medium length arrows. Weaker forces are represented by short arrows.

The force field analysis for the list of barriers and drivers in Table 8.3 is shown in Figure 8.2.

In this case, the force field analysis suggests that the plan is likely to be implemented, as the drivers look at least as powerful as the barriers. However, the path to implementation will be smoothed if the key account manager can reduce two key barriers: his lack of understanding of the key account and his Managing Director's scepticism about KAM. Change could be brought about more readily in this organization if the key account manager could persuade the MD of the benefits of KAM and improve his understanding of the key account. The key account manager should also aim to improve his/her planning skills.

Clearly, the forces that are of most interest to the key account manager are those drivers and barriers that he/she can influence. Sometimes, a force field analysis will reveal forces that the manager cannot influence. However, this is still valuable information because it may be possible to "go around" some of the obstacles that are revealed by the force field analysis.

As a result of drawing up a force field analysis, this key account manager might choose to add some actions to his/her action plan. The actions might address one or both of the following questions (Table 8.4):

1 How to overcome the barriers?
2 How to strengthen the drivers?

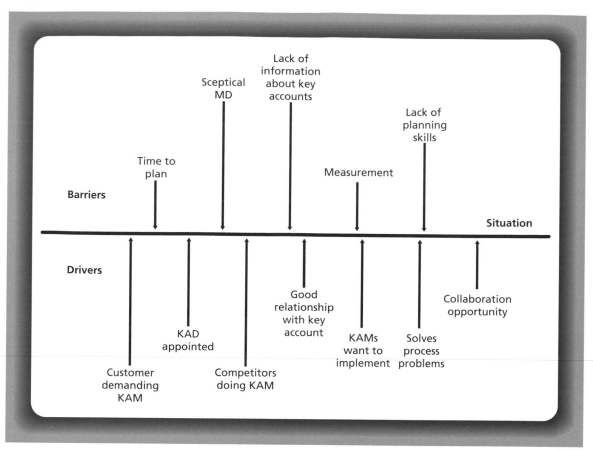

Figure 8.2
Force field analysis.

Table 8.4 Additional actions from force field analysis			
Issue	**Action**	**Who**	**When**
"Sell" KAM internally to MD	Presentation on benefits of KAM, including case studies of success	KAD	March
Information about key account	Research key account and its industry	KAM	January–March

Developing clear objectives and strategies, and then linking these to tactics and action plans, make plan implementation straightforward. Careful action planning also enables the key account manager to monitor progress towards the achievement of the key account goals.

However, key account managers are also project managers. In fact, key account managers typically spend most of their time in their own companies, sorting out problems and issues on behalf of the customer so that the relationship runs smoothly. Force field analysis can help in changing situations where there are barriers to the implementation of a KAM plan. The force field analysis will not only help the key account manager to identify what the barriers are; it will also help him to see what the drivers for change are, which may, in turn, suggest ways that the drivers could be used to help overcome the barriers.

This brings us to some of the supplier organizational factors that affect the success of KAM, such as KAM teams, structures and processes for KAM, and motivation and reward of key account managers. These factors are vital in enabling an organization to deliver world-class KAM, which is the subject of our next section.

Key account managers are also project managers.

Delivering World-Class KAM

In the previous chapters, we have laid the foundations for excellence in key account management (KAM) planning. These are: setting clearly defined key account goals; carefully selecting and analysing key accounts; understanding the profitability and managing the risks of key accounts; developing key account objectives and strategies; and action planning for implementation.

In this second section of the book, we turn to some of the organizational and strategic issues that suppliers need to address, if they are to deliver world-class KAM. Some of these may be outside your role as a key account manager. However, they are issues that effective key account managers need to be aware of. More importantly, they are issues that key account managers should bring to the attention of their directors. In addition to its importance for the KAM performance of the organization overall, reading this section of the book will help you increase your understanding of your role, and the reasons that delivering KAM successfully may be harder than you think.

To deliver world-class KAM, suppliers have to have the following: structures and processes for delivering world-class KAM: measurement of the effectiveness of KAM plans; understanding of how customers categorize suppliers and what they expect from them; and, finally, the knowledge, skills, and attitudes that key account managers need to be world-class planners.

CHAPTER 9

Organizing for KAM

One of the fundamental requirements for world-class key account management (KAM) is that the supplier organization is committed to KAM. This means that the organizational structure, systems and processes needed to support the key account manager exist. It also entails that key account managers are measured and rewarded appropriately.

Too many organizations pay lip service to KAM. They think that all they have to do to introduce KAM is simply to get some new business cards printed for the sales force that say "key account manager", and perhaps send them on a training course or two. If that is the sum total of the commitment that the organization makes to KAM, it is doomed to failure; and yet it is how some suppliers behave. Even worse, if customers have been told they are getting KAM, and all they get is the same service and the same face with a different title, they will understandably be disappointed.

Suppliers need to understand that KAM is not just something that is done by the key account manager; it is a management system for the entire organization. The key account manager can no more deliver KAM on his/her own than deliver the products and the profit alone. There have to be organization structures, systems and processes to support KAM.

> KAM is a management system for the entire organization.

In this chapter, we discuss three of the most important organizational elements of KAM: the structure and management of KAM teams; the systems and processes that support KAM; and the measurement, motivation and reward of key account managers.

■ Fast track

- World-class KAM demands the commitment of the organization, not just the key account manager.
- Three crucial organizational issues that suppliers need to get right for world-class KAM are: the structure and management of KAM teams; the systems and processes that support KAM; and the measurement, motivation and reward of key account managers.
- About 50% of key account managers now work in KAM teams, and the proportion is growing.
- KAM is supported by specific processes such as IT-based planning, e-business, extension of existing CRM (customer relationship management) systems, systems that support customization of products and services, and sometimes the development of tailored KAM systems.
- Two technological developments are of particular relevance to key account managers: Extranets, through which suppliers can share information and planning with a single customer; and exchanges, through which relationships with many key accounts can be managed.
- There are two dominant trends in e-business: standardization and collaboration. Standardization offers advantages in terms of lower unit costs and longer runs, as well as simplicity, but it is unlikely to result in sole supplier relationships. Collaboration pays off for both sides, but requires initial investment.

- The measurement and reward of key account managers is an important issue. A higher proportion of basic salary is appropriate for key account managers who manage long-term relationships where there will have to be a considerable investment of time before results can be seen. A higher proportion of commission or other variable pay is more appropriate where the key account relationship is more tactical.

■ The KAM team

Almost half of all key account managers work in KAM teams, and the proportion is increasing. Team working ranges from the informal, where the team is hardly recognized as such, through the ad hoc team that is put together for a specific issue, to a formalized team. Many of these teams are cross-functional. Team working adds additional complexity to the KAM role. Its increasing prevalence means that key account managers need to understand how KAM teams function, how they are composed, and what they do. This will enable the key account manager to assemble, and run, a successful KAM team.

Scope and structure of KAM teams

> KAM teams are particularly prevalent where a company is managing a relationship with a global client.

KAM teams are more prevalent where a company is managing a relationship with a global client. Fifty per cent of KAM teams describe themselves as internationally or globally based. One role of the international or global KAM team can be to ensure harmonization and consistency, as described by a consumer products manufacturer who supplies private label products to international retailers:

> "For the private labels, the client branded products, we have a global approach to key account management. It has to be this way because the client is looking for consistency for their brand across all their outlets. Our key account management reflects that global aspect".
>
> Key account manager, consumer products manufacturer

More than 71% of KAM teams manage more than one customer. It is more unusual, although far from unknown, for a KAM team only to manage a single customer. The third type of KAM team is "ad hoc". These are KAM teams that are put together for a single piece of work, such as the installation of a major piece of enterprise software.

> The core KAM team typically consists of people from Sales, Marketing or Commercial, and Customer Service departments.

KAM teams are drawn from the functions within the supplier that are appropriate for the client at that time. Many KAM teams have a core of permanent members but also draw on other functions from time to time. The core composition of a KAM team relates to pre-, during, and after-sales and consists of people from Sales, Marketing or Commercial, and Customer Service departments. Typically, however, a KAM team will also draw on expertise from Operations and Logistics, Finance, and Legal as needed. IT and R&D people may also have links to KAM teams.

The average number of people in a KAM team will depend on the size of the supplier organization and the international scope of the key account. Teams range in size from 2 to 200 people, but the average seems to be about 7 people. The team is usually led by a key account manager or director, to whom team members report.

In some cases the KAM team does not report solely to a key account director, but instead operates in a matrix structure where team members have a reporting line to their functional heads, or to local country managers, as well as to the team leader. This latter structure is often seen in industries where there are strong product structures, such as manufacturing, chemicals, etc. It has the benefit of ensuring that the KAM team retains its links to the product side of the business and maintains its technical expertise. The downside is that key account managers may find themselves reporting to a product or country manager who puts the interests of his business unit above those of the relationship as a whole.

It can be seen that there are many varieties of KAM team. KAM teams can be ad hoc or permanent; they can be regional or international; they can be specialist or cross-functional. These differences mean that there is no single way in which KAM teams operate, although successful KAM teams tend to share some particular characteristics.

> The average number of people in a KAM team is seven, although teams managing global customers can be much bigger.

How KAM teams operate

There are some wide variations in the way that KAM teams operate. Meeting frequency, for example, varies widely between KAM teams. Many teams meet monthly, but just as many say they meet only when they need to. Quite a few teams meet weekly, but some meet several times a week and others meet only quarterly.

What is common across a large majority of KAM teams is the spread of their activities. Almost all KAM teams are involved in six main activities:

The six main activities of the KAM team

1. Winning new business from existing customers
2. Working in project teams with customers
3. Key account planning
4. Delivering day-to-day business for customers
5. Winning new key accounts
6. Working in internal project teams on customer issues

The most important activity for a KAM team is retaining and managing the customer, with at least 80% of the team's time typically spent on this. However, most KAM teams are also tasked with winning business from new customers. This may include developing existing non-key customers to key account status.

> Eighty per cent of the KAM team's time is spent on retaining and managing the customer, although most KAM teams are also tasked with winning business from new customers.

What makes a good KAM team?

The main factor that underpins good KAM team performance is communication between team members.

The main factor that underpins good KAM team performance is communication between team members. This includes openness with information, exchange of assistance (team members help one another), and respect for each other's roles. These behaviours promote learning from one another within the team, and enable teams to accept change and accountability. Open teams are also more accepting of others outside the team, which again helps them to learn.

Team performance is also affected by the level of motivation, which is in turn influenced by how the team is rewarded (for instance, what proportion of compensation is based on team performance) and also by whether the team is fun to work in.

Characteristics of a good KAM team

- Openness, honesty, inclusive, supportive, and culturally aware
- Experts, well trained, astute, close to the customer
- Senior management buy-in and external support for the team
- Enthusiastic, team players, slightly crazy people!

Organizations can influence the performance of their KAM teams not only in the way that the team is paid. Appointing a good team leader will make a difference; the team leader should be someone who has a high emotional intelligence, which is the ability to understand how others are feeling and to manage people on an emotional as well as on a practical level. Training is also an important determinant of KAM team performance. Training in KAM, in planning skills, and in how to analyse and understand the customer, will improve team members' performance in front of customers. The team should also build its general business skills and acumen.

The main barriers to KAM team performance relate to the "hygiene factors": reward; working conditions; lack of proper management; lack of high-level support within the company; and bureaucracy. The other factor that undermines the performance of a KAM team is aggressively individualistic behaviour by KAM team members:

The barriers to KAM team performance: some comments from KAM team leaders

The dominance of some personalities – people who want to do their own thing and not share the information and reward – conflict between marketing and sales. Everyone wants to be top dog; people don't know their own role or respect the roles of other people.

> Internal politics and bureaucracy
> The fact that KAM is not highly regarded in the organization.
> ... no leadership involvement, and a lack of processes and systems.
>
> *Source*: Ryals et al. (2005).

Previous research suggests that good KAM teams exhibit certain behaviours that support and enhance the relationships within the team, which include exchanging information freely, learning from each other, accepting change, accepting accountability and responsibility, and trust. Effective KAM teams are also characterized by five factors that improve their performance with customers: empowerment to make decisions, customer understanding, planning, training, and reward.

A first step to developing a better-performing team is analysing the strengths and weaknesses of the existing team. If you work in a KAM team, you might like to complete Table 9.1 (KAM team audit) before you move on to the next section.

Table 9.1 KAM team audit

For each factor, give your KAM team a score out of 5, where 1 = very weak and 5 = very strong. Complete the pro-forma by adding your own notes about any actions you will take, as a result of your audit.

Factor	Score (1–5)	Notes/Actions
Behaviours that support and enhance team relationships		
Exchanging information freely		
Learning from each other		
Accepting change		
Accepting accountability		
Trust		
Factors that enable the team to build successful relationships with key accounts		
Empowerment to make decisions		
Customer understanding		
Key account planning		
Training		
Motivation and reward systems support KAM		

Underpinning the operation of the key account manager or of the KAM team is a series of organizational systems and processes that support KAM. Even the best team will be undermined if the systems and processes do not work properly.

In the next section, we will look at some of the main systems and processes that support KAM, and examine case studies of successful KAM delivery.

> Even the best KAM team will be undermined if the organization's systems and processes do not work properly.

■ Systems and processes that support KAM

There are two types of systems and processes that support KAM: the underlying organizational processes; and KAM-specific processes. Underlying organizational processes include tendering, order processing, production, invoicing and financial controls, HR, corporate strategy and planning, investor relationships, etc. These organizational processes have to perform well, with or without KAM, for the supplier to succeed. They will therefore not be considered here. Instead, we will look more closely at some KAM-specific processes. KAM-specific processes are processes that assist specifically in the delivery of KAM and would not exist – or not in the same form – if the supplier did not offer KAM.

In this section, we will look at some crucial KAM-specific processes:

- IT systems for KAM planning
- Key relationship management (using the CRM system to support KAM)
- Customizing the offer to key accounts
- E-business
- IT support for key account relationships

IT systems for KAM planning

It takes around 50 hours to create a detailed key account plan for the first time.

Our previous research has found that it takes around 50 hours (i.e. a long working week) to create a detailed key account plan for a single key account for the first time. This is a heavy call on the key account manager's time. Part of the KAM planning process involves communication with other parts of the company, particularly with other team members if the key account is managed by a team. These team members could be located in different environments, time zones, and language zones, adding to the complexity of the KAM planning task.

An additional problem is that senior managers have to aggregate all the different KAM plans that they receive. They need to be able to compare the plans with one another and make decisions about resource allocation based on this comparison. This task can be all but impossible to do effectively if the KAM plan formats are different, and if the KAM plans contain different amounts of data.

As well as sharing the KAM plan with colleagues and with senior managers, parts of KAM plans are often shared with the key account itself. The closer the relationship, the more likely it is that some or all of the supplier's KAM planning process will be carried out jointly with the key account.

Some of the problems that suppliers face in developing and sharing KAM plans are as shown.

IT systems that support KAM planning can help overcome many of the problems in developing and sharing KAM plans. The IT solutions that suppliers have bought or developed for their KAM planning range from

Problems for KAM planning systems

- KAM teams widely dispersed and unable to hold regular meetings
- Need for consistency in format and content across plans
- Ensuring plans are accurate and kept up-to-date
- Insufficient information or information inaccessible
- Progress tracking
- Accessibility for interested parties
- Multi-lingual
- Protection and security for sensitive information

straightforward sets of templates in Word, Powerpoint, or Excel, through bespoke or off-the-shelf planning software packages, to shared Extranets. The key is to find a system that everyone will support; the more useful it is, the more likely it is to be kept up-to-date.

Key relationship management (using the CRM system to support KAM)

CRM systems are associated with business-to-consumer markets and the management of relationships with thousands or millions of customers. Where customers are so numerous, technology offers an attractive alternative to expensive, slower, and fragmented traditional relationship management.

However, some CRM functionality can be applied in a KAM context. This can be thought of as key relationship management (KRM).

One of the most interesting areas in which CRM technology can support KAM is in the area of customer profitability and customer lifetime value calculation, which we discussed in Chapters 5 and 6. Customer profitability analysis is now an accepted element in enterprise-wide CRM, and several data mining tools are useful in forecasting customer lifetime value. Good information systems can provide data on the cost of managing a key account which are very useful to the key account manager's profitability calculations. More sophisticated systems also have data mining tools which can help predict customer behaviour. Although these work better with larger amounts of data (i.e. larger portfolios of customers), data mining might provide the key account manager with some useful insights into the factors driving future revenues and risks.

> Customer profitability analysis is now an accepted element in enterprise-wide CRM.

Another major area in which CRM systems can support KAM is in the area of centralization of procurement and what we might term "customer memory". It is increasingly common for customers who want to centralize their procurement of even small items, so that purchasing can be done more cheaply and efficiently. The problem is that procurement directors find it hard to manage and to enforce centralized procurement. Local managers frequently have their local suppliers and will circumvent or ignore instructions from the centre to deal with the preferred supplier. One office technology products supplier is working with a key customer to improve procurement efficiency:

Competitive advantage through data management

A UK-based supplier of office technology products sells through retail outlets and call centres. It also has a small KAM team. Its biggest key account is a large conglomerate, which has a number of different business units in dispersed locations around the UK. Analysis of the purchasing data for this customer showed that it did some buying centrally for the higher-ticket items, but also spent surprisingly large amounts on small value purchases by individual employees through multiple local buying points.

In support of the procurement manager, who wanted to introduce greater procurement centralization, the supplier began by analysing purchases across the entire group and supplying the new procurement manager with an overview of the buying patterns for technology products across his whole organization. This service secured the account for the supplier on a long-term contract.

Next, the new account manager at the supplier travelled around to many of the individual customer sites, explaining to local managers why adherence to the central procurement policy was advantageous to the customer's company as a whole. Conformance went up, and the supplier's share of customer spend increased as a direct result.

A further step in the relationship came when the supplier developed a sophisticated web-based reporting system that allows managers at individual sites to see their customer records and manage local procurement in real time. The system provides customers with information about products they have purchased recently (up to the previous hour) and product mix, as well as offers ordering for next-day delivery.

The customer and supplier now consider themselves to be partners. The supplier is not the single source, but it has a large majority of market share. The customer is beginning to talk to the supplier about joint development of other procurement and management systems.

As well as supporting procurement centralization and providing useful information to customers, KRM can support other KAM functions:

- *Analytical*: creating information and knowledge to support strategic and tactical decision-making.
- *Operational*: sales force automation (SFA), marketing systems, customer service and call centre systems, technical support.
- *Channel management*: real-time and instantaneous updates to customer information, and consistent information between channels such as key account managers, websites, call centres, email/text messaging, etc.

- *Collaboration*: supporting shared systems and multi-channel access across organizational boundaries. Team interaction tools (video conferencing, teleconferencing, document sharing). May also provide shared metrics.

Analytical systems can provide information support, for example, in calculating customer profitability and in customer analysis. Operational systems can be a considerable support to the key account manager. A KAM-friendly SFA system, for example, will enable the key account manager and others who have access to it, to track the progress of negotiations, relationship development, etc. and support the development of attractive propositions and winning tenders. Integrated channel management is particularly important with larger and more international key accounts, where the KAM team is likely to be bigger and where desk-based account management has to integrate with field operations. Finally, KRM processes may span the boundary between the supplier and the customer. This can take the form of shared ordering or delivery information systems, or shared planning.

> Key relationship management processes may span the boundary between the supplier and the customer. An example would be a KAM plan on a shared Extranet.

As this summary suggests, IT systems that support KAM offer more than merely day-by-day operational support for the relationship. KAM support systems also offer innovative ways in which suppliers can customize their offer to key accounts.

Customizing the offer to key accounts

As we have seen, business-to-business sales are characterized by their complexity and by the degree of customization. This is particularly so in KAM relationships, where customers expect that both products and services can be tailored to their organizational needs.

> In KAM relationships, customers expect that products and services can be tailored to their needs – but customization creates hidden costs that may not be recovered in the price.

Customizing products and services, however, can be dangerous. Customization creates hidden costs, such as longer selling and order-taking processes, retooling, reworking, customer-specific stock, production bottlenecks, and delivery issues. These costs may not be recovered in the price, particularly as pricing customized products is more complex and time consuming than pricing standard products.

Many of these problems have been addressed by suppliers who have created "on-line stores" in which customers can browse, configure their own products, check prices, and place orders.

On-line configuration

A leading international engineering company has applied configuration technologies to support its web-based services. The customer can access an on-line webstore containing an electronic catalogue. Once in the webstore, the customer can specify a sub-assembly or customize the fittings on a standard product.

When the customer submits the specification, it is automatically checked against a CAD package to ensure that the design is workable. At this stage, the webstore recommends any necessary

> changes to the specification, the design, and/or to the components list that the customer also submits online.
>
> Once the design is evaluated and the customer is satisfied, the webstore produces a price. The customer can submit his/her order online.
>
> The webstore provides customers with a fast and flexible service that enables customers to evaluate the workability and cost of customization. In addition, the webstore is an efficient way for the supplier to supply and for the customer to purchase, since it reduces the need for input from designers in both companies.

The engineering company's webstore indicates the importance that other channels have in KAM relationships, even though the main point of contact is the key account manager or KAM team.

This brings us to the more general topic of e-business, which is playing an increasing role in the delivery of KAM.

E-business

> E-business in KAM is the use of the Internet and other related electronic media to improve the organization's competitiveness across the full supply chain.
>
> Mouncey et al. (2004).

The field of e-business is a huge one, but the focus in this section is on the core e-business applications that support KAM. There are three main aspects of e-business that are affecting the way that key accounts and suppliers do business:

- Websites
- Extranets or customer portals
- Electronic exchanges

Websites are (generally) open to all. This does not mean that they are standard; they can be customized to reflect the current and previous interests of the customer, and to present specific offers to returning customers based on their previous purchase history. By contrast, Extranets are secure, protected private sites that connect one organization to another for the purposes of exchanging information (such as a shared KAM plan) or carrying out transactions (such as on-line ordering). Extranets typically connect one supplier to one key account. This makes them different from electronic exchanges, which connect one key account to many suppliers (or, occasionally, connect many-to-many) for the purposes of trading. E-auctions, which are making an often unwelcome appearance on the KAM stage, are a form of electronic exchange.

Research shows that there are two overall trends within e-marketplaces: standardization and collaboration. The trend towards standardization is more dominant in the one-to-many relationship found in electronic exchanges; the trend towards collaboration is more dominant in the one-to-one relationships supported by Extranets.

The trend towards standardization

Standardization can relate to products and service. Product standardization is found in one-to-many business-to-business relationships in which the key account has a policy of multiple sourcing but requires the product to be standardized for reasons of consistency, interchangeability, and price transparency. There may be substantial power differentials between the key account and its supplier. IKEA, the international furniture and household goods retailer, has a strong standardization policy as part of its IWAY supplier management programme. Suppliers have to conform or lose IKEA's business, although they (and IKEA) gain from the economies of scale that come through longer runs of standard products. Service standardization might include common definitions and data standards that facilitate exchange; here, the supplier to lead the way will gain a "first-mover" advantage, but this is soon lost as the new standard becomes the market-dominant approach.

That said, suppliers with low market power, or who make heavy use of exchanges for e-business, can find standardization an attractive option. Standardization tends to simplify transactions, which is an important success criterion for selling online to customers with whom the relationship element is lower. Standardization also brings supply chain and operational benefits, and makes it easier to develop e-catalogues and to set up online purchasing with standard prices.

> Standardization tends to simplify transactions. It also brings supply chain and operational benefits.

The benefits of standardization are considerable, but standard products may not meet the needs of the key account or promote a closer collaborative relationship.

The trend towards collaboration

In a close key account relationship, a supplier can gain considerable advantage from collaborating with a key customer. Collaboration is, in many ways, the opposite of standardization. Through collaboration, the supplier may produce products or services which are more closely aligned with the needs of the customer. Again, collaboration can refer to shared product collaboration or shared innovation; for example, recent research advocates very early involvement of the customer in the new product development process, perhaps even at the concept stage.

Key suppliers have also realized considerable benefits for themselves and their key accounts through process collaboration. This may range from information sharing, through joint planning and forecasting, to process benchmarking. However, collaboration leading to customization may be more costly for the supplier, at least in the short term.

The benefits of collaboration for the key account are that it receives a product and service that is particularly tailored to its needs, although this will often be more expensive than a standard approach. The supplier has greater control over a collaborative relationship than a standard one, and may gain from being able to spot opportunities faster.

However, collaboration increases the switching costs to both sides. Switching costs are the costs that would be incurred by switching out of the relationship to an alternative supplier or customer. The supplier's switching costs increase if collaboration results in a product or service that has been developed specifically for one key account and cannot be easily transferred to another. Moreover, the supplier has invested in the development of the relationship, and those investment costs will be lost if the relationship terminates.

From the customer's point of view, there are switching costs associated with finding, testing, and getting to know a new supplier. There may also be learning costs associated with the switch to an alternative product.

Generally, suppliers benefit from switching costs. The higher the switching costs, the more likely the customer is to stay with them. So, high switching costs to the customer are associated with high customer retention for the supplier. This does not mean that high switching costs are necessarily bad for the customer. There are gains from stability of supply and learning curve effects in longer-term relationships, and much research has found that both sides benefit from long-term KAM collaboration.

An example of how technology has been used to enhance and customize KAM relationships comes from the fast-growing management education sector:

> *Research shows that both sides benefit from KAM relationships.*

Collaboration and customization in management education

A world-leading management education centre provides bespoke management development programmes to business. Traditionally, the development and administration costs of customizing such programmes are very high and the programmes are specific to the customer so they cannot be sold elsewhere. Each programme typically consists of a number of courses which may be delivered a number of times in multiple international locations over a period of several years.

In collaboration with its key clients, this centre now builds bespoke Extranet sites to support management development programmes. The Extranets developed for these multi-million pound programmes are designed not just to administer each course as it runs, but to create a cohort of trained and knowledgeable professionals within the customer company and to act as a vehicle for delegates to continue to develop themselves through further reading and discussion with others. The site provides access to learning support materials, course materials, administration information, the "Round Table" (a virtual discussion forum to enable past and present students to share knowledge and discuss issues), links to other sites, both internal and external, and contact details for all delegates past and present, and for course administrators and development professionals within the client and the provider.

The benefits to the customer include:

- Infrastructure for continuous learning rather than a one-off experience.
- Effective and consistent management of an international programme world-wide.
- Lower administration costs.
- More effective measurement of the returns on the investment in the management training.
- Fosters a spirit of shared learning.
- Updated materials available to all past and present delegates via the knowledgebase; delegates can also register to receive automatic email alerts when there is an updated posting on a topic of interest to them.

The benefits to the training provider include:

- Differentiation of its offer at relatively low cost.
- Creates customer switching costs.
- Lower administration costs.
- Builds the provider brand name.

The management education example is a one-to-one example of collaboration and customization. Other companies may collaborate as networks of suppliers serving one or a network of key accounts, as in the case of Global Healthcare Exchange (GHX).

Global healthcare exchange (GHX)

Healthcare is a multi-billion dollar business and is growing fast.

Big global pharmaceutical companies notwithstanding, healthcare supply is highly fragmented and complex. There are many suppliers of specialist products and services and procurement is complex. The picture in the UK is complicated by restructuring in the NHS, the largest single customer, and the emergence of substantial private providers. Still worse, different providers use different software packages. With all these layers of complexity, it is perhaps not surprising that traditional order systems generate an estimated 25% error rate.

This is where GHX comes in. Founded in the USA in 2000 by a consortium of medical suppliers, GHX is an electronic exchange that aims to simplify procurement processes for customers and provide a common set of standards for suppliers. Multiple suppliers are connected to multiple customers through GHX's hub. At its heart sits GHX's AllSource™ catalogue which standardizes the many and varied descriptions that individual suppliers give their products, into a simple and easy-to-search standard description. GHX insists that entries in the AllSource™ catalogue must conform to its own style guide but, in return, it provides good data quality and keeps the information updated. Suppliers and customers can continue to use their existing order processing system, or can use GHX's own e-business tool. Prices remain subject to negotiated arrangements between supplier and customer.

GHX's success has been immediate. Product returns, an inevitable consequence of the high order error rates of the previous system, have plummeted to close to zero. Hospitals have also been able to gain procurement efficiencies through order consolidation and, consequently, fewer deliveries. Suppliers have also benefited from more efficient supply chain management and the dramatic reduction in returns. Still better, because the number of day-to-day disputes has fallen, key account managers can focus on the long-term strategic aspects of their relationships with key customers.

Source: Based on Mouncey et al. (2004).

The GHX example shows how a KAM support system freed the key account managers from sorting out day-to-day problems and enabled them to focus on relationship development. Our final look at systems and processes for KAM considers how IT can support the management and development of key account relationships. This goes beyond the use of existing CRM systems, discussed earlier, to consider the advantages of specific KAM-related systems.

IT support for key account relationships

> IT systems play an important role in determining the profitability of key accounts and the payback to a supplier's investment in KAM.

As the field of KAM has developed and become more sophisticated, suppliers are starting to ask more searching questions about their commitment to KAM and the payback on their considerable investments in customization, people, and support for their key accounts. At the same time, customers are looking to their key suppliers for a greater level of support than ever before. At a strategic level, senior key account managers and key account directors find themselves considering how they can establish the profitability of individual key customers and how they can decide whether their investment in KAM provides a higher rate of return than simple transactional selling.

A KAM system for a global office equipment manufacturer

A leading global office equipment manufacturer has developed an account management system for its key accounts. The system was built and implemented in modules. First, basic P&L (profit and loss) information was provided, customer by customer. Then the P&L information was extended and enriched. The next module gave invoice details, the one after that provided activity reporting, another module gives legal and financial status information about the customer, and so on. The difference between this system and the existing CRM system is that this system allocates detailed product and service costs at individual customer level. The KAM system also contains "Virtual Sales Accounts" that allow the different costs by channel to be identified (enabling the key account manager to see the impact that managing a client via the web would have versus desk-based or face-to-face KAM).

In addition to its financial capabilities, the KAM system acts as the supplier's organizational memory about its key accounts. Although the average length of service for the US key account managers is about 10 years, the UK and European key account managers tended to move on more quickly. The impact on the customer relationship has been reduced thanks to this system, and a separate programme to develop, motivate, and retain key account managers is under way.

The office equipment manufacturer measures the success of its KAM system by its share of key account spend. The system has also helped provide the information that led this company to identify KAM as a critical business process, on a par with production management.

This is where IT support for key account relationships comes in. In an effort to address strategic questions about the success of KAM, some suppliers have developed KAM systems that will manage and measure the relationship. An example is the global office equipment manufacturer.

So far, we have seen ample evidence of the importance of the systems and processes for KAM that support the key account manager in delivering best practice KAM. However, the case of the global office equipment manufacturer also illustrates another issue in the delivery of world-class KAM, which is that systems and processes are only as good as the people who use them. Even the best and most sophisticated KAM systems will only help a supplier to deliver world-class KAM if the key account manager is measured, motivated and rewarded appropriately. In the final section of this chapter, we turn to the issue of how key account managers are motivated and how they can be appropriately rewarded.

■ Measurement, motivation and reward of key account managers

The vexed question of how key account managers should be measured, motivated and rewarded has not kept pace with the rapid emergence of KAM. Too many key account managers are still measured and rewarded as though they were traditional sales people with a focus on short-term revenue generation rather than as team leaders managing complex long-term relationships. The truth is that suppliers still pay lip service to KAM but carry on measuring their people in ways that undermine best practice.

So, how are sales people different from key account managers? It is not so much a question of the job title – it seems possible that many sales executives are in fact fulfilling KAM roles, and vice versa – but of the function that the sales person/key account manager actually performs. Complete

Table 9.2 Are you truly a key account manager?						
Consider each factor and circle the number (1–5) which represents where you are in your current role, not where you would like to be. For example, the first factor is customer contact. Circle "1" if you usually have high levels of customer contact; "5" if your customer contact is usually confined to specific opportunities; or 2–4 if your role is somewhere in between. Then add up your total score and turn to the scale in Table 9.3 to find out the degree to which you are a key account manager.						
Factor						**Factor**
High levels of customer contact	1	2	3	4	5	Customer contact when a specific opportunity presents itself
Majority of time spent in own company	1	2	3	4	5	Majority of time spent with customers
Planning is an important feature of job	1	2	3	4	5	Getting out and doing it is key role
Strategic focus	1	2	3	4	5	Practical focus
Measured on customer profit	1	2	3	4	5	Measured on customer volume or revenues
"Farmer"	1	2	3	4	5	"Warrior"
Nurture multiple contacts at customer	1	2	3	4	5	Tend to have a main contact
Manage a team	1	2	3	4	5	Mainly work alone
Work closely with operations	1	2	3	4	5	It is operation's job to deliver what I sell
Mainly paid on salary	1	2	3	4	5	Mainly paid on commission
Have fewer than 7 clients	1	2	3	4	5	Have more than 30 clients

Table 9.3	Results: Are you truly a key account manager?	
Use your tota score for the questions in Table 9.2 to find out the degree to which you are a key account manager.		
Score	**Your role**	**Advice**
5–19	Definitely a key account manager	Based on this profile, you are definitely a key account manager. Ensure you are paid on long-term results, not short-term sales. Build your team-leading skills. Work closely with operations to deliver customer service. Above all, resist pressures to spend more time "on the road". Your job is back in your company, ensuring the smooth running of the relationship.
20–30	Probably a key account manager	Your role profiles like that of a key account manager, but includes some tactical elements. It is possible you are a business development manager. You can play an important role in a KAM team by identifying opportunities.
31–40	Probably a sales executive	Your role is relationship-based selling. Build your skills in customer portfolio manag ement, figuring out where you can spend your time for the best returns. Resist the temptation to spend too much time with small, friendly customers who will not bring you incremental business.
41–55	Definitely a sales executive	Your role is going out and winning business. All businesses need sales people. If this is your role, make sure that the company does not cloud the picture by setting long-term relationship targets. Think about growing your territory or your target accounts.

the quick quiz in Table 9.2 to see how closely your role matches that of a key account manager.

Selling is part of a key account manager's role, but more important is that key account managers are standard bearers for their company, relationship managers who will build long-term relationships, solve problems, and manage complexity. Selling, whilst still part of the role, is less urgent.

The differences between the sales and the KAM role are reflected in the different ways they are measured. Sales people are most often (although not always) measured on a volume or revenue basis, against quota. Key account managers are far more likely to be measured against customer profitability or lifetime value and also to have "soft" relationship factors such as customer satisfaction included in their performance appraisal, alongside "hard" financial factors.

> Key account managers are likely to be measured against customer profitability or lifetime value, and to have "soft" relationship factors such as customer satisfaction included in their performance appraisal.

One factor that links key account managers and sales people is variable pay – that is, pay with some performance-related element to it. However, the salary component typically forms a higher proportion for key account managers (70% or more), because their focus is on the longer term. Sales people have in the past been paid entirely on commission, although it is increasingly common for the sales executive now to have a smaller (50% or less) salary element to their remuneration. In fact, previous research shows that paying a sales force purely on salary, without commission, is actually a bad idea; sales force retention and performance both go up when commissions or bonuses are introduced.

However, that does not mean that performance continues to increase as the commission percentage increases. In fact, paying a sales force purely on commission does not increase its performance. Nobody likes large monthly income fluctuations, and highly competitive pay structures create more losers than winners, undermine team working, and encourage manipulative behaviour by sales people. Examples of manipulative behaviour include *channel stuffing*, in which the customer is persuaded to take goods on trial, only to return them in a later period; or *sandbagging*, in which the sales person brings forward delivery dates to raise results in a particular period. Interestingly, research into the link between reward and satisfaction has found that the most highly rewarded sales people are the most dissatisfied.

For key account managers, the focus has to be on salary and fringe benefits, because the results of the key account manager's efforts are difficult to measure in the short term. Activities such as developing contacts, seeking information, learning, planning, and delivering service, do not produce short-term results but are vital in KAM. There are also team- and strategic business unit (SBU)-based elements to KAM, and it is not uncommon for a proportion of the key account manager's overall compensation package to be linked to the performance of others.

Key account managers with long-term relationships with their customers place more importance on salary. Their motivators include job satisfaction, meeting customer needs, job retention, recognition, promotion, training, and better job content. Some researchers have suggested that key account manager packages should be based on 75% basic salary and 25% variable pay, the latter linked to key account profitability rather than sales.

> Key account managers with long-term relationships with their customers place more importance on salary.

Other objectives that may be used to measure key account manager performance include:

- Renewal of customer contracts
- Sales results over a number of years
- Share of customer spend
- Account growth
- Customer satisfaction/relationship management effectiveness

Of these, share of spend is an interesting performance measure. It indicates the quality of the relationship. If share of spend is declining, this may signal a deteriorating relationship position even before the financial numbers confirm it. An increasing share of spend generally indicates an improving relationship. For this reason, share of spend should be measured alongside the financial results when evaluating key account manager's performance. Care must be taken, however, not to set too high a target for share of spend. Some key accounts have a policy to multiple source, in which case unrealistically high share of spend targets will never be met. Additionally, the supplier should take a view about the share of spend that it actually wants to achieve. Hundred per cent share of spend is not necessarily a desirable objective, if it cannot be attained profitably.

An interesting finding from previous research is that the role of the sales person or account manager in creating customer satisfaction may be smaller than some would like to believe. It seems that service may have twice the impact on customer satisfaction that the account manager or sales person does. This again underlines the need for some form of team-based remuneration, since service to a key account is largely a matter of team performance rather than delivery by a single individual. Some commentators have even argued the case for an index-based system to allocate rewards between team members according to their contribution to the result.

All of these approaches are based on the role, rather than the type of customer relationship. However, the customer portfolio matrix could be used as a basis for determining the measurement and reward of the key account manager.

> A declining share of spend may signal a deteriorating relationship position even before the financial numbers confirm it.

■ Rewarding key account managers using the customer portfolio matrix

A rather different approach to the measurement and reward of key account managers is to identify the type of customer relationship according to the customer portfolio matrix, and then to design a reward system around the supplier's strategic positioning vis-à-vis that particular relationship (Figure 9.1). Key accounts can be categorized as investment accounts, selective investment accounts, maintenance accounts, and tactical management/sales accounts.

Where the relationship is attractive to both the supplier and the customer (investment accounts), it may be appropriate to reward the key account manager with a high salary element, perhaps 70–80% or more. If the investment accounts are managed on a team basis, the compensation package should include an element of team performance. Hewlett Packard practices this approach for its largest accounts, which are served by teams. The pay of sales managers and executives working on such accounts is largely team based.

Where the relationship is attractive to the supplier but less developed (selective investment accounts), the situation regarding recognition and reward is very different. There is a need for "missionary selling" to acquire or develop new accounts, which calls for considerable individual effort. Here, a higher proportion of commission is called for, but the commission should reflect the current investment of time for future results. One US software company, Mathworks, offers its sales people 35% of their

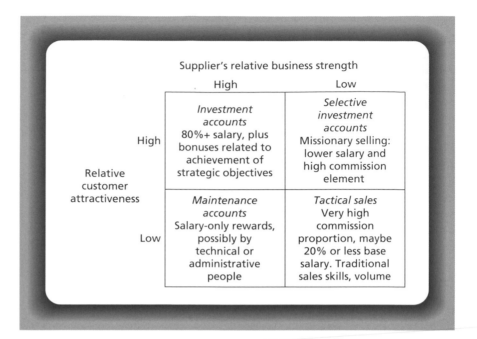

Supplier's relative business strength

	High	Low
High Relative customer attractiveness	*Investment accounts* 80%+ salary, plus bonuses related to achievement of strategic objectives	*Selective investment accounts* Missionary selling: lower salary and high commission element
Low	*Maintenance accounts* Salary-only rewards, possibly by technical or administrative people	*Tactical sales* Very high commission proportion, maybe 20% or less base salary. Traditional sales skills, volume

Figure 9.1
The customer portfolio matrix and KAM rewards

package in commission for these types of accounts, compared with 20% for maintenance or tactical sales accounts.

Maintenance accounts are those where the key account is relatively less attractive, but has a high degree of loyalty to the supplier. Here, non-sales or KAM staff might be used to manage the relationship. Hewlett Packard uses teams comprised of managers from research, HR, and technology, amongst other non-traditional client management backgrounds, for these types of clients.

Tactical sales accounts are those where the relationship with the supplier is less warm and the key account is less attractive. This could still be a high-volume account, but perhaps one that takes a tactical or transactional stance to its supplier relationships. In these circumstances, the key account manager should have traditional sales skills such as negotiation and handling objections. A high proportion of commission is usually an appropriate method to reward managers handling tactical accounts. Some companies supplement this method with smaller but more regular celebrations of sales performance. Enbridge Gas Distribution in the US supplements its rewards to sales people with tickets to sporting events or with a free dinner for two. It does this several times a year, to ensure that the tactical account managers make the link between short-term performance and its reward.

The measurement, motivation and reward of key account managers is an area that is underexplored but which is important in the delivery of world-class KAM. The customer portfolio matrix can be used to determine measurement and reward strategies for different types of key account.

> The measurement, motivation, and reward of key account managers is a vital area in the delivery of world-class KAM. The customer portfolio matrix can be used to determine measurement and reward strategies for different types of key account.

This approach serves as a reminder that not all key accounts are the same, that different management and measurement approaches may be necessary, and that this may affect the appropriate motivation and reward package for the key account manager. There is no particular reason why all of a firm's key account managers should have the same motivation schemes and the customer portfolio approach suggests why that might be.

The measurement, motivation and reward of key account managers signals another essential area for delivering world-class KAM, which is how firms measure the effectiveness of their KAM plans. In this chapter, we considered the measurement of key account managers. In the next chapter, we will turn our attention to the effectiveness of KAM plans and how key account managers can improve their planning for key accounts.

References

Mouncey, P., McDonald, M. and Ryals, L.J. (2004) *Key customers: Identifying and implementing IT solutions for KAM*. Report by the Cranfield Key Account Management Best Practice Club, Cranfield, July 2004.

Ryals, L.J., Bruce, L. and McDonald, M. (2005) *Managing KAM relationships*. Report by the Cranfield Key Account Management Best Practice Club, Cranfield, September 2005.

CHAPTER 10

What needs to
be measured,
managed, and
reported;
critiquing plans;
barriers to
successful key
account
planning

■ Introduction

Once again, as in the spirit of this book, let us get straight to the point and share with readers the evaluation guidelines we have used for many years with some of the world's leading multinationals, who are always keen to establish the effectiveness of the strategic plans produced by their top key account managers. Those guidelines are given in Table 10.1. Table 10.2 provides other crucial points to watch out for.

Also, early in this chapter, we feel it would be useful to provide a simple case history of just one way in which key account managers are measured and motivated in a leading, global business-to-business company.

Mini Case

Figure 10.1 shows a "spidergram" for one key account. The perimeter labels of the web spell out each of the factors considered to be of importance in achieving an improved relationship over a 3-year period with this particular account. The inner points are where the supplier's performance is considered to be currently. The outer points are the targeted position to be reached in 3 years time.

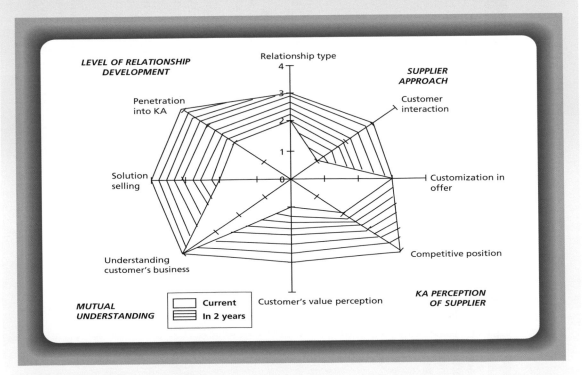

Figure 10.1
Current versus target performance.

Table 10.1 Evaluation guidelines for key account strategic plans

Key account attractiveness (KA) planning process	Reference sections	Level 1	Level 2	Level 3	Level 4	Level 5
Phase 1 Goal Setting	Mission statement Financial summary	Clear, coherent	Good	Acceptable	Poor	Not attempted
Phase 2 Situation review 1 for the customer	Key account overview	• Excellent understanding of KAM • Complete, coherent • Addresses key issues • Comprehensive and effective use of tools • Valid conclusions drawn • Deep understanding of the customer • Deep understanding of customer's objectives and strategy • Creative	• Good understanding of key account • Mostly complete, some visible coherence • Addresses key issues • Significant and effective use of tools • Illustrates main points of customer situation • Good understanding of customer's objectives and strategy • Clear	• Acceptable understanding of key account • Essential components • Some use of tools • Elucidates key issues facing customer • Acceptable understanding of customer's objectives and strategies • No significant contradictions or omissions	• Weak understanding of key account • Little use of tools • Does not draw valid conclusions • Little understanding of customer's objectives and strategies • Significantly incomplete or incoherent	• Little or no understanding of key account • Little or no use of tools • No conclusions • Poor understanding of the customer • Poor understanding of the customer's objectives and strategies • Incomplete and/or includes major contradictions

Situation review (ii) for the supplier	Supplier overview	• Excellent alignment of supplier's strengths and weaknesses with issues facing the customer	• Good alignment of supplier's strengths and weaknesses with the issues facing the customer	• Acceptable alignment of supplier's strengths and weaknesses with the issues facing the customer	• Poor alignment of supplier's strengths and weaknesses with the issues facing the customer	• Little or no alignment of supplier's strengths and weaknesses with the issues facing the customer
Phase 3 Strategy Formulation	Supplier's objectives	• Realistic. Joined up with customer situation, customer and supplier strategies	• Realistic. Connects current situation and supplier strategies	• Statement building form current situation	• Unclear or not well connected to situation	• Not stated, or just sales targets
	Supplier's strategies	• Clearly stated. Targeted. Added value for customer Feasible, clear resource requirement Consistent with objectives	• Clearly stated. Targeted. Added value for customer Feasible clear resource requirement Consistent with objectives	• Clearly stated. Targeted. Added value for customer	• Strategy simply stated	• Strategy not stated, and/or stated strategies are outcomes or actions
Phase 4 Resource Allocation	Resource Requirments/ Budget	• 12 month development 3 year major action Matched with strategy Thorough measurement framework	• 12 month development 3 year major action Matched with strategy Focused measurement framework	• 12 month development Limited measurement framework	• Short-term action Measurement is just sales targets	• Short-term action No control mechanism

Table 10.2 Further points to watch in evaluation key account strategic plans

Key Account Overview	• Enough written to be clear to any reader, not excessive, unfocused prose. Information included is necessary and sufficient. • Is punchy and contains all essential facts and points. • Conclusions drawn: not just undigested 'stuff'. • Joined-up thinking: logical progression from analysis to objectives to strategies and actions. • Major business and market issues recognized and given appropriate level of focus, not hidden in sub-text.
Market Structure	• Market maps: quantified. Mapped as segments at all levels, customer not the centre of the universe.
Summary	• Conclusions drawn. • Right amount of material: not a presentation dump. • Customer's customer segments recognized, understood and given appropriate degree of importance
Objectives	• Customer wallet is defined, and defined appropriately. • Objectives match analysis, including downturns
Strategy	• Clear, explicit and explained, especially customer value proposition. • Answers "Why us?" • Not "wish-list" of sales outcomes. • Not simple actions. • Consistent with analyses: origins are clear. • Resources are realistic. • More than "business as usual". • Acknowledges importance of customer's customer.
Your plans	• Does not run out of steam in 6 months. • Identified "big" actions, not "set up meeting" etc. • Includes metrics.

It is an interesting side observation that this particular key account manager's reward and remuneration package will include movement towards these goals and will not be related solely to revenue targets. In this particular case, such goals constituted up to 30% of the manager's remuneration.

Clearly, measurement of these non-revenue-related goals requires an element of subjectivity and will neither be measured nor reported monthly, but senior managers in this company know what to look for in each of these dimensions and agree the parameters with the key account manager before setting the objectives. They also agree how and when they will be reviewed during the planning.

We have included this mini case here to establish up front that world-class sophisticated companies do not just measure revenue and profit. Our research at Cranfield has proved conclusively that if a supplier pays its key account manager only on revenue and profit, it inevitably produces poorer performances, for reasons we will explain now.

Take, for example, the complex and intricate information sets and associated diagnosis required to be conducted on a key account (spelled out in detail in Chapter 3). Without any financial incentive to engage in such processes, key account managers tend to concentrate only on selling and negotiating, something we know sophisticated customers detest and reject (see the research results from a 2001 USA Survey in Figure 10.2).

Sophisticated and continuously successful suppliers always have a remuneration package based around the agreed key account strategic plan (the contents of a key account strategic plan will be spelled out in Chapter 14). Thus, whilst on average 70% of remuneration packages are based on revenue, costs, and return on sales, such companies understand that these are *lag* indicators (i.e. outcomes) and that *lead* indicators also have to be measured and rewarded (i.e. the actions that *cause* the financial outcomes). A later section of this chapter deals with lead and lag indicators in more detail.

■ Measurement systems for key accounts must match the objectives set for them

Figure 10.2 shows a portfolio of key accounts for a company (for a detailed explanation refer back to Chapter 2).

"Status" accounts (bottom left) are normally big, loyal customers who provide regular, low-risk revenue to suppliers, but who are unlikely to

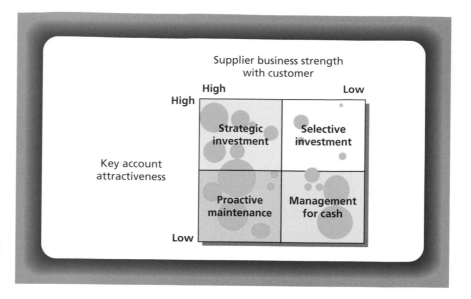

Figure 10.2
The key account portfolio.

The Buyers' View of Sellers (78%)

- The enemy
- Untrustworthy
- Pushy
- Aggressive
- Manipulative

- Unreliable
- Devious
- Opinionated
- Arrogant
- Poor Listeners
- Big Talkers

Only 18% saw the salesperson in positive terms

Source: Negotiation Resource International 'Buyer Behaviours', 2001
(2000 purchasers over 2 years)

Cranfield UNIVERS
School of Managem

provide a source of growth in the future. Such customers are normally very profitable and loyal. In such cases, measurement should not normally focus on *growth* in revenue, but *costs* should be carefully measured. In other words, the whole measurement package should revolve around *maintenance* and *net free cash flow*.

"Streamline" accounts (bottom right) will be similar, but there will be a greater focus on *costs to serve* and *net free cash flow*. Here, relationship issues and measurement will be much less important than in "status", "strategic", and "star" accounts.

"Strategic" accounts (top left) represent a supplier's future and it is crucial that measurement and reward systems are appropriate. For example, a system that overemphasized immediate growth in revenue and profits may damage the relationship and the supplier may fail to make sufficient investments in products, services, processes, people, etc. to ensure a continuing and long-term successful relationship. Such a policy may well be good for short-term profits, but, as we shall demonstrate later in this chapter, would probably contribute to the destruction of shareholder value. So, for "streamline" accounts, relationship issues such as those outlined in the mini case earlier in this chapter form a crucial part of measurement systems and 3-year plans which measure net present value are also important.

"Star" accounts (top right) are equivalent to the "Question Mark" box of Bruce Henderson's Boston Matrix of 1969. There may well be half a dozen accounts which are attractive (in the sense that they have excellent potential for growth in profits for the supplier over the next 3 years), but the supplier is not yet as competitive as some of its competitors. The choice facing the supplier, then is either to invest in these accounts in order to build competitive position to enjoy greater revenue and profitability in the future, or to manage them for cash and probably thereby become even less competitive in the future. The issue is how to make this decision, for it will be obvious that forward-looking companies who want to build long-term shareholder value added will be prepared to invest in at least some of such accounts, whilst recognizing that they just do not have sufficient financial, physical, and human resources to invest in all such customers.

The methodology for making such decisions is simple and logical. First, the costs of resources required to build a competitive position are assessed. These costs are deducted from the forecast revenue over the planning period (usually this is a 3-year period). These revenues are reduced probabilistically according to the assessed risks (for a detailed explanation of this, see Chapter 6). For each of the accounts in this top right-hand box, it is now possible to select those with the most promising net present values.

Using this method, suppliers now know which accounts to invest in and which to manage for cash.

In the context of measurement, however, there is a potential problem here, because measurement/accountability systems in most companies are financially driven. In other words, there is a proclivity for companies to measure the net profit generated by each account in each period and if it doesn't reach the forecast level, either prices are raised, or costs are reduced, or both, inevitably making the competitive position with the customer worse.

However, in the case of those accounts referred to above which have been selected as investment accounts, it would clearly be foolhardy to manage them for profit maximization. It would be a bit like putting a plant in the garden at Springtime in the knowledge that it will look beautiful in early Summer, only to have an "accountant" pull it up by the roots every day to check whether it was growing properly.

However far fetched this analogy might sound, there would clearly be little point in trying to maximize profit in those accounts selected for investment. In these accounts, measurement should focus not only on revenues and costs, but on those actions that appear as "strategies" in Forms 21 and

22 in Chapter 14. Such strategies and actions will depend on what is to be achieved in each account, but will also include the measurable elements of multi-disciplinary projects, as well as progress towards the personal relationships specified in Form 22 in Chapter 14. The frequency of such measurements is a matter of managerial judgment.

■ Key account metrics in the context of marketing accountability

There follows a very brief review of marketing accountability as a precursor to describing a state-of-the-art methodology for assessing whether key accounts create or destroy shareholder value.

As we have repeatedly stressed throughout this book, in world-class organizations where the customer is at the centre of the business model, marketing as a discipline is responsible for defining and understanding markets, for segmenting these markets, for developing value propositions to meet the researched needs of the customers in the segments, for getting buy-in from all those in the organization responsible for delivering this value, for playing their own part in delivering this value, and for monitoring whether the promised value is being delivered.

Indeed, this definition of marketing as a function for strategy development as well as for tactical sales delivery, when represented as a map (see Figure 10.3), can be used to clarify the whole problem of how to measure the

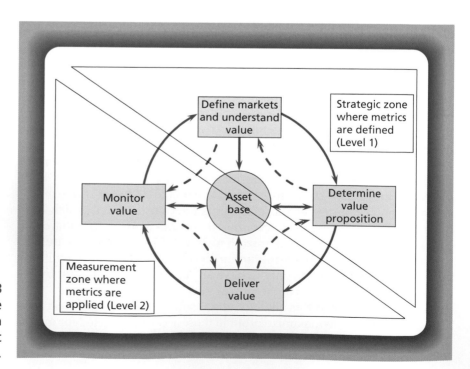

Figure 10.3
Map of the marketing domain and measurement fields.

effectiveness of all commercial activities related to marketing, including key account management (KAM).

From this map, it can be seen that there are two levels of measurement or metrics.

■ Level 2: Effectiveness

When one of the authors was Marketing Director of a fast-moving consumer goods (FMCG) company 30 years ago, there were many well tried-and-tested models for measuring the effectiveness of marketing promotion expenditure. Indeed, some of these were quite sophisticated and included mathematical models for promotional campaigns, for advertizing threshold and wear out levels, and the like.

Indeed, it would be surprising if marketing as a discipline did not have its own quantitative models for the massive expenditure of FMCG companies. Over time, these models have been transferred to business-to-business and service companies, with the result that, today any organization spending substantial sums of shareholders' money on promotion should be ashamed of themselves if those responsible could not account for the effectiveness of such expenditure.

But, at this level, accountability can only be measured in terms of the kinds of effects that promotional expenditure can achieve, such as awareness or attitude change, both of which can be measured quantitatively.

Likewise in the case of KAM, all those strategies and actions referred to above are *lead* indicators which will, if implemented efficiently, lead to the desired sales and profit levels, which are, of course, *lag* indicators. We have discussed these lead indicators in the first part of this chapter.

■ Level 1: Shareholder value added

Level 1 is the most vital of the two, however, because this is what determines whether or not the marketing strategies for the longer term (usually 3–5 years) destroy or create shareholder value added. At the corporate level, it is justified to use the strategic plan for assessing whether shareholder value is being created or destroyed because, as Sean Kelly agrees:

> The Customer is simply the fulcrum of the business and everything from production to supply chain, to finance, risk management, personnel management, and product development, all adapt to and converge on the business value proposition that is projected to the customer.
>
> (Sean Kelly, *The Customer Information Wars*, Wiley, 2005).

Thus, corporate assets and their associated competences are only relevant if customer markets value them sufficiently highly that they lead to sustainable competitive advantage or shareholder value added. This is the justification for evaluating the strategic plan for what is to be sold, to whom, and with what projected effect on profits as a route to establishing whether shareholder value with be created or destroyed.

A supplier's share price, the shareholder value created, and their cost of capital are all heavily influenced by one factor: risk. Investors constantly seek to estimate the likelihood of a business plan delivering its promises, whilst the boards try to demonstrate the strength of their strategy. What is certain is that in capital markets, success is measured in terms of shareholder value added, having taken account of the risks associated with future strategies, the time value of money, and the cost of capital.

How much is a company really worth? We all know about the huge discrepancy between the tangible assets and the share price; there are innumerable tools that try to estimate the true value of intangibles and goodwill. However, these mostly come from a cost-accounting perspective. They try to estimate the cost of re-creating the brand, intellectual property, or whatever is the basis of intangible assets. That approach is flawed, because what matters are not the assets, but how they are used. We need to get back to the basics of what determines company value.

We should never be too simplistic about business, but some things are fundamentally simple. A supplier's job is to create shareholder value, and their share price reflects how well they are thought to be doing that. Whether or not they create shareholder value depends on creating profits greater than investors might get elsewhere at the same level of risk. Supplier's business plans make promises about profits, which investors then discount against their estimate of the chance they will deliver. So it all comes down to that. A supplier says it will achieve $1 billion, investors and analysts think it is more likely to be $0.8 billion. The capital markets revolve around perceptions of risk. What boards and investors both need therefore is a strategic management process that gives a rigorous assessment of risk and uses that to assess and improve shareholder value creation. Just such a process has emerged from many years of research at Cranfield, a process we have called, appropriately, Marketing Due Diligence.

Marketing Due Diligence begins by looking for the risk associated with future strategy. Evaluation of thousands of business plans suggests that the many different ways that companies fail to keep their promises can be grouped into three categories:

1   The market wasn't as big as they thought.
2   They didn't get the market share they hoped for.
3   They didn't get the profit they hoped for.

Of course, a business can fail by any of these routes or a combination of them. The risk inherent in a plan is the aggregate of these three categories, which we have called, respectively, market risk, strategy risk, and implementation risk. The challenge is to accurately assess these risks and their implications for shareholder value creation.

A full description of the methodology for calculating whether future strategies will result in shareholder value added can be found in *Marketing Due Diligence – Reconnecting Strategy to Share Price"* (Butterworth-Heinemann, Oxford 2005).

Yet we have also found that for those companies who have a very large percentage of its sales accounted for by a small number of key accounts (what is often referred to as the 80/20 rule), the methodology for calculating whether strategies for key accounts create or destroy shareholder value, is very similar.

The only difference is that instead of assessing the risk associated with markets, strategies, and profit pools, each individual key account is risk-assessed according to factors such as the longevity of the relationship, the number of possible product/service lines bought, etc., as detailed in Chapter 6.

This methodology is now described in Tables 10.3–10.5 and Figure 10.4.

Table 10.3 Valuing key accounts

Background/facts
- Risk and return are positively correlated (i.e. as risk increases, investors expect a higher return).
- Risk is measured by the volatility in returns (i.e. the likelihood of making a very good return or losing money). This can be described as the quality of returns.
- All assets are defined as having future value to the organization. Hence assets to be valued include not only tangible assets like plant and machinery, but intangible assets, such as key accounts.
- The present value of future cash flows is one of the most acceptable methods to value assets including key accounts.
- The present value is increased by:
  - increasing the future cash flows
  - making the future cash flow "happen" earlier
  - reducing the risk in these cash flows (i.e. improving the certainty of these cash flows) and, hence, reducing the required rate of return.

Table 10.4 Suggested approach

- Identify your key customers. It is helpful if they can be classified on a vertical axis (a kind of thermometer) according to their attractiveness to your company. "Attractiveness" usually means the potential of each for growth in your profits over a period of between 3 and 5 years (see the attached matrix).
- Based on your current experience and planning horizon that you are confident with, make a projection of future net free cash flows from your key customers. It is normal to select a period such as 3 or 5 years.

(Continued)

Table 10.4 (Continued)

- These calculations will consist of three parts:
  - revenue forecasts for each year;
  - cost forecasts for each year;
  - net free cash flow for each key customer for each year.
- Identify the key factors that are likely to either increase or decrease these future cash flows. These factors are risks.
- These risks are likely to be assessed according to the factors shown below.
- Now recalculate the revenues, costs, and net free cash flows for each year, having adjusted the figures using the risks (probabilities) from the above.
- Ask your accountant to provide you with the overall SBU cost of capital and capital used in the SBU. This will not consist solely of tangible assets.
- Deduct the proportional cost of capital from the free cash flow for each key account for each year.
- An aggregate positive net present value indicates that you are creating shareholder value – that is achieving overall returns greater than the weighted average cost of capital, having taken into account the risk associated with future cash flows.

Table 10.5

Relationship risk factors	Minimum value	Maximum value	Assigned probability
Overall relationship with the company			
1 Number of relationships with other business units.	0	3	0 = 40%, 1 = 60%, 2 = 80%, >2 = 90%
2 Number of business lines with in this business unit.	3	10	1 = 40%, 2 = 50%, 3 = 60%, 4 = 70%, 5 to 10 = 80%, >10 = 90%
3 Longevity of relationship (in years).	0.5	16	<3 = 40%, 3 = 60%, 4 = 70%, 5 = 80%, >5 = 90%
Account relationship			
4 Company's relationship with broker. (where 1 = very poor, 2 = poor, 3 = fair, 4 = good, 5 = excellent)	1	5	1 = 40%, 2 = 60%, 3 = 70%, 4 = 80%, 5 = 90%
5 Quality and warmth of company/client relationship (where 1 = very poor, 2 = poor, 3 = fair, 4 = good, 5 = excellent).	1	5	1 = 40%, 2 = 60%, 3 = 70%, 4 = 80%, 5 = 90%
6 Number of relationship contacts company has at client.	2	8	1 = 50%, 2 = 60%, 3 = 80%, More than 3 = 90%
7 Number of relationship contacts client has at company.	3	10	1 = 50%, 2 = 60%, 3 = 80%, More than 3 = 90%

(Continued)

Table 10.5 (Continued)			
Relationship risk factors	Minimum value	Maximum value	Assigned probability
Understanding of client			
8 How good was our understanding of their company (where 1 = very poor, 2 = poor, 3 = fair, 4 = good, 5 = excellent).	1	5	1 = 40%, 2 = 60%, 3 = 70%, 4 = 80%, 5 = 90%
9 How good was our understanding of their industry (where 1 = very poor, 2 = poor, 3 = fair, 4 = good, 5 = excellent).	1	5	1 = 40%, 2 = 60%, 3 = 70%, 4 = 80%, 5 = 90%

A detailed explanation of the calculation in Table 10.5 was given in Chapter 6.

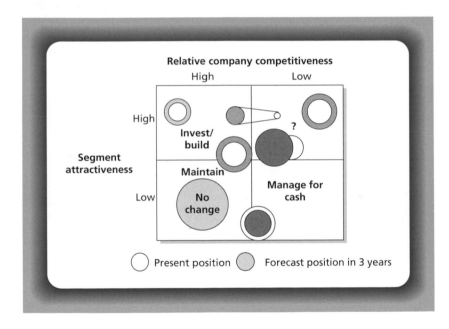

Figure 10.4
Portfolio analysis – directional policy matrix (DPM) (Note: Suggested time period – 3 years).

■ Barriers to the preparation and implementation of world-class key account plans

The key account planning process is quite rational and proposes nothing which, on the surface at least, is risky or outrageous. It is extremely surprising, therefore, that when confronted by an unfriendly economic environment, a majority of business people perpetuate an essentially parochial and short-term strategy as a coping mechanism.

By their own admission 80% of companies in recent research studies did not produce anything approximating to an integrated, co-ordinated and internally consistent plan for their marketing activities. It is even greater for their key account activities.

KAM's contribution to business success lies in its commitment to detailed analysis of future opportunities to meet customers' needs: in other words, identifying what products or services go to which customers. World-class companies reward those managers with a sense of vision who realize that there is no place for "rear view mirror" planning (i.e. extrapolations from past results). Of course, it is wise to learn from history, but fatal for businesses to attempt to relive it.

It is clear that any attempt to introduce formalized key account planning systems will have profound implications for the business in terms of its organization and behaviour. Until these implications are recognized and addressed, it is unlikely that strategic key account planning will be effective. Moreover, the task of designing and implementing sensible planning systems and procedures becomes progressively more complex as the size and diversity of the company grows.

The authors' research has identified the items in Table 10.6 as the most frequently encountered barriers to successful key account planning.

Table 10.6 Barriers to the preparation and implementation of key account strategic key account planning

- Weak support from the chief executive and top management.
- Lack of a process for planning.
- Lack of line management support due to any of the following, either singly or in combination:
  - hostility
  - lack of skills
  - lack of information
  - lack of resources
  - inadequate organizational structure.
- Confusion over planning terms.
- Numbers in lieu of written objectives and strategies.
- Too much detail, too far ahead.
- Once-a-year ritual.
- Separation of operational planning from strategic planning.
- Failure to integrate key account planning into the total corporate planning system.

We will now elaborate on each of these.

Weak support from chief executive and top management

Since the chief executive and top management are the key influencers in the company, without their active support and participation any formalized key account planning system is unlikely to work. This fact emerged very clearly from the authors' research. Their indifference very quickly destroyed any credibility that the emerging plans might have had, led to the demise of the procedures, and to serious levels of frustration throughout the organization.

There is a depressing preponderance of directors who live by the rule of "the bottom line" and who apply universal financial criteria indiscriminately to all products and markets, irrespective of the long-term consequences. There is a similar preponderance of technical people who see KAM as an unworthy activity and who think of their products only in terms of their technical features and functional characteristics, in spite of the existence of overwhelming body of evidence that these are only a part of what a customer buys. Not surprising, in companies headed by people like this, key account planning is either non-existent, or where it is tried, it fails. This is the most frequently encountered barrier to effective key account planning.

Lack of a plan for planning

The next most common cause of the failure or partial failure of key account planning systems is the belief that, once a system is designed, it can be implemented immediately. One company achieved virtually no improvement in the quality of the plans coming into headquarters from the operating companies over a year after the introduction of a very sophisticated system. The evidence indicates that a period of around 3 years is required in a major company before a complete key account planning system can be implemented according to its design.

Failure, or partial failure, then, is often the result of not developing a timetable for introducing a new system, to take account of the following:

1 The need to communicate why a key account planning system is necessary.
2 The need to recruit top management support and participation.
3 The need to test the system out on a limited basis to demonstrate its effectiveness and value.
4 The need for training programmes, or workshops, to train the management in its use.
5 Shortage of resources in some parts of the world.

Above all, a resolute sense of purpose and dedication is required, tempered by patience and a willingness to appreciate the inevitable problems which will be encountered in its implementation.

This problem is closely linked with the third major reason for planning system failure, which is lack of line management support.

Lack of line management support

Hostility, lack of skills, lack of data and information, lack of resources, and an inadequate organizational structure, all add up to a failure to obtain the willing participation of operational managers.

Hostility on the part of line managers is by far the most common reaction to the introduction of new key account planning systems. The reasons for this are not hard to find, and are related to the system initiators "lack of a plan for planning".

New systems inevitably require considerable explanation of the procedures involved and are usually accompanied by pro formas, flow charts, and the like. Often these devices are most conveniently presented in the form of a manual similar to that described in detail in Chapter 14. When such a document arrives on the desk of a busy line manager, unheralded by previous explanation or discussion, the immediate reaction often appears to be fear of their possible inability to understand it and to comply with it, followed by anger, and finally rejection. They begin to picture headquarters as a remote "ivory tower" totally divorced from the reality of the marketplace.

This is often exacerbated by their absorption in the current operating and reward system, which is geared to the achievement of current results, while the new system is geared to the future. Also, because of the trend in recent years towards the frequent movement of executives around organizations, there is less interest in planning for future business gains from which someone else is likely to benefit.

Allied to this is the fact that many line managers are ignorant of basic key account principles, have never been used to analysing their key accounts in the detail suggested in this book, nor of collecting meaningful information about them.

Confusion over planning terms

Confusion over planning terms is another reason for the failure of key account planning systems. The initiator of these systems, often highly qualified, frequently use a form of planning terminology that is perceived by operational managers as meaningless jargon.

Those companies with successful planning systems try to use terminology which will be familiar to operational management, and where terms such as "objectives" and "strategies" are used, these are clearly defined, with examples given of their practical use.

Numbers in lieu of written objectives and strategies

Most managers in operating units are accustomed to completing sales forecasts together with the associated financial implications. They are not accustomed to considering underlying causal factors for past performance or expected results, nor of highlighting opportunities, emphasizing key issues, and so on. Their outlook is essentially parochial, with a marked tendency to extrapolate numbers and to project the current business unchanged into the next fiscal year.

Thus, when a key account planning system suddenly requires that they should make explicit their understanding of the customer's business, they cannot do it. So, instead of finding words to express the logic of their objectives and strategies, they repeat their past behaviour and fill in the data sheets provided without any narrative.

It is the provision of data sheets, and the emphasis which the system places on the physical counting of things, that encourages the questionnaire-completion mentality and hinders the development of the creative analysis so essential to effective key account strategic plans.

Those companies with successful planning systems ask only for essential data and place greater emphasis or narrative to explain the underlying thinking behind the objectives and strategies.

Too much detail, too far ahead

Connected with this is the problem of over planning, usually caused by elaborate systems that demand information and data that headquarters do not need and can never use. Systems that generate vast quantities of data are generally demotivating for all concerned.

The biggest problem in this connection is undoubtedly the insistence on a detailed and thorough key account audit. In itself this is not a bad discipline to impose on managers, but to do so without also providing some guidance on how it should be summarized to point up the key issues merely leads to the production of vast quantities of useless information. Its uselessness stems from the fact that it robs the ensuing plans of focus and confuses those who read it by the amount of detail provided. This is why we have encouraged users of this book to summarize the audit sheets in Chapter 14 on the accompanying planning forms.

The trouble is that few managers have the creative or analytical ability to isolate the really key issues, with the result that far more problems and opportunities are identified than the company can ever cope with. Consequently, the truly key strategic issues are buried deep in the detail and do not receive the attention they deserve until it is too late. This is the reason that we have suggested categorizing issues facing the customer as low/medium/high in Chapter 14.

Not surprisingly, companies with highly detailed and institutionalized key account planning systems find it impossible to identify what their major objectives and strategies are. As a result they try to do too many things at once and extend in too many directions, which make control over a confusingly heterogeneous portfolio of projects and actions extremely difficult.

In companies with successful planning systems, there is system of "layering". At each successive level of management throughout the organization, lower-level analyses are synthesized into a form that ensures that only the essential information needed for decision-making and control purpose reaches the next level of management.

It can be concluded that a good measure of the effectiveness of a company's key account planning system is the extent to which relevant senior functional managers in the organization can make a clear, lucid, and logical statement about the major problems and opportunities a particular key account faces, how they intend to deal with these, and how what they are doing fits in with the overall objectives for the key account.

Once-a-year ritual

One of the commonest weaknesses in the key account planning systems of those companies whose planning systems fail to bring the expected benefits, is the ritualistic nature of the activity. In such cases, key account managers treat the writing of the key account plan as a thoroughly irksome and unpleasant duty. The proformas are completed, not always very diligently, and the resulting plans are quickly filed away, never to be referred to again. They are seen as something which is required by headquarters rather than as an essential tool of management. In other words, the production of the key account plan is seen as a once-a-year ritual, a sort of game of management bluff. It is not surprising that the resulting plans are not used or are relegated to a position of secondary importance.

In companies with effective systems, the planning cycle will start in month 3 or 4 and run through to month 9 or 10, with the total 12-month period being used to evaluate the ongoing progress of existing plans by means of the company's intelligence system. Thus, by spreading the planning activity over a longer period, and by means of the active participation of all levels of management at the appropriate moment, planning becomes an accepted and integral part of management behaviour rather than an addition to it which calls for unusual behaviour. There is a much better chance that plans resulting from such a system will be formulated in the sort of form that can be converted into things that people are actually going to do in order to create value for the key account.

Separation of operational planning from strategic planning

Most companies make long-term projections. Unfortunately, in the majority of cases these are totally separate from the short-term planning activity that takes place largely in the form of forecasting and budgeting.

The detailed operational plan should be the first year of the long-term plan, for each key account and key account managers should be encouraged to complete their long-term key account strategies and get them approved internally and by the customer before making their short-term projections. The advantage is that it encourages managers to think about what decisions have to be made in the current planning year, in order to achieve the long-term projections.

Failure to integrate key account planning into a total corporate planning system

It is difficult to initiate an effective key account planning system in the absence of a parallel marketing and corporate planning system. This is yet another facet of the separation of operational planning from strategic planning. For unless similar processes and time scales to those being used in the marketing and key account planning system are also being used by other major functions such as distribution, production, finance, and personnel, the sort of trade-offs and compromises that have to be made in any company between what is wanted and what is practicable and affordable, will not take place in a rational way. These trade-offs have to be made on the basis of the fullest possible understanding of the reality of the company's multifunctional strengths and weaknesses and opportunities and threats.

One of the problems of systems in which there is either a separation of the strategic corporate planning process or in which key account planning is a separate, formalized system, is the lack of participation of key functions of the company, such as engineering or production. Where these are key determinants of success, as in manufacturing companies, a separate key account planning system is virtually ineffective.

■ Conclusions

Consultants have learned that introducing change does not always mean forcing new ideas into an unreceptive client system. Indeed, such an approach invariably meets resistance for the organization's "antibodies" whose sole purpose is to protect the status quo from the germs of innovation.

A quicker and more effective method is to remove or reduce the effect of the barriers which will stop the proposed improvement from becoming effective. Thus, any attempt to introduce systematic strategic key account planning must pay due concern to all the barriers listed in this section.

Of course, not all of them will be the same for every organization, but without a doubt the most critical barrier remains the degree of support provided by the chief executive and top management. Unless that support is forthcoming, in an overt and genuine way, key account planning will never be wholly effective.

Strategic key account planning, when sensibly institutionalized and driven by an organization's top management, can make a significant contribution to the creation of sustainable competitive advantage. It is, however, important to distinguish between the *process* of key account planning and the *output*. Indeed, much of the benefit will accrue from the process of analysis and debate amongst relevant managers and directors rather than from the written document itself.

Finally, there are many human organizational and cultural barriers which prevent an organization deriving the maximum benefit from strategic key account planning. Being aware of what these are will go some way to helping organizations overcome them.

Mini Case

The Chief Executive Officer of a global engineering company recognized early in his tenure that, in each of his five strategic business units, there was a growing trend towards very large customers accounting for the bulk of sales revenue.

He started a process to tackle this problem by making himself familiar with the research outputs on global best practice in KAM from the KAM research club at Cranfield. He quickly realized that it would be totally pointless to initiate a development programme for his key account managers without the full support of his colleagues. So, he began the process by getting the authors to run a 2-day KAM appreciation workshop for his corporate board of Directors. This was followed by a 3-day KAM appreciation workshop for all the senior executives of every function in the company from around the World. This was followed by a series of 5-day skill programmes for every key account manager in the company. During these programmes, tentative key account plans were produced which were to be properly completed later and evaluated by the authors of this book.

Subsequently, planning systems were introduced.

The main point, however, was that the group CEO attended the beginning of every workshop over a 2-year period in order to demonstrate his and the board's full commitment to the process. It is not surprising that this company now has one of the best KAM programmes in the world and is reaping the benefits by outperforming the FTSE 100 average and outperforming its sector consistently.

CHAPTER 11

Knowing how customers think about their suppliers will make you a better key account planner

The purpose of this chapter is to explore key account management (KAM) from the customer's point of view. This chapter will spell out to key account managers precisely what it is that their key accounts are looking for from their suppliers. The more that the key account manager understands about the customer, the greater the chances that they can win new business and manage the existing relationship successfully.

In this chapter, we consider how customers select their suppliers, how they categorize them, and how they measure them. In some cases, the customer even has a plan for the supplier relationship; this chapter will offer the key account manager a peek behind the curtain to see how customers manage their key supplier relationship. We will explore:

- How to make sure you appear on the customer's radar
- Understanding customer's supplier selection criteria
- The buying motive
- Strategic intent in the relationship
- The customer's strategic plan for their suppliers

■ Fast track

- The supplier selection process has three broad phases: first, the customer has to be aware of the supplier; then, the customer has to consider the supplier seriously; finally, the customer has to choose the supplier.
- It is possible to differentiate the supplier offer even in the initial awareness stage through better communication with the customer.
- Only 1–2% of their suppliers are actually viewed as strategic by customers. This affects both the supplier selection and the supplier management process.
- The transaction cost (the price) may not be the best way for a supplier to present its offering. Instead, total cost of ownership (TCO) or even total cost of relationship (TCR) may be a better way of demonstrating how the supplier can add value.
- The supplier must understand the decision-making unit (DMU) and the decision-making process (DMP) of its key accounts. The earlier the supplier is involved in the DMP, the more likely it is eventually to win the business.
- Sophisticated customers will have a supplier management strategy according to the strategic importance of that supplier (the "strategic purchasing matrix"). However, even "commodity" suppliers can add value to their key accounts.

■ Introduction

The purchase of goods and services can account for 50–70% of a company's costs, so procurement is increasingly an area of strategic concern.

Key customers may be engaged in two aspects of strategic procurement: reduction of the supplier base and improving the ways that they manage the suppliers that remain. Establishing long-term relationships with fewer suppliers tends to increase *efficiency*; improving supplier management tends to increase *effectiveness*. Research has shown that supplier performance improves by 25% once customers put a supplier performance management programme in place. This performance improvement is a powerful incentive for customers to rationalize and manage their supplier base. Thales, the global defence and aerospace company, discovered that whilst the firm accounted for 20% of the total global market, it had over 50% of the suppliers. This example makes it easy to understand how a supplier rationalization project can save substantial sums of money.

> Supplier performance typically improves by 25% when customers put a supplier performance management programme in place.

The trend towards fewer, more managed supplier relationships can be both good news and bad news. Some suppliers – the weaker ones – will lose out as they are relegated to second tier or below. The stronger suppliers will benefit from increased customer closeness and an increased share of customer spend.

To grasp the opportunity, and in order not to lose out to competitors, key account managers need to understand what key accounts look for in a supplier relationship. This means four things: knowing how to appear on the customer's radar; understanding the selection criteria and process that will get your company selected over the competition; understanding the customer's strategic intent for the relationship; and appreciating what customers want from a longer-term supplier relationship.

> To be considered as a key supplier partner:
> 1 Register on the customer's "radar"
> 2 Understand the supplier selection criteria
> 3 Understand the customer's strategic intent
> 4 Appreciate what customers want from a longer-term supplier relationship.

■ Registering on the customer's radar screen

Like a nation's early warning system, customers have radar screens on which a number of competing suppliers appear. When they are choosing or switching suppliers, they first create an awareness set; then a much smaller consideration set from which the final supplier will be selected; finally, they choose their preferred supplier.

The first task for potential suppliers is to appear on the radar as a member of the customer's awareness set. The awareness set consists of all the suppliers the customer is aware of, which might be able to supply that particular product or service. If your company does not appear on the customer's radar, there is no way that you can be selected to supply. Sometimes this problem of failing to appear on the radar results in a supplier only hearing about an order when it has already been awarded to the competition. At that point, the key account manager thinks indignantly to himself, "we could have done that, but nobody asked me".

> The selection process has three phases: first, the customer has to be aware of the supplier; then, the customer has to consider the supplier seriously; finally, the customer has to choose the supplier.

Generally, suppliers have a good understanding of what they need to do to appear in the awareness set. Sadly, the factors which get suppliers into the awareness set tend to be more or less the same for competitors as well. In many markets quality, delivery performance, and continuous improvement are taken as given by the customers. So too is the ballpark price. To progress to the next stage, the consideration set, suppliers need to do more.

One of the factors that differentiates the suppliers in the consideration set (those who are being seriously considered), is communication with the customer. This will include demonstrating processes for handling the relationship, and for keeping customers informed of any product or delivery issues. Another factor that makes a consideration set supplier stand out from the competition is being proactive about suggestions for improvement and implementing these. A demonstrable track record of "going the extra mile" for customers can be an invaluable aid to selection. The BUPA example illustrates the basis on which a sophisticated procurement operation selects its key suppliers.

Key supplier selection: BUPA

BUPA is the largest private health insurer in the UK, with more than 4 million members. It operates 36 hospitals, 270 care homes, and 34 screening centres. It employs 40,000 staff and has some 5000 consultant partners, 3000 dentists, and 400 fitness centres. It is also an international organization, having operations in Spain, Ireland, Thailand, and Hong Kong.

It is clear from the description of its activity that BUPA is a major spender in the healthcare market. It is also an example of excellent practice in the selection and management of its key supplier relationships. In fact, BUPA has a strategy to build world-class suppliers that is part of its purchasing best practice process. BUPA's strategy for building world-class suppliers is:

- segment suppliers;
- focus the supply base;
- build relationships;
- continuously improve.

BUPA views procurement with a process focus rather than a product focus. It has also adopted a "total cost" approach in which it considers its purchased equipment and services in terms of acquisition costs, possession costs, and usage costs. Acquisition costs include the product price, but also the cost of evaluating products and correcting supplier mistakes. Possession costs include quality control and obsolescence, as well as storage and financing. Usage costs include disposal and environmental issues as well as training time, usage defects, product longevity, and waste.

Suppliers to BUPA who want to make the leap from preferred suppliers to performance partners will have to provide quality and innovation at the same time as cost control. BUPA looks for certain qualities in partner suppliers, which clearly include trust, common goals, and the expectations of both parties. However, BUPA is also interested in continuity of key staff and the length of the relationship.

Interestingly, BUPA tends not to commit itself exclusively to a single supplier. In its procurement policy, it explicitly prefers the freedom to purchase elsewhere.

The purpose of BUPA's procurement function is to manage all interactions with suppliers for requisitioning, authorization, ordering, receipt, and payment. The procurement function carried out purchasing, category, and supplier management.

BUPA also makes use of e-auctions. It views e-auctions as having advantages for both buyers and suppliers. From the buyer's point of view, e-auctions provide transparency, competitive prices, are quick and inexpensive, and can help identify efficient new suppliers. However, BUPA also argues that there are advantages for suppliers in e-auctions. These include transparency and valuable benchmarking information, more business for the most efficient suppliers, fairness, and a level playing field.

Like other customers who have key supplier relationships, BUPA believes that there is an effective relationship level and also a natural relationship lifetime. Suppliers need to recognize that their key customers have expectations about the relationship level and how they are managed. However, there will also be a relationship lifetime. Eventually, the relationship may come to an end; and no customer will preserve a relationship that has reached the end of its useful life, just for historic or sentimental reasons.

■ Supplier selection criteria and process

Only 1–2% of their suppliers are actually viewed as strategic partners by their customers.

Suppliers contemplating a relationship with a key account or a potential key account always aspire to be a strategic partner. However, only 1–2% of their suppliers are actually viewed as strategic partners by their customers. The largest category, which accounts for 70% of suppliers to a company, is its "arms' length" relationships. Thus, many suppliers need to resign themselves to having a relationship with the customer that is not as close as they would like. The mismatch between supplier and customer strategic intent will be considered in the next section.

What does a supplier have to do, to be considered as a strategic partner? First, it probably has to supply something that is strategically important to the customer. Second, it has to be difficult for the customer to replace the supplier. So, with the best will in the world, a small supplier of relatively unimportant products is unlikely to establish itself as a strategic partner in the way that a supplier of important and unique products might. That said, it is still possible to make good profits from such a relationship as long as it is handled correctly, as we shall explain later in this chapter.

Figure 11.1 illustrates a method that is widely used by sophisticated customers to categorize their suppliers. It analyses the supplier base according to the attractiveness of the supplier and the value of the business. The bottom left box (the "Nuisance" box) represents suppliers from whom they buy little and where the customer can buy similar goods or services from many similar suppliers. These relationships are almost invariably price-driven.

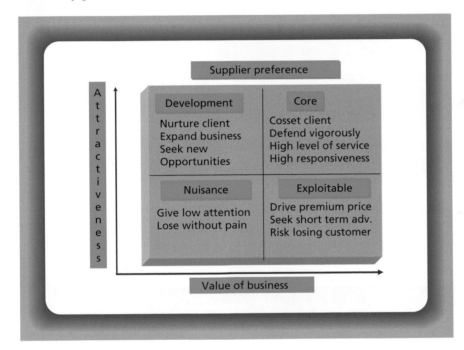

Figure 11.1
The strategic purchasing matrix. (*Source*: PMMS Consulting Group).

The top left box ("Development") is unusual in that, although the customer doesn't buy a lot, the relationship is important to them. It could, for example, be an ingredient that gives one of their products a unique taste, so the supplier is important to them.

The bottom right box ("Exploitable") is the most common cause of problems to suppliers, because the customer buys a lot, but has a wide choice of suppliers, so purchases tend to be made on price. E-auctions are frequent in such cases. Nonetheless, as we said above, there is a way in which suppliers can escape the commodity trap and become a strategic supplier.

To be in the top right box ("Core" supplier) is a much-coveted goal of most suppliers, because not only is it big business, but it tends to be very profitable, as customers work closely with you to get costs down and value up and often both parties share the benefits. There is a mutual dependency that ensures respect on both sides. Moreover, even companies who use e-auctions for other types of supplier relationship are sometimes prepared to pay substantial premiums to deal with preferred suppliers in the top right box.

Figure 11.2 is kindly supplied by a global leasing company. It shows the percentages of suppliers likely to fall into the boxes described in Figure 11.1 and indicates that most suppliers must inevitably fall into the "commodity" category, a fact which is well worth bearing in mind by those suppliers who do not take marketing seriously as a route to differential advantage.

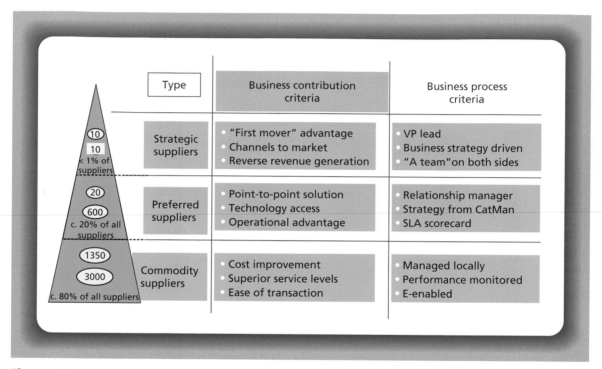

Figure 11.2
Supplier relationships as a source of business advantage.

Figure 11.3 sets out the criteria used by a global company in selecting their strategic suppliers. Supplier selection is the first stage in supplier relationship management (SRM). Most world-class companies have criteria similar to these.

Supplier relationship management

SRM is the practice of determining, developing, and maintaining the optimal business relationship with each supplier to achieve maximum long-term value from doing business with each supplier and from the supply base as a whole.

The first step in understanding how customers think about suppliers is for the key account manager to understand the key account's supplier

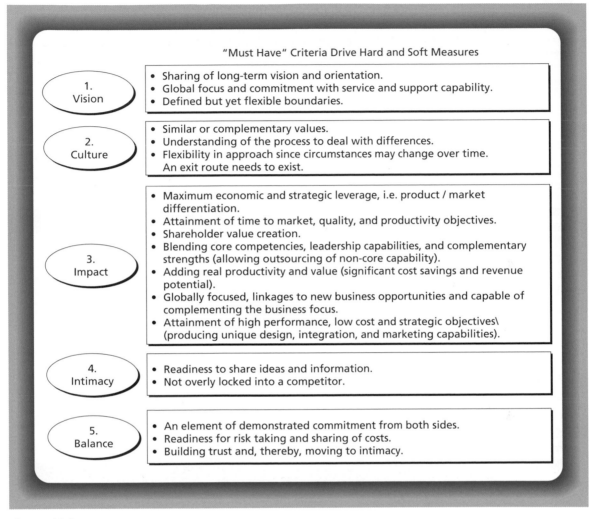

"Must Have" Criteria Drive Hard and Soft Measures

1. Vision
- Sharing of long-term vision and orientation.
- Global focus and commitment with service and support capability.
- Defined but yet flexible boundaries.

2. Culture
- Similar or complementary values.
- Understanding of the process to deal with differences.
- Flexibility in approach since circumstances may change over time. An exit route needs to exist.

3. Impact
- Maximum economic and strategic leverage, i.e. product / market differentiation.
- Attainment of time to market, quality, and productivity objectives.
- Shareholder value creation.
- Blending core competencies, leadership capabilities, and complementary strengths (allowing outsourcing of non-core capability).
- Adding real productivity and value (significant cost savings and revenue potential).
- Globally focused, linkages to new business opportunities and capable of complementing the business focus.
- Attainment of high performance, low cost and strategic objectives\ (producing unique design, integration, and marketing capabilities).

4. Intimacy
- Readiness to share ideas and information.
- Not overly locked into a competitor.

5. Balance
- An element of demonstrated commitment from both sides.
- Readiness for risk taking and sharing of costs.
- Building trust and, thereby, moving to intimacy.

Figure 11.3
Supplier selection criteria.

selection and SRM processes. The next step is to develop a deeper understanding of how the customer actually makes purchasing decisions. In the next section, we will examine the characteristics of business-to-business purchasing decisions and show how to analyse who is making decisions and what motivates them.

Characteristics of business-to-business purchasing decisions

Business-to-business purchasing decisions are very different from consumer buying. There are fewer, larger customers in business-to-business markets, whereas retailers may have hundreds of thousands, even millions,

Business-to-business purchasing is characterized by a DMU (decision-making unit) and a formal DMP (decision-making process).

of customers. Perhaps, more importantly, the decision about which supplier to use and which product to purchase is made by a number of people (the DMU) and often follows some formal or semi-formal process (the DMP) which can take weeks or months rather than days. As the products and decisions are complex, there are closer relationships between supplier and customer than in business-to-consumer markets, which means that personal selling plays a more important part. Moreover, the products are often customized; prices are negotiated; there may be a requirement for considerable technical support and advice from the supplier, including post-sale installation and training; and there may be specialist logistics (Table 11.1).

Table 11.1 A comparison of business-to-business purchasing and consumer buying

	Business-to-business purchasing	Consumer buying
Customer base	Few	Many
Buying process	DMU, formal, long-lasting	Individual or small group; informal; usually short
Relationship	Often close and long-lasting. Personal friendships may form	Usually short and impersonal
Product	Often complex/customized	Usually standard or modular
Price	Negotiated; often complex discount or rebate arrangements	Standard price
Promotion	Personal selling predominates	Multi-channel
Place (accessibility/ logistics)	Delivery; or through wholesalers or distributors	From stock. Often collected, or through retailers/delivery companies
Information requirements	Significant technical support expected	Low

Suppliers who are involved earlier in the DMP are more likely to win the order.

An important difference between business-to-business purchasing and consumer buying, as Table 11.1 shows, is that the DMP tends to be much longer and more complex in business-to-business situations than it is in consumer buying decisions.

Key account managers need to inform themselves about the DMP of their customers. Research shows that suppliers who are involved earlier in the DMP are more likely to win the order. The later in the process that the supplier gets involved, the less likely they are to win the order.

The DMP

Although we discussed the Decision making process in Chapter 3, we feel that it is of such importance that it needs to be revisited here.

Business-to-business purchasing decisions often pass through a formal DMP, which can take months or even years for larger purchases. Although it is not universally true, a general rule of thumb is that larger customers, such as key accounts, have bigger DMUs than smaller customers; and larger and newer purchases have more complex and formal DMPs than smaller, routine, or replacement purchases.

The DMP varies from customer to customer, but in outline terms it may have eight steps, sometimes more. The first step is problem recognition. Suppliers can help identify business issues for their key accounts. This may then lead to the recognition of a more general need. For example, issues with customer complaints might lead to the identification of a more general need for a customer relationship management (CRM) system. Then, there will usually be a process of specification which sets out exactly what the product or service should do and the standards it should meet. This is followed by a period of supplier search. Customers will sometimes issue requests for proposal (RFPs) or requests for information (RFIs) as early as the specification stage, to help them develop their own specification. It is vital that the supplier is firmly on the customer's radar at this point, and is considered to be a credible supplier of this particular good or service, as otherwise the chances of winning the order are vanishingly small.

This step may be followed by a separate and formal invitation to tender (ITT), after which the supplier is selected. The process does not end here, though, as there is very often a need for further specification of the order.

Finally, there is likely to be a process of supplier evaluation and performance review that takes place during and after delivery. In some key account relationships, the supplier performance review is conducted jointly with the customer. Some suppliers are proactive on this, and collect data on their performance themselves. In other cases, the customer carries out the performance review and feeds back some or all of the results to the supplier. This performance appraisal is in turn fed back into the DMP and may affect the supplier's chances of winning future orders.

> Generally, larger customers have bigger DMUs than smaller customers; and larger and newer (to the customer) purchases have more complex and formal DMPs than smaller, routine, or replacement purchases.

The DMP

1 Problem recognition
2 Formulation of general need
3 Specification
4 Supplier search
5 Proposal/tender submission
6 Supplier selection
7 Order specification
8 Performance review

Factors affecting the DMP

As we have seen, not all these phases are followed in every buying decision. When something is being bought for a new project, all the phases would be followed. Where it is a case of simply reordering something which has been bought before, the search and even tender processes may not be necessary. The newness of the decision to the buying organization also determines which types of people and how many are involved at each stage. Newness is a function of:

- the complexity of the product;
- the commercial uncertainty surrounding the outcome of the purchase.

The higher the "newness" on both these dimensions, the more people are involved and the higher their status. If product complexity is high, but commercial uncertainty is low, then the more important role is that of the design engineer and technologist. If newness is low on both dimensions, purchasing officers tend to dominate the process.

When faced with a new buy situation, the key account manager will be involved with a large number of people over a long period, helping, advising, and informing, always trying to influence the decision process and to build up a growing commitment towards their product.

A typical example of this process at work can be seen in the following example of the purchase of a telecommunications system:

The DMP for a large telecoms system purchase

1 The managing director proposes to replace the company's telecommunications system.
2 Corporate purchasing and corporate telecommunications departments analyse the company's needs and recommend likely matches with potential selling organizations.
3 Corporate telecommunications department and data processing managers have an important say about which system and firm the company will deal with. Other company directors also have a key influence on this decision.
4 Employees who use the telecommunications equipment are consulted.
5 The director of administration selects, with influence from others, the supplying company and the system.

The reason for going into such detail about the business-to-business buying process is simply to illustrate that it is not possible to determine the precise role of advertising versus, say, personal selling, until a company fully understands how its potential customers buy, and who are the important people that have to be contacted at the different stages in the buying process. Clearly, financial and administrative people will be involved at a different stage from, say, the engineers, and they will also require different kinds of information. For example, price, performance characteristics, delivery, before and after sales service, reputation/reliability, guarantees, payment terms, and so on, are not relevant to all people at all stages in the buying process.

The first point, then, is that a key account manager must understand the buying process of the markets which he/she addresses. Moreover, it is important to identify the people with significant influence on the purchase decision and the specific benefits each influencer wants (Figure 11.4).

There are many models for helping with this process, but essentially we should use a simple model which answers these questions:

- Who are the people with a significant influence on the purchase decision?
- What specific benefits does each important influencer want?

Figure 11.4 provides a logical approach to analysing an organization. As can be seen, it can be used equally effectively in either a product or service company.

> It is not possible to determine the precise role of advertising versus, say, personal selling, until a company fully understands how its potential customers buy and who are the important people that have to be contacted at the different stages in the buying process.

Key account:		
	Who, at client?	Their "hot buttons"
Buyer		
User		
Specifier		
Influencer/ Policymaker		
Gatekeeper(s)		
Decider		

Figure 11.4
DMU analysis form.

How customers measure and evaluate suppliers

Suppliers can sometimes forget that customers consider the performance review to be part of the purchasing process. It is all too easy to think that the process has finished when the product or service is delivered. In fact, smart key account managers will find out how their key accounts measure and evaluate their suppliers and will then put considerable effort into ensuring that their company delivers against the customer's targets and measures.

> Smart key account managers will find out how their key accounts measure and evaluate their suppliers.

As well as order-by-order performance, the type and closeness of the key account's relationship with the supplier affects the way the supplier is measured and evaluated. Standard suppliers are likely to be evaluated on a number of measures: quality, on-time delivery, service, price, total cost, contract compliance, lead times, and responsiveness. Strategic partners, on the other hand, are more likely to be evaluated on their ability to create value for the key account.

> Strategic partners are likely to be evaluated on their ability to create value for the key account.

Typically, strategic partners are selected and evaluated on both hard (financial) and soft (relationship) factors. Hard factors are the objectively measurable aspects such as delivery performance. Soft factors have to do with culture, values, and relationship factors, such as the warmth of a relationship or the supplier's ethical stance.

> Strategic partners are selected and evaluated on both hard and soft factors.

Financial aspects of supplier evaluation

Customers who practice strategic procurement are tending to move away from measuring their suppliers in terms of each individual transaction, and are increasingly thinking in terms of TCO or even TCR.

TCO evaluates a purchase in terms of its transaction cost, plus the cost per year of ownership, minus any residual value. So, a car fleet buyer will look at the purchase of the cars but will add on running costs, insurance costs, maintenance and repair costs, etc. The second-hand value at which the cars can be sold at the end of the contract (this measures how well they keep their value) will be deducted to give the TCO.

TCO calculations can reveal that the cheapest initial transaction price may not be the best deal for the customer. There are many examples of transactions where the cheapest product or service turns out to be of poorer value than buying a more expensive product which lasts longer and requires less maintenance. Sometimes the true cost of ownership is hidden from an organization because the costs of the transaction are borne by one department and the costs of servicing and maintenance are borne by another. The department bearing the transaction costs will try and keep these costs as low as possible, so might be tempted to buy the cheapest product on offer; whilst the maintenance or IT department then has to carry higher costs to look after a troublesome purchase.

> There are many examples of transactions where the cheapest product or service turns out to be of poorer value than buying a more expensive product which lasts longer and requires less maintenance.

Mini Case:

TCO

An interesting example was given to one of the authors by a director of a specialist construction company which built and fitted out hospital operating theatres. The customer's procurement guidelines initially resulted in the cheapest suitable light bulbs being specified in the operating theatres. However, a TCO analysis after the theatres had been in use for a while revealed that these light bulbs blew more frequently than the more expensive ones. This meant the expense and disruption of shutting down the operating theatre, calling in a maintenance contractor, and then re-sterilizing the operating theatre – all to change a light bulb!

TCO is a more sophisticated tool than cost comparison, but some customers go still further and measure TCR. As well as taking into account transaction costs and cost of ownership, TCR measurement may include cost of management time, communications costs, cost of quality, and even the cost of additional supply chain relationships that might be needed.

Both TCO and TCR are more likely to be used by larger customers. They are approaches that are increasingly employed before a customer makes a decision to rationalize its supplier base, so that it can figure out which suppliers to keep. Generally, both approaches are welcomed by good suppliers. Both help to demonstrate the true performance to the customer. Moreover, they can show suppliers where they are losing out with a key customer, and this may not be on the invoice price.

Relationship aspects of supplier evaluation

The relationship aspects of supplier evaluation often include measures of customer satisfaction and the general warmth of the relationship. Customer-focused measures might also include communications and speed of problem resolution. Strategic partners might also be evaluated on their internal processes, and on the opportunities they provide for joint projects and shared development which leads to improved productivity.

An important issue for the supplier to bear in mind is that relationships develop relatively slowly over time. Suppliers can make the mistake of underrating the importance of the non-financial aspects of the relationship to the customer. A common problem is that suppliers move key account managers from account to account, undermining the process of relationship building. It is clearly difficult to put a cost on the additional time and disruption involved when suppliers keep changing key people on the key account team. But it will be evident, however, that a company that has good employee retention and robust succession plans for its key account team will cause less disruption to ongoing projects in which learning and productivity are an important part of cost reduction and value creation for both parties.

■ Managing the relationship and its strategic intent

Over time, it is normal for relationships between supplier and buyer firms to pass through periods of strain and adjustment. Some research has even suggested that conflict can *increase* rather than reduce as the relationship endures and deepens. Key account managers need to be aware that, from time to time, their key accounts may question the relationship. In times of uncertainty, there is a tendency for customers to internalize functions and to draw back, even from interdependent or integrated relationships.

Important indicators of relationship continuity under pressure are:

- Trust and fairness
- Flexibility
- Absence of opportunism in the relationship

Trust is repeatedly cited by key customers as one of the most important factors in supplier selection, and it undoubtedly plays a major role in the perceived success of the relationship. Perceived fairness in the way that the supplier treats the customer is important in building trust. Those customers who have reduced their supplier base have created a new problem for themselves, that of supplier dependency. Supplier dependency makes the customer vulnerable to exploitation by, or being let down by, its suppliers. Perceived fairness of treatment (e.g. in terms of scheduling of production orders or availability of key people) influences the degree to which the customer feels they can trust the supplier. Note that fairness of treatment is not the same as "customer obedience", just doing everything the customer wants. Fairness of treatment may sometimes require a key account manager to say no to a key account, but if there are good reasons and those reasons are carefully explained to the customer, the relationship may not be damaged. It may even be enhanced, as the customer comes to respect the key account manager's judgement.

> Trust is repeatedly cited by key customers as one of the most important factors in supplier selection.

Having said that, flexibility and responsiveness to the customer's needs play a vital role in the development of relationships. A customer which has been assured that it is a key account is entitled to expect that its treatment by the supplier will be differentiated from the treatment received by ordinary customers. Flexibility and responsiveness is one of the characteristics that customers like in their suppliers; customers sometimes use phrases like "going the extra mile" to describe this. A supplier who takes real pains to help out a customer may gain not just a loyal customer but also an advocate, someone who tells others about their experiences. Key accounts are unlikely to be impressed by a key account manager who says that he can't help because "our systems don't allow it", or who can't make a decision on the spot. On the other hand, suppliers who are fast and flexible at responding to customers tell us that they often find customers reciprocating, so that the speed of decision-making increases. In turn, this accelerates cash flows to the supplier.

> Flexibility and responsiveness to the customer's needs play a vital role in the development of the relationship.

Linked to trust and fairness in the customer's mind is the absence of opportunism in the relationship. As we have seen, customers can be concerned about possible exploitation by their suppliers. A typical example is where the customer feels that the supplier might be making excessive profits out of the relationship. This can lead the customer to introduce e-auctions into its procurement function; the purpose of an e-auction is often to check whether the incumbent supplier is pricing its goods or services opportunistically. Frankly, the results of some e-auctions would tend to confirm the customer's suspicions. Some firms have secured price reductions of over 30% through e-auctions. On the positive side, the absence of opportunism can lead to reciprocity on the part of the customer. Research has shown that the benefits from a joint investment, for example, are often shared, even where the power asymmetries are considerable.

■ How customers manage their key suppliers

Key supplier plans

Key account managers are sometimes astonished to discover that their key accounts have similar management processes for the relationship as the key account managers do. They should not be. KAM is for customers as well as suppliers. In fact, where the relationship is valuable to the customer, there may be another plan – a key supplier plan – that sets out how the customer will manage the relationship on their side.

Supplier account plan

A forward-thinking UK financial services company has had a key supplier plan for some years. The plan contains six sections:

1 Introduction, indicating that, in this case, the plan was produced through a collaborative planning process between the customer and its key supplier, and a statement of how progress on the plan will be regularly reviewed at meetings between the customer's and key supplier's teams.
2 Information about the customer including its brand profile, organization structure, vision and strategy, and budgets.
3 Information about the supplier, including its products and services, objectives and strategy, market position and competitors, analysis of the revenue that the key supplier was getting from the customer and projecting how that revenue might change in the future, also indicating how important that made the customer to the supplier, plus supplier accreditations.
4 Overview of the relationship covering its history, the key contacts on both sides, the perception of the attractiveness of the relationship by both sides, where the supplier's decision-making authority is, and the supplier's perception of its opportunities with the customer.
5 A list of current projects between the customer and its key supplier.
6 A discussion of the customer's future requirements and potential projects.

The level of detail within the plan is impressive, as is the openness that this plan reveals in the relationship between this customer and its key supplier. Section 3, in particular, is remarkable for its statements of revenues and also of the analysis of the importance of the customer to the supplier. This analysis strengthens the customer's hand in supplier negotiations.

The detail in this key supplier plan is possible because the plan was produced in a joint planning exercise between the customer and its key supplier. However, other customer plans for suppliers exist even where these have not been developed collaboratively; it could be bad news for a supplier if there is a plan in existence but they are not aware of it.

■ The buying motive: What customers want from supplier relationships

What customers want: BT

With a turnover of £20.2 billion and employing just over 100,000 employees, BT is a large global organization. It serves more than 20 million business and residential customers in the UK and delivers service in 170 countries. BT offers local, national and international telecoms, broadband, internet products and services, mobility, and IT solutions.

Every year, BT spends more than £10 billion with its suppliers. Its procurement team consists of some 350 people who manage relationships with more than 22,000 suppliers.

Of its suppliers, BT regards less than 10% (2000) as key suppliers. However, only 20 or so of these are genuinely considered to be BT's supply partners.

BT says that it wants partners that it can trust; it also looks for innovation and mutual gain, not just "trying the hard sell". It is important for BT that suppliers recognize their relative importance to BT and adapt their contact strategy accordingly. High levels of contact are not welcomed from less important suppliers. Finally, BT warns that sometimes both parties need to recognize when the relationship is over.

BT finds itself engaged in some complex relationships where its suppliers are also its customers, and its collaborators are also sometimes its competitors. Of necessity, it has developed a clear view of how to categorize its key suppliers depending on business risk and business opportunity or benefit. The majority of key suppliers are viewed as commodity vendors, where BT's exposure (business risk) is low, as is the business benefit. Another 10–15% of key suppliers are categorized as specialist, which is high business risk but low opportunity. A smaller proportion is referred to as strategic suppliers, who offer high opportunity but low business risk. Finally, there are 20 or so group partners where there is major business opportunity but higher risk if things go wrong.

How to avoid becoming a commodity supplier

As suggested earlier in this chapter, it is possible to become a strategic supplier to a major customer even when the category of goods and services may be considered by the customer to be of low strategic importance. An aerospace company first split its €1.4 billion of purchases in Europe into strategic and non-strategic, as shown in Figures 11.5 and 11.6.

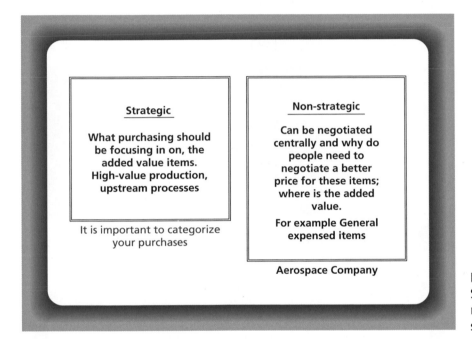

Strategic

What purchasing should be focusing in on, the added value items. High-value production, upstream processes

It is important to categorize your purchases

Non-strategic

Can be negotiated centrally and why do people need to negotiate a better price for these items; where is the added value.

For example General expensed items

Aerospace Company

Figure 11.5
Strategic versus non-strategic suppliers.

It then analysed the true cost of buying items. A summary of its findings is shown in Figure 11.7 below. Figure 11.8 shows another analysis that made the customer realize that 90% of its non-strategic suppliers fell into the bottom left box and they determined to look for reliable suppliers using the criteria in Table 11.2 below.

At the same time, perspicacious suppliers of items such as computers, office supplies, shelving, ladders, and the like were able to approach this customer with fully researched propositions incorporating such value-added services as vendor-managed inventory (VMI), having worked out the cost savings to the aerospace company.

VMI involves the coordinated management of finished goods inventories outbound from a manufacturer, distributor, or reseller (the vendor) to a retailer or other merchandizers.

The vendor is given the responsibility for monitoring and controlling inventory levels at the retailer's depot and in some instances at the retail store level as well. Specific inventory targets are agreed and it is the responsibility of the manufacturer to ensure that suitable inventory is

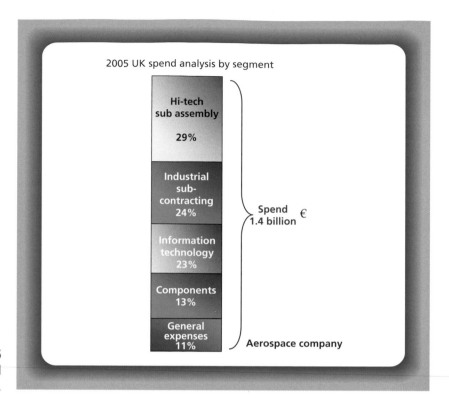

Figure 11.6
Customer's spend
analysis by category.

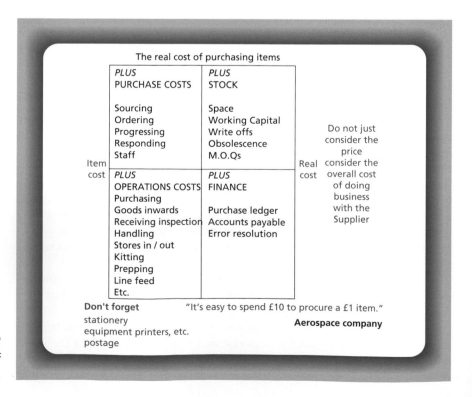

Figure 11.7
The real cost of
purchasing items.

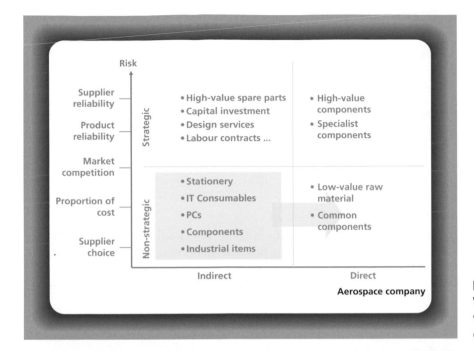

Figure 11.8
Where the company
was using
e-procurement.

Table 11.2 Selection criteria for non-commodity suppliers

Selection criterion

1 Companies who are technically advanced
2 Forward-thinking
3 Happy to partner
4 Best practices adopted
5 Radical
6 Open and honest relationship
7 Preferably global
8 Can offer more than what is seen in the catalogue
9 One stop shop

always available. The VMI proposition can be highly attractive to customers, as the true cost of holding stocks (inventory) can be substantial. The main elements of inventory costs are shown in Table 11.3.

The net result of this was a strategic alliance with five suppliers who took on the responsibility for managing all the processes associated with supplying those 90% of non-strategic goods and services that were previously costing the aerospace company far too much in terms of the effort involved. Even more important, however, is the fact that not only did costs reduce for the customer, but service improved, whilst the profitability of the suppliers also improved considerably.

Table 11.3 The true cost of inventory

Selection criterion

1 Cost of capital
2 Storage and handling
3 Obsolescence
4 Damage and deterioration
5 Pilferage/shrinkage
6 Insurance
7 Management costs

The moral of this case study is clear. For a sophisticated supplier of so-called commodity items, it is possible to become a strategic supplier to large customers who are open to such approaches.

To see where your company might be on your key account's strategic purchasing matrix, complete the audit in Table 11.4.

Table 11.4 Auditing your relationship with the key account

First, identify up to five factors that make suppliers of products or services such as yours attractive to the key account. Enter these in the right-hand column. In the left-hand column, enter the *acceptable* level of performance (as judged by the key account) for this factor. An example relating to delivery performance has been given to help you.

Once both columns are full, circle the number that corresponds to your company's performance on a scale from weak to excellent. Continue down the list, circling your company's score as viewed by the key account.

If you want to use this for benchmarking against the competition, join up your scores into a line. Then, using a different colour, circle the corresponding scores for a competitor and join these up. If your line tends to lie to the left of the competitor line, you will be viewed as a less attractive supplier by this key account. If your line lies all or mostly to the right of the competitor line, you are outperforming your competitor in the eyes of this key account.

If you are really brave, you could even ask the key account to complete this about your company and its competitors.

Factor (acceptable)	Performance (1 = weak, 5 = excellent)					Factor (attractive)
Reliable delivery into 1-hour delivery slots	1	2	3	4	5	Highly reliable delivery into 15-minute delivery slots
	1	2	3	4	5	
	1	2	3	4	5	
	1	2	3	4	5	
	1	2	3	4	5	
	1	2	3	4	5	

CHAPTER 12

How to evaluate your suitability as a key account manager

Summary

Are you the right kind of person to be a great key account manager?
There are certain indicators that can help predict whether an individual will make a good key account manager. In descending order of importance, these are:

● Biodata (especially, rate of promotion in previous jobs)
● Personality type (particularly signs of Conscientiousness and Extraversion)
● Emotional intelligence (empathy and understanding)

Up to this point in the book, we have focused on the planning and process aspects of key account management. These are vital aspects of world-class KAM. However, the people factor is also important. Previous research into business-to-business purchasing has found that people buy from people they know and like. This often gives the incumbent supplier an advantage over a new supplier. Moreover, when key accounts themselves are asked about what they want in a key account manager, they talk about trust and integrity, not about product knowledge and selling skills. Therefore, to complete your development into a world-class key account planner, we need to look at the people factor.

For some time now, companies managing long-term business-to-business relationships have recognized the need for a relationship manager to take responsibility for the successful development of the relationship. This chapter examines the experience and personality type that is required of a key account manager, to help you examine your strengths and weaknesses in the role.

Then, in Chapter 13, we will look at the skills and competencies required of a key account manager and show you how to develop into a world-class KAM planner.

■ Fast track

● To decide on whether a manager will make a good key account manager, the most important factors are biodata (life history) and personality type. The conventional job interview is not a good indicator of likely success.
● The very best sales people may not make great key account managers.
● Extraversion and Conscientiousness are associated with success in sales and KAM roles.
● Fast track promotion is a good indicator of likely future success, even where the prospective key account manager comes from a very different (i.e. non-sales) background.
● Higher EQ (Emotional Intelligence) is associated with success as a KAM team leader.

■ Do great sales people make good key account managers?

A major issue that companies face when they adopt KAM is who they should appoint into the key account manager roles. The obvious place to look first is amongst the sales force, and in many companies the key account managers are drawn exclusively from sales (in fact, a KAM role is seen as a "promotion" from a sales role and is based on sales success).

Clearly, the policy of appointing key account managers from the sales force has its merits. Good sales people tend to have better than average interpersonal skills; they have experience in customer contact; they are skilled at making presentations; they are persuasive, good at presentations, and not afraid of asking for the order.

However, the best sales people do not necessarily make great key account managers. Consider the comparison between sales and KAM presented in Table 12.1.

> The best sales people do not necessarily make great key account managers.

Table 12.1 A comparison of sales and KAM

The centre column shows a scale. For each row, put a cross against the box indicating which end of the scale your current job is. The more crosses there are towards the left side, the more strongly your role is sales focused. The more crosses to the right -hand side, the more the job is KAM focused.

This scale can also be used to rate whether a new job should be advertised as sales or as account management, and will help you to check that KAM job descriptions are appropriately written and that performance measures have been set correctly for the two different types of role.

Sales focus	Your current job role	KAM focus
Obtaining the order (short term)	☐ ☐ ☐ ☐ ☐	Developing value (long term)
Customer acquisition	☐ ☐ ☐ ☐ ☐	Customer retention and management
Multiple customers	☐ ☐ ☐ ☐ ☐	Small number of customers
Time spent with customer	☐ ☐ ☐ ☐ ☐	Time spent in office ensuring processes work smoothly for the customer
Mostly pre-sale	☐ ☐ ☐ ☐ ☐	Pre-, during- and after-sale
Measured by revenues	☐ ☐ ☐ ☐ ☐	Measured by profits
High percentage of compensation is commission	☐ ☐ ☐ ☐ ☐	High percentage of compensation is base salary

Having completed Table 12.1, you should consider whether your role currently profiles as a KAM role and, if it does, whether that fact is recognized. If your role profiles to the left (i.e. as more of a sales than a KAM role), you should consider whether you would be more comfortable in a KAM role or whether you would, in fact, prefer to continue in sales.

Admittedly, the picture presented in Table 12.1 is black and white, representing the extreme ends of the spectrum. In the real world, the distinction between sales and KAM is less clear-cut. Many sales people managing business-to-business relationships have a role in customer retention and relationship management. Many key account managers are measured by revenues and receive commission. But both sales people and key account managers recognize the general truth that there is a difference of emphasis in the two roles. It is less often acknowledged that this difference of emphasis also implies a different skill set.

When appointing key account managers, a company needs to consider the skill set it requires the key account manager to have or to develop. The most popular recruitment tool is the job interview, but it is widely recognized that job interviews are a poor method of evaluating an applicant's suitability for a job. Increasingly, companies are turning to a battery of other evaluation techniques that, used in conjunction with a job interview, improve the likelihood that they will appoint the right person. Four additional tools can be used to assess the suitability of an applicant for a key account manager role. In descending order of usefulness for KAM roles, these are: biodata; personality type; emotional intelligence; and cognitive ability (Table 12.2).

Table 12.2 Tools to assess suitability to a KAM role

Tool	Definition	Measured by	Suitability
Biodata	Life experience	Experience, work history, rate of promotion, age, education.	Clearly predicts job success.
Personality type	The way an individual interprets the world and interacts with it.	Psychometric tests. There are many of these, some far more predictive than others.	Predictive, if correct psychometric approach is used.
Emotional intelligence	EQ: The ability to detect and deal with the emotions of oneself and others. Has become very popular as a managerial tool.	EQ tests; can also be observed in interaction behaviour.	Moderately predictive. Most important for team leaders.
Cognitive ability	IQ.	IQ tests; can also be inferred from educational record.	Not strongly predictive.

As each of these four tools has some predictive ability for key account manager role success, each will be considered in turn.

Biodata

Biodata is the longest-established selection devise used when recruiting managers of all kinds, although it is used more systematically in the US and the UK than in other parts of Europe. Typical biodata elements include:

BIODATA

- Gender*
- Age**
- Education history and attainment, awards, prizes, etc.
- Work history and experience
- Rate of promotion in previous jobs
- Interests and spare-time activities
- Cultural background

* Discrimination on the basis of gender is illegal in many countries.
** There are moves to ban ageism (job discrimination on the basis of age) in the US and UK.

> Men are no more or less likely than women to find sales-related jobs attractive.

There is no gender difference in job attraction. Men are no more or less likely than women to find sales-related jobs attractive. However, men and women find different things about the job appealing. Generally, men enjoy the product servicing and travel aspects of KAM roles, whereas women tend to enjoy people-related aspects of their role, such as recruitment and training. When it comes to team leadership, there are some gender differences in sales. Sales teams led by women tend to have higher sales unit effectiveness and higher-growth sales areas; sales teams led by women also exhibit higher job satisfaction.

Age is a sensitive topic for most of us, but is an interesting issue in KAM roles. Essentially, the people who call for the banning of "ageism" have got it right, at least from a KAM perspective. There is no proven relationship between age and selling ability. However, there is a tendency for senior managers to perceive older key account managers as more effective. This tendency explains why many bright and able younger managers feel that they cannot get the recognition they deserve in their own companies and they move into higher status jobs elsewhere. Sometimes, these people even move back to their previous employers, but now in the better job they were turned down for a few months previously! The message for key account directors is to look at the record of the person applying for the job, not their age.

> There is a tendency for senior managers to perceive older key account managers as more effective.

Education history and attainment, to some extent, signals intelligence. However, there may be reasons to do with poor schooling or home life, or factors such as dyslexia, which mean that bright people may not do well at school, so it should not be taken as an invariable guide. Education history can also signal characteristics such as motivation, conscientiousness, and determination, especially if the individual has struggled against adversity to complete an education or has gained qualifications in their spare time. Evidence for educational attainment should always be checked, as there are surprising numbers of people who are holding down jobs for which they are not, in fact, qualified. In most organizations, false claims about qualifications are grounds for instant dismissal.

Work history and experience is used by many key account directors to "weed out" applicants who have either no relevant experience or who seem to "job hop", having many different jobs in a short period of time. However, key account directors should be aware that people not from sales or marketing backgrounds could make excellent key account managers. Operations and project managers, for example, often have useful skills that can be applied to the smooth running of a KAM relationship. Former HR managers may have useful people skills and are often knowledgeable about marketing and sales because they have commissioned courses and hired sales people for their former employers.

Rate of promotion in previous jobs is a good indicator of probable success in the future. Someone who is able in one role is likely to be able in another. The key account director should, however, allow for the age factor discussed above – a younger manager may not have progressed as fast as he/she should, because they were perceived as less able than older colleagues. Personal factors (likes and dislikes) can also play a role. Overall, though, rate of promotion is a good indicator and, of course, it is particularly helpful in evaluating a candidate with no previous KAM experience.

> Rate of promotion in previous jobs is a good indicator of probable success in the future. Someone who is able in one role is likely to be able in another.

Interests and spare-time activities are thought by some managers to provide useful insight into personality and motivation. For example, someone who is interested in competitive sports may tend to have a competitive personality. Outside interests can also provide indications of administrative capability, preferences for team versus individual working, leadership, sociability, attitude to detail, risk-taking, and many other useful pointers.

Cultural background may be taken into account when a candidate is interviewed. Some cultures, for example, frown on making a direct challenge to authority; in others, it is acceptable to do so. The style of questioning the key account director uses, could affect the outcome if the questioner is not sensitive to cultural differences. Where the applicant is not from the home country of the company, language and cultural references need to be considered; international applicants may simply not understand jargon or cultural references, or could find them offensive. With appropriate adjustment, biodata performs well across cultures, allowing comparisons between very different candidates to be made. Interestingly, research has also shown that biodata has a low adverse impact against ethnic minorities. In other words, biodata tends not to discriminate on racial or ethnic grounds.

Gathering biodata

The commonest way in which biodata is obtained is through a candidate's curriculum vitae (CV, called a résumé in the US and parts of Europe).

As biodata is predictive of job success, it is worth studying the CV with some care. Sadly, some applicants make claims on their CVs that are not, in fact, correct. These are chiefly about qualifications or previous job experience or success. They do this in the full confidence that many employers do not check the "facts" presented to them on the CV, and some do not even take up references. References should always be taken up and, for key positions, the CV should be checked. There are firms which offer CV checking services if it cannot be done by the company's HR department.

What biodata predicts

Properly used, biodata is a good indicator of probable success in a KAM role.

> Biodata strongly predicts job success in middle management roles such as that of the key account manager.

In addition, biodata has been found to predict an astonishing range of other aspects of performance. Amongst others, these include:

- proficiency (skill at the role, clearly associated with success);
- promotion and achievement;
- training success;
- propensity to leave;
- substance abuse;
- accidents.

Evaluating suitability for KAM using a CV

So far, we have seen that biodata is useful at predicting job success and other aspects of performance because of the evidence it provides of previous performance and of approach, capability, and personality. Most companies use biodata in its "raw" format, perhaps simply based on the candidate's CV or perhaps by ticking off various elements on a checklist that allows them to compare a number of candidates.

A few companies use a slightly more advanced checklist to try and make the biodata even more predictive. This is to combine biodata with a checklist that is weighted for task criticality. Table 12.3 shows a hypothetical example of a task criticality analysis for a key account manager role.

In this case, the KAM role has been broken down into a series of key tasks (column A). The key account manager will be expected to spend 50% of their time on internal management on behalf of the customer, 20% on ongoing relationship management, and the rest in a variety of different activities, including KAM planning and meetings (column B). Each task has been evaluated according to its difficulty (column C) and importance (column D). Task criticality is calculated using the simple formula:

$$\text{Task criticality} = \text{Time spent} + (\text{Difficulty} \times \text{Criticality})^1$$

[1] Adapted from Altink (1991).

Table 12.3 Biodata and task criticality

A	B	C	D	E	1	2	3
		Task				**Candidate**	
Task	Time spent (%)	Difficulty	Importance	Task criticality (C × D) + B	Rating	Rating	Rating
Selling new products	5	5	2	9	*	*	*
Collecting customer satisfaction data	5	1	5	10	*	*	*
Ongoing relationship management	20	3	5	35	**	**	***
Analysis of customer and markets	10	3	4	22	**	**	**
Developing KAM plan	5	2	5	15	**	**	**
Internal management	50	4	5	59	***	**	**
Other meetings	5	2	1	7	***	***	***

1 = very low; 2 = low; 3 = moderate; 4 = high; 5 = very high.

There are three short-listed candidates for this job, and they are all closely matched. Using their biodata, a straightforward star rating can be given. On this basis, the job would be awarded to candidate number 1, a former operations manager, who has the better performance at the critical task of internal management, rather than to candidate 3, a former sales person, who has a better track record in client-facing relationship management.

Personality type and the KAM role

Personality testing is a big business. Personality tests are used in at least 50% of all US manager selection. Finding the right personality test is confusing: personality testing is a huge and disparate field and there are some 5000 different personality tests in use in the US. However, the difference in predictive power between the best and the poorest is three times, so it is important to use the right test.

Personality, or "psychometric", tests are based on the assumption that there are a small number of different but fundamental personality types. The psychometric test aims to establish which personality type an individual falls into. Proponents argue that personality typing is a useful tool, not just in appointing someone who is likely to be successful in a job, but also in understanding how people operate.

In this section, we will consider two widely used psychometric tests – the Myers–Briggs Type Indicator (MBTI), and the Five Factor personality type.

Myers–Briggs Type Indicator

The MBTI is said to be the most popular and widely used of all psychometric tests. It is based on the psychology of Carl Jung, who built on Freud's work. It is widely available, straightforward to complete, has memorable results, and managers say that they find it gives them insight.

The MBTI uses reactions to a series of statements to categorize people by their preferences along four dimensions, described in terms of their anchors at each end.

MBTI dimensions

Extravert to Introvert
Intuitive to Sensing
Feeling to Thinking
Judging to Perceiving

The four MBTI dimensions are described in Table 12.4.

Table 12.4 MBTI dimensions

From	Anchor	Description	To	Anchor	Description
E	Extravert	Gains energy through interaction with others	I	Introvert	Gains energy through individual contemplation
N	Intuitive	Gathers data through intuitive, soft, people-based methods	S	Sensing	Prefers hard facts and evidence
F	Feeling	Processes information through people factors and "gut feel"	T	Thinking	Processes information through logic
J	Judging	Prefers reaching individual decisions	P	Perceiving	Prefers collective decision-making

Because there are four dimensions, there are 16 (4×4) MBTI types. There is no right or wrong here; the MBTI questionnaire simply elicits the individual's preferences on each of the four dimensions and profiles them accordingly. MBTI profiles are known by the identifying letters for the preference, so the results are expressed as, for example, "ENTJ" for an Extravert/Intuitive/Thinking/Judging type, or "ISFP" for an Introvert/Sensing/Feeling/Perceiving type. Note that the definition of Extravert and Introvert in MBTI is not the same as the everyday use of the term.

What MBTI predicts

Proponents of MBTI claim that it is helpful for putting people into the best job role for them. Extraverts, for example, are said to like stimulation and change in their job roles and will embrace challenging roles that involve high levels of interaction with others, so they are placed in managerial roles where they help others. Introverts prefer developing technical skills. Intuitive types prefer stimulation and self-direction, whereas Sensing types prefer comfort, belonging, and helping others; so Intuitive types might prefer to work alone or lead a team, whereas Sensing types might prefer to work in a caring role within a team. Feeling types are said to be more sociable comfort oriented than Thinking types; they might make judgements based on gut feel or people issues, rather than logic, so they might be more inclined to give people the benefit of the doubt, whereas Thinking types would ask for proof. Judging types enjoy decision-making and also belonging and security, so are likely to find themselves in managerial positions in organizations, compared to Perceiving types who value autonomy and freedom in their careers and might prefer to freelance.

There are also combinations of MBTI dimensions that are said to be of particular interest to businesses. For example, NT types (as in ENTJ, INTP) like innovative action and creativity. When combined with Extraversion and Judging, this type – ENTJ – is said to be an important profile for business leaders and managing directors. It is said that ISJ types, as in ISTJ, are managers who are interested in productivity improvements and might find careers as Finance Directors or company doctors. Although businesses prefer to appoint EST types (as in ESTP or ESTJ) into middle manager roles, N is creative and the percentage of Ns increases, the higher the managerial rank.

Using MBTI

As described above, its supporters argue that MBTI can be used to help put the right person into the right job. However, the right MBTI profile in as KAM job could vary depending on the precise conditions of the job. For example, E types might be preferred over I types if the job was team based. NF types might be preferred if the company thought that soft factors were important; ST factors might be preferred if hard performance data were what won clients. A J type might be preferred for a role as a KAM team leader, whereas a P type might be preferred as an assistant. Some attempts to profile the roles of key account managers, particularly for key account managers who lead global teams, have suggested that these roles are akin to that of a managing director running a business unit, in which case an ENTJ profile might be very successful.

In a KAM or sales role, MBTI may have some uses. For example, N (Intuitive) types are more likely than S (Sensing) types to intuit how the customer is feeling and to respond. If adaptation is considered to be a key skill in relationship management, which it usually is, N types may be preferred over S types. In addition, people who profile as T (Thinking and logic) rather than F (people factors) are more likely to adapt to changes in customer situations or responses. This is because T types are more responsive to the facts they are being told, than F types who are more influenced by who is telling them. T types might be preferred for key account manager roles. Thus, NT types (such as ENTJ or ENTP) might be preferred for a KAM role.

MBTI: Popular but less useful

Before appointing a key account manager using MBTI, however, companies should be aware of the drawbacks. In spite of – or, perhaps, because of – its alluring simplicity, MBTI has attracted some criticism. One criticism is that the dimensions tend to overlap. Critics argue that, for example, N–S and F–T partly measure the same things. More seriously, MBTI is not particularly stable over time. Up to 44% of people retaking MBTI will change on at least one dimension. This criticism is borne out by the personal experience of one of the authors, whose profile apparently changed from ENTJ to ENTP on retesting within 5 years. If the MBTI profile can change, it is argued, it must be measuring something less fundamental than personality type, which would not be expected to change at all, let alone within a comparatively short period. On consulting with an independent MBTI expert, who had not been involved in either test, the expert advised that the author's ENTJ profile had been suppressed in favour of ENTP "because of your current job environment". If the MBTI profile can change depending on one's work environment, its ability to predict how someone will perform in different roles or in a different work environment must be limited.

The conclusion is that MBTI, which is a widely used personality profile mechanism, should be used with caution in a KAM context. However, there is another approach to psychometric testing which does seem to offer useful guidelines to key account directors looking to appoint key account managers. This is the Five Factor Model.

The Five Factor Model

Until the mid-1990s, research indicated that key account manager performance was determined by experience and history (biodata), skill, and knowledge, rather than by personality type. Even today, most organizations do not use personality type when recruiting key account managers. However, the evidence that certain personality types are correlated with success in sales and KAM roles is growing. The Five Factor Model is currently regarded as the most valid of the many personality typologies. Although the five personality factors profiled in the Five Factor Model are quite broad, they seem to perform well in explanatory power. In fact, the influence of the Five Factor Model is now so great that psychologists now divide the various personality typologies into "Five Factor" and "non-Five Factor". The basic Five Factor Model has been developed into numerous approaches such as the popular 16PF. MBTI is a non-Five Factor approach.

> The evidence that certain personality types are correlated with success in sales and KAM roles is growing. The Factor Model is currently regarded as the most valid of the many personality typologies.

As the Five Factor Model seems to be predictive of key account manager success, it should be taken seriously by key account directors. The Five Factors and their explanations are set out in Table 12.5.

Table 12.5 The Five Factor Model	
Personality trait	**Description**
1 Extraversion	Talking, active, assertive, self-confident
2 Emotional stability	Low worrying; not subject to major mood swings; opposite of Neuroticism (pathological worrying)
3 Friendliness	Agreeableness, getting on with others
4 Conscientiousness	Self-starting, personal motivation, will to achieve, striving for targets
5 Openness to experience	Flexibility, willingness to learn, adaptability, intelligence

Table 12.5 lists the "Big 5" personality traits. The only one in common with MBTI is Extraversion. Proponents of the Five Factor Model argue that the Big 5 accounts for most of the variability in human personalities.

Long-term studies have found that the Five Factor Model is very stable. People taking Five Factor tests tend to profile the same way, repeatedly. This makes the results of the Five Factor approach more reliable. It is also claimed that it is less amenable to biased responses than MBTI. The factor that can change somewhat is factor 3, Friendliness. A person's friendliness can be temporarily affected by circumstances such as life problems or uncongenial employment, although the essential characteristic does seem to reassert itself over time.

The link between personality and key account manager performance

Personality type is predictive of job performance. If used in combination with biodata, it is strongly predictive.

> The best results for predicting job performance are achieved by combining biodata and personality type. The latter is best evaluated using the Five Factor Model.

Overall, taking all types of occupation into account, factors 1 and 4 (Extraversion and Conscientiousness), seem to be the most powerful predictors of success. People with higher Extraversion and Conscientiousness tendencies are more likely to be employed in the first place, and are more likely to be successful at work.

Two of the Five Factors are more predictive of sales-related roles such as KAM. These are Conscientiousness and, to a lesser extent, Extraversion.

As already outlined, these two factors are generally associated with success in other jobs. However, there are specific aspects of Conscientiousness and Extraversion that are correlated with success in KAM-type roles; these detailed aspects are shown in Table 12.6.

Table 12.6 Detailed aspects of Conscientiousness and Extraversion associated with KAM success

Conscientiousness	Extraversion
Drive for competence	Sociability
Feelings of personal control	Influence
Achievement orientation/competence striving	Energy
Independence	
"Can do" mentality	
Goal setting	

Other elements of the Big 5 that are linked to success in KAM roles include:

- emotional stability/an optimistic outlook;
- empathy and imagination.

Conscientiousness is a strong predictor of job performance, whatever be the job. It also includes the will to achieve and, hence, drive and internal motivation. It affects performance through goal setting; research has repeatedly found that people who set goals, particularly if they write them down, achieve more than people who do not set goals. Also, conscientious people are less likely to engage in counterproductive behaviours such as feigning illness.

Interestingly, there is no relationship between Conscientiousness and intelligence. Clever people are not necessarily more conscientious. For any given level of ability, conscientious people will outperform less conscientious people.

Extraversion does not predict success as strongly as Conscientiousness, but Extraversion is particularly associated with success in jobs with high social contact such as key account managers.

If Extraversion and Conscientiousness are definitely predictive of success, two other factors (factors 3 and 5, Friendliness and Openness to experience) may have a role to play in key account manager's performance. Friendliness is correlated with performance in jobs that involve substantial interpersonal interactions, such as KAM. Essentially, research has

Extraversion does not predict success as strongly as Conscientiousness, but Extraversion is particularly associated with success in jobs with high social contact such as key account managers.

shown that buyers have a tendency to buy from people they like. Openness to experience, factor 5, is not directly correlated to success, although people who have this characteristic get more out of training and learn faster, which might be important in KAM roles.

So, Extraversion and Conscientiousness are definitely associated with KAM success, and Friendliness and Openness to experience are in some measure associated with KAM success. The only personality factor in the Five Factor Model that does not correlate with job performance is Emotional stability; this means that worriers are no more likely to make good key account managers than non-worriers.

Career success and personality type

The measurement of career success can take two forms – extrinsic and intrinsic. Extrinsic success is the usual measure of job success and examines measures such as salary, number of promotions, total pay (including commissions and bonuses), and status. These measures are extrinsic because they can be seen by the outside world. Intrinsic success is job satisfaction, which is a subjective measure of success. This measure is intrinsic because it cannot readily be observed directly by the external world but is more a matter of internal attitude and feelings.

Conscientiousness is a strong predictor of both extrinsic and intrinsic success. In terms of extrinsic success, Conscientiousness specifically predicts promotion success. Conscientious people are more likely to be promoted. They are also more likely to have high job satisfaction (intrinsic success).

> Conscientious people are more likely to be promoted. They are also more likely to have high job satisfaction.

It is fascinating to find that earnings are also linked with Extraversion. Extraverts are likely to have higher earnings. This may also be linked with the self-confidence that leads Extraverts to apply for higher-paying jobs.

> Extraverts are likely to have higher earnings.

Emotional Intelligence

Emotional intelligence (EQ) is defined as emotional literacy, being able to handle one's own emotions; and social literacy, which is sensing what others are feeling, and handling relationships effectively. EQ has achieved remarkable recognition as a management tool in a relatively short time because it is thought to measure important managerial skills. Some personality profiling tools, such as 16PF, now incorporate measures of emotional intelligence.

EQ measures an individual's ability to interact with others, called interpersonal competencies. These include: managing people; persuasiveness; assertiveness; decisiveness; sensitivity; and effective oral communication. These are desirable traits in general managers, but also in key account managers.

The development of EQ was, to some extent, in response to the failure of cognitive intelligence (IQ) to explain differences in job performance. Having a higher EQ is associated with career success. In particular, two specific aspects of emotional intelligence, Influence and Adaptability, are associated with EQ. Good team leaders tend to have higher EQ than other

> Good team leaders tend to have higher EQ than other team members.

team members, although they may not be more conventionally intelligent as measured by IQ tests.

Proponents of EQ suggest that combining it with a measure of IQ will give better predictability of job performance than either measure on its own.

Cognitive ability (IQ) and KAM

General cognitive ability (IQ) has only a small direct effect on job performance, beyond a threshold level of intelligence that is required to carry out the role. Two specific aspects of IQ, Risk-taking and Creativity, do have some predictive power for job success.

In fact, research into IQ in a sales context found that IQ is not a good predictor of sales success. Curiously, sales managers with higher IQs are rated more highly by their bosses, even though their higher IQ does not translate into better sales success.

IQ may also have an indirect effect on job performance through its effect on job knowledge (how to perform the job, what to do and how to do it). Job knowledge comes with experience, but people with high IQs tend to develop better job knowledge.

> IQ is not a good predictor of sales success, despite the fact that sales managers with higher IQs are rated more highly by their bosses.

References

Altink, W.N.M. (1991). Construction and validation of a biodata selection instrument. *European Work and Organisational Psychology*, 1(4), 245–270.

See also: Ryals, L.J., Bruce, L. and McDonald, M. (2005). Managing KAM relationships. A report for the Cranfield KAM Best Practice Research Club, Cranfield, September 2005.

CHAPTER 13

How to be a world-class key account planner

The purpose of this chapter is to spell out the knowledge and skill sets required by key account managers through an analysis of the various roles that key account managers have to fulfil. It is based on years of research at Cranfield School of Management and on many key account management (KAM) development programmes for major multinationals. This chapter looks at the roles, knowledge and skills of key account managers and global account managers. Finally, the chapter considers a new development in world-class KAM planning, which is to match the key account manager to the key account.

The purpose of this chapter is to identify the roles and skills of the key account manager; to show how these might be different in different types of relationship; to show how to audit your key account manager skills; to look at the different preferences that different key account managers have for managing in different styles and to show that this can be turned to a positive advantage in the management of a portfolio of key accounts.

■ Fast Track

- The roles of the key account manager are: boundary spanning, strategist, entrepreneur, team leader, information provider, relationship manager, and negotiator. Different types of relationship may call for greater or lesser amounts of certain roles. For example, in strategic partnerships the key account manager may spend more time on boundary-spanning and strategic roles, whereas in basic relationships the negotiation role may be more important.
- The core competencies of the key account manager are those competencies which key account managers must have, although they will be stronger in some competencies than in others. The seven core competencies of the key account manager are: product knowledge; knowledge of the customer; knowledge of the customer's industry; ability to inspire trust; project management; interpersonal skills; and negotiating and selling skills.
- Closer and more complex KAM relationships demand more advanced competencies from the key account manager. These advanced competencies are: commercial awareness/strategic vision; consultancy skills and business performance improvement; advanced KAM planning; internal management; team leadership; advanced marketing techniques; and finance.
- All key account managers have a wide range of skills, but most have a preference for a certain work style. The four styles are business manager, entrepreneur, project manager, and tactician.
- Matching the key account manager style to the type of key account based on its position in the customer portfolio is more likely to result in optimizing the relationship. Allocating key accounts to key account managers by territory or geographical convenience may not be the best way.

■ The roles of the key account manager

One of the most challenging things about the key account manager's role is that it is complex and varies according to relationship circumstances. Unlike the sales role, which is mostly concerned with informing, negotiating, and closing, the KAM role is about complex relationship management. The particular role played and the skills needed may vary over time. At certain times, the key account manager may need to focus on negotiation; but at other times, the role may be problem solving, co-ordinating, providing information and advice, or even managing corporate politics! Generally, the roles of the key account manager are thought to be boundary spanning, strategist, entrepreneur, team leader, information provider, relationship manager, and negotiator.

> The roles of the key account manager are boundary spanning, strategist, entrepreneur, team leader, information provider, relationship manager, and negotiator.

Boundary spanning: One of the most important roles of the key account manager is known as "boundary spanning". This is a co-ordinating role between the two organizations and also within the supplier. Between the two organizations, for example, the key account manager may work with the procurement manager to ensure that the customer's local factories buy from the approved supplier. Perhaps, even more importantly, the key account manager works within his/her own company to solve problems and ensure that the service to the customer is seamless. Because of the importance of this role, key account managers may spend 60–70% of their time in their own companies, ensuring that the internal processes run smoothly, rather than with the customer.

> Key account managers may spend 60–70% of their time in their own companies, ensuring that the internal processes run smoothly and resolving problems.

Strategist: Key account managers have an important role in developing strategy for the key account. In many instances, this involves working with the key account to identify shared goals, advise on future developments in products and markets, undertake joint planning with the key account, ensure strategic alignment, and discuss joint projects.

Entrepreneurial: The entrepreneurial role is about locating the kinds of opportunities that are then developed through the strategist role. Wearing an entrepreneurial hat, the key account manager will be on the lookout for possible areas in which the supplier can extend the product range it supplies to the key account, can extend the geographical scope of the relationship, or can engage in shared projects. One example would be proposing new stock-holding arrangements to the customer, or perhaps identifying an opportunity for the customer to reduce costs and improve efficiency by switching to category management, a service that the supplier can provide. The key account manager is uniquely well placed to identify new opportunities because of the closeness of his/her relationship with the key account.

Team leader: At least 50% of key account managers now work in teams, and the proportion is rising. KAM teams may also be geographically dispersed, which makes them more difficult to manage.

Information provider: Information provision about products and services provided by the supplier is one of the classical sales roles. However, the information that the key account manager may provide is generally broader. For example, the key account manager may report on the supplier firm's delivery performance. Or, the report may be a progress report on a shared project or on the achievement of shared goals. In addition, some key account managers are good at identifying trends in the key account's own markets, which are then reported back in the context of a discussion about the relationship.

Relationship manager: The role of relationship manager is about developing trust between the two companies; it is also a troubleshooting role. In a KAM relationship, the customer will not expect to have to sort out problems for themself; that is seen as the role of the key account manager. The key account manager acts as the key account's representative within the supplier company. This can sometimes lead to frictions between the interests of the client and of the supplier. Relationship management will also comprise communication with the customer; it may also involve social functions.

> The key account manager acts as the key account's representative within the supplier company.

Negotiator: Key account managers still need to be able to sell, although in some larger companies the selling role is separated from the relationship management role.

The key account manager's job is likely to involve some of each of these roles, although not all at the same time. Some relationships need less of certain roles, and some relationships need more. For example, some key accounts are less willing to share their strategic plans, so the strategist role is reduced. In other situations, the key account is not managed by a team, so the key account manager does not need to perform a team leader role. That said, the job of the key account manager is a multifaceted one and most people are more comfortable with some roles than with others.

Table 13.1 provides a quick assessment tool for thinking about which roles you are most comfortable with.

To be able to fill the seven roles listed in Table 13.1, key account managers have to have a wide knowledge and skill set. In the following section, we will take a look at the knowledge and skills (competencies) needed by key account managers. These are divided into core competencies and advanced competencies. Then, we look at the emerging role of the global account manager, who manages an international or global customer, and examine the additional competencies needed for global account management (GAM).

■ Knowledge and skills of the key account manager

The knowledge and skills ("competencies") required by a key account manager fall into three categories. First, there is the essential knowledge and skill set required for all key account managers to carry out a basic KAM role. Second, there are advanced KAM competencies that a key account manager needs in order to manage more complex types of key account relationship. Third, there are competencies that are important for global account managers.

Table 13.1 Audit of role importance and confidence level

Think of a particular key account that you manage; this will help to make the audit relevant to your needs. For each role, indicate its importance and your confidence level on a scale of 1–5 where 1 is low and 5 is high. Consider the results. Ideally, you should be more confident with roles that are important in that relationship; so, if the importance score is high, the confidence score should also be high. If this is not the case, you may like to consider whether you need to undertake some reading or training to build your confidence; this can be noted in the final column. If the role importance is low, then it does not matter that your confidence level is low, although you might want to consider some longer-term personal development in these areas .

Key account:

....

Role	Importance with this client (1–5)	My confidence level with this role (1–5)	Notes on personal development
Boundary-spanning Strategist Entrepreneurial Team leader Information provider Relationship manager Negotiator			

Core KAM competencies

The core competencies of the key account manager are those competencies that the key account manager needs to manage both exploratory and basic (bow tie) type relationships with a key account. These are: product knowledge; knowledge of the customer; knowledge of the customer's industry; ability to inspire trust; project management; interpersonal skills; and negotiating and selling skills.

The core competencies needed by a key account manager

- Product knowledge
- Knowledge of the customer
- Knowledge of the customer's industry
- Ability to inspire trust
- Project management
- Interpersonal skills
- Selling and negotiating skills

Product knowledge: Key customers expect that the key account manager appointed by their supplier will have an in-depth knowledge of the supplier's products.

Knowledge of the customer: As well as extensive knowledge of the supplier's products or services, the key account manager should be able to identify how those products or services fulfil a need for that customer. This requires the key account manager to understand the customer and the customer's industry in depth.

> As well as extensive knowledge of the supplier's products or services, the key account manager should be able to identify how those products or services fulfil a need for that customer.

Inspire trust: In addition to the knowledge and application requirements, it is very important for key account managers to establish their own – and their firm's – integrity and to demonstrate that they can be trusted. Key customers overwhelmingly declare trust and integrity to be the most important factors in their selection of suppliers. In early stages of the relationship, establishing trust can be difficult as there may be very few or no transactions to back up the claims made by the key account manager. Other evidence, such as case studies or the endorsements of other customers, guarantees, market research, etc. may be helpful to establish trust. The key account manager must also think carefully about what he/she is promising; these promises must be credible. Further, the key account manager's behaviour and general demeanour should underline the trust and integrity message.

Project management: As part of the "delivering what we promised" issue, key account managers need to develop project management skills which help them to ensure that undertakings given to the customer are actually met. The role of the key account manager is to ensure that things get done and that what is promised is delivered. Like the sales role, the key account manager works on developing the customer value proposition but, unlike most sales roles, he/she is also instrumental in ensuring delivery to the customer. Thus, project management skills are important. These include problem analysis and solving, planning, resource allocation, and change management skills.

> The role of the key account manager is not just to develop the customer value proposition, but also to ensure that what is promised is delivered.

Interpersonal skills: Research shows that customers do more business with people that they like, so interpersonal skills are important. World-class key account managers establish rapport, demonstrate empathy, listen well, and are likeable people. They tend to be slightly extraverted and are "people people" because it's easier to like someone who likes you.

Selling and Negotiating: Even when the relationship is well developed, there is still a need for selling skills. This is even more the case with basic (bow-tie) relationships. Basic relationships tend to have transactional characteristics, so the key account manager needs to have essential sales skills (such as solution selling, going for the close, presentation skills, etc.). Moreover, there are often frictions in KAM relationships that require the key account manager to exercise negotiation skills. In fact, the very closeness of the relationship means that the customer is more exposed to the supplier and, therefore, is more likely to notice failures of performance and communication. In addition, the key account manager has an important internal role as the customer's advocate; he/she often has to negotiate with other departments in the supplier firm to ensure that the appropriate levels of service are delivered to the customer.

Now use Table 13.2 to evaluate your KAM skills against the checklist and to note any actions you should take to build up your skills.

Table 13.2 Audit of KAM core competencies

For each competence, consider how good you are at it and circle a number on the 1–5 scale where, where 1 is weak and 5 is world class. Consider the results: these are all core competencies where your score should be high or very high; so are there any actions you need to take with respect to your personal development?

Competence	How good are you?	Personal development actions
Product knowledge	1 2 3 4 5	
Knowledge of the customer	1 2 3 4 5	
Knowledge of the customer's industry	1 2 3 4 5	
Ability to inspire trust	1 2 3 4 5	
Project management	1 2 3 4 5	
Interpersonal skills	1 2 3 4 5	
Negotiating and selling skills	1 2 3 4 5	

The core competencies are those which all key account managers would be expected to have to a reasonable degree; they are also competencies that most key account managers would use on a regular basis.

However, more complex and closer relationships and strategic partnerships or alliances with key accounts require additional skills from the key account manager. These will now be discussed.

Advanced KAM competencies

In closer relationships, the key account manager is expected to operate at a higher level and take a more strategic view than in basic relationships.

To manage key account relationships that are co-operative, interdependent, or integrated, key account managers need all the basic competencies plus some additional ones. Co-operative, interdependent, and integrated relationships are progressively closer than the bow tie type and the key account manager in closer relationships is likely to be expected to operate at a higher level and take a more strategic view than in basic relationships.

In co-operative relationships, the key account manager must be able to establish higher-level contacts and fulfil a consultancy role. The key account manager should also have the authority and the ability to make decisions; key accounts become frustrated if they perceive that their key account manager is not able to make decisions in situ. As interdependent and integrated relationships develop, the consultancy and strategy skills of the key account manager become more important, as do KAM plans and the development of relationship strategy.

As we have already seen, key account managers actually spend most of their time (estimates range between 60% and 80%) in their own businesses, co-ordinating the delivery to the customer. The closer the relationship, the more important becomes the internal management of the supplier's performance by the key account manager. The skills of internal management include overcoming conflict, influencing, and team leadership. So too do advanced marketing techniques such as scenario planning and customer portfolio management, and financial analysis.

Advanced competencies of a key account manager

- Commercial awareness/strategic vision
- Consultancy skills and business performance improvement
- Advanced KAM planning
- Internal management
- Team leadership
- Advanced marketing techniques
- Finance

Table 13.3 suggests some ways in which a key account manager can develop and strengthen his/her advanced skills.

Table 13.3 How to develop advanced KAM competencies

Advanced competency	Key aspects	Methods for building skill
Commercial awareness/ strategic vision	High-level contacts; operating at Board level; strategic view	1 Mentoring and coaching (external mentor*) 2 Shadowing other top key account managers
Consultancy skills and business performance improvement	Advising on problem management and solutions; identifying areas for efficiency improvement; identifying market trends	1 Training in consultancy skills 2 Liaise with others in the supplier, for example, market research department
Advanced KAM planning	Scenario planning; contingency planning; shared goal setting; development of relationship strategy; evaluation of relative attractiveness of different key accounts; resource allocation	1 Training in planning skills 2 Additional reading
Internal management	Influencing skills; negotiation; advanced project management; overcoming conflict	1 Mentoring (external mentor) 2 360° feedback 3 Training, especially using role play

(Continued)

Table 13.3 (Continued)

Advanced competency	Key aspects	Methods for building skill
Team leadership	Managing teams; motivation; leadership; developing others; succession planning	1 Additional reading 2 Mentoring (external mentor) 3 Psychometric profiling
Advanced marketing techniques	Scenario planning; customer portfolio management	1 Training 2 Additional reading 3 Getting feedback on draft plans (internal mentor) 4 Shadowing advanced planners
Finance	Ability to read customer balance sheet and profit and loss; customer profitability analysis; customer lifetime value analysis; risk analysis	1 Training 2 Additional reading 3 Short secondment to Finance

*An external mentor is one who does not work for the supplier; an internal mentor works for the supplier. Increasingly, senior managers have internal mentors who can advise them on career progression within the firm and external mentors who take a more holistic view and who can also advise on sensitive issues, work/life balance, etc.

> People from business backgrounds other than sales and marketing can do very well as key account managers. They may already have useful competencies such as project management, finance, or planning skills.

The set of competencies needed by a senior key account manager is extensive because the role itself is a broad one. Advanced KAM is as much about people and project management, finance, and planning as it is about selling and negotiating. For this reason, people from business backgrounds other than sales and marketing can do very well as key account managers.

A new role that is emerging as distinct is that of the global account manager. GAM is about the internationally co-ordinated management of a company's biggest global customers. In many companies, KAM is operated at a business unit or national level. The global account manager operates at a company-to-company level. For this reason, there are fewer global account managers than key account managers, and the demands on them are even greater. We will now take a look at the competencies required from the global account manager.

■ Knowledge and skills of the global account manager

Many business-to-business markets have been affected by the phenomenon of globalization. This phenomenon has witnessed the emergence first of international, then of global, markets and companies. This trend can be seen in markets as diverse as banking, car manufacturing, and pharmaceuticals.

Typically, along with globalization comes consolidation, where fewer larger firms emerge, often through takeovers of smaller and less successful rivals. The pattern of consolidation has some serious consequences for suppliers. Global companies, by virtue of their size, have greater bargaining power, which they can use to drive down prices and drive up service levels. They may have centralized purchasing processes or internal structures that are different from those the supplier is used to. Global customers may demand international price harmonization. They may also require consistent and co-ordinated international or global servicing. If a supplier is not able to meet these needs, it may find itself demoted to "Tier 2" status. Tier 2 suppliers do not deal with the global customer directly; instead, they have to deal with a Tier 1 supplier, part of whose role is to co-ordinate the offer of a series of Tier 2 suppliers.

GAM has emerged as a way for suppliers to manage their relationships with global customers. Just as KAM is different and more complex than standard account management, so is GAM different and more complex than KAM. Global account managers need skills and competencies over and above those of the key account manager.

> Global account managers need skills and competencies over and above those of the key account manager.

Additional issues for global account managers

Global account managers need the skills of a key account manager. However, they face additional issues in their GAM role, including:

- Cultural
- Systems and processes
- Managing dispersed teams
- Managing conflicts between global and local interests
- Global logistics and service
- Location
- Communication

The additional issues faced by global account managers are reflected in the additional competencies that they need.

How GAM roles differ from KAM roles

There are five broad roles that global account managers undertake.[1] These are the goal role (target setting), customer role (interaction with the customer), internal role (managing the relationship with the customer within their own organization), account planning role (account planning and forecasting), and complex boundary-spanning (cultural and communication) role. Fundamentally, these roles are common to most key account managers, but the complexity and extent of the issues are greater for global account managers than for their KAM counterparts. In particular, the boundary-spanning role in GAM can be very complex and difficult, and the goal role tends to be more important and strategic than for the key account manager.

The *goal role* of the global account manager is concerned with the objective that the global account manager sets himself/herself in their role. Some goals will be financial, relating to revenues and profits from the key account. Share of spend is a key measure of both KAM and GAM performance, although it can be more difficult to measure in a GAM context

> Share of spend is a key measure of both KAM and GAM performance, although it can be more difficult to measure in a GAM context where the customer operates in multiple countries and may deal with the supplier under many different subsidiaries.

[1] This section draws on the innovative work of our colleague Dr. Sue Holt.

where the customer operates in multiple countries and may deal with the supplier under many different subsidiaries. The global account manager might also set non-financial goals, perhaps relating to supplier performance, customer satisfaction, level and seriousness of complaints, etc.

How goal setting in GAM differs from that in KAM

Setting goals for a global account relationship is more difficult than for a key account relationship. One problem is economic: in a global relationship, the global account manager has to consider currency movements and different local economic conditions when setting goals. This will also have an impact on the profitability of business generated from different global locations.

The role of the global account manager is to set goals that will maximize the value of the customer's total global business to the supplier. This brings the boundary-spanning role into play, as the global account manager may have to make decisions that will impact negatively on some of the supplier's business units.

Take the example of a furniture manufacturer based in Denmark and supplying an international retailer which has strong market penetration in the UK and the US. This retailer opens a small store in Germany and the global account manager determines that it should initially be supplied from the supplier business unit in Germany. The German country manager objects, because his plant is working close to full capacity and there are more profitable opportunities for him to supply local clients. In fact, the distance from the supplier plant and the customer depot means that the current small orders from this customer are unattractive and will reduce the business results for Germany for the next 18 months or so. The global account manager has to have the vision – and the authority – to act in the overall best interests of the supplier, even though this is opposed by local interests.

Another way in which goal setting is more complex in GAM is the problem of the customer with multiple subsidiaries, many of which have different names from their parent companies. This makes it difficult to identify and to track share of spend with a global customer. The supplier needs to have a customer relationship management (CRM) system that will help it identify orders coming from a small subsidiary of a global customer.

A third problem for goal setting in GAM relates to the complexity of customer profitability analysis when the customer is global. This problem can be exacerbated by management information systems that run along country or business unit lines, and by differences in supplier invoicing policies between different countries. Some suppliers admit that they have only a hazy picture of the profitability of their global customers.

The *customer role* relates to how the global account manager interacts with the customer. This includes developing a deep understanding of the customer, which is particularly complex in a global relationship. From this deep understanding of the customer, part of the global account manager's role is to identify opportunities and threats. More generally, the global account manager has to facilitate the contract agreed between buyer and supplier. This can be demanding in an international or global context where local interests can conflict with those of the global contract.

The *internal role* of the global account manager is about how the global account manager manages the relationship between the supplier and the customer within his/her own company. In both KAM and GAM, the majority of the relationship manager's time is typically spent within the supplier company, implementing the customer's requirements, sorting out problems, and avoiding service failures. This involves the manager in multiple relationships within the company, ensuring that systems and processes, logistics and services, and internal communications, all work as smoothly as possible.

Again common to KAM and GAM is the *account planning* role. However, developing a successful GAM plan is a complex activity which may involve both other members of the GAM team and also liaison with, and the involvement of, the customer.

A unique feature of the GAM role is the *complex boundary-spanning role*, relating to communications and cultural management. This role underpins the other roles. It relates to communication between the supplier and customer, and also within the supplier. Global account managers face particularly difficult communications problems because their responsibilities typically span regions with different languages, cultures, and time zones.

The complex boundary-spanning role

The complex boundary-spanning role of the global account manager is about managing communication and managing culture. Both issues are bigger and more complex for global account managers than for key account managers.

Managing communication: Information and co-ordination is more difficult in GAM because the global account manager has to co-ordinate internationally as well as between different business units. The sheer volume of communication makes the task a demanding one, and there are also issues of language and time zones to be taken into account. In a global account relationship, the global account manager may be managing a virtual GAM team which is located in different time zones and may never physically meet. One downside found in previous research is that virtual teams take longer to reach a consensus than conventional teams do. However, team members participate more equally in discussions and express their views more frankly than their conventional counterparts.

> *Managing culture:* Culture is an important, but slippery, concept. Much has been written about issues of personal behaviour in different national cultures, which we will not repeat here. However, for the global account manager, it is likely that business and corporate culture are at least as important as national culture.
>
> Business culture is the way that business is conducted in that country or industry. This covers topics such as attitudes towards meetings, verbal versus contractual arrangements, corporate entertainment, and soft commissions.
>
> Corporate culture is possibly the most important factor in business-to-business relationships. Corporate culture is about the style of an organization, the way it does business, its behaviour towards its customers and people, its beliefs, etc. More and more key customers are putting "corporate culture" or "cultural fit" onto their list of what makes a good supplier.

The issue of corporate culture is a substantial field in its own right. The focus here is on helping the key account manager understand the possible implications for the success of KAM relationships. Table 13.4 sets out a simple cultural evaluation tool that will help you see the degree of cultural fit between you as the supplier and your global account. You are asked for two sets of responses: one based on the culture of your own company and the other based on the culture of your key account.

If the two sets of scores are close, it is likely that there will be a good cultural fit between the organizations. There may still be problems that the key account manager, acting in his/her boundary-spanning role, must resolve. However, the cultural frictions and the chance of misunderstandings are likely to be much reduced.

If the two sets of scores are very different, there may be cultural difficulties that the key account manager has to contend with, as well as the day-to-day issues. Cultural difficulties can range from simple misunderstandings, through to customer irritation and even damage to the relationship. For example, a key account that has a culture of very tight managerial control processes may feel uneasy when dealing with a supplier that has strategic vision but a more easygoing style. In these circumstances, the relationship may break down just because the two sides don't understand one another. The purpose of Table 13.4 is to help the key account manager gain some insight into the potential difficulties or areas of unease.

> The key account manager may have to contend with cultural difficulties that cause unease and friction between the two companies, as well as the day-to-day relationship management issues.

Our discussion of the global account manager's function indicates the complexity of GAM. In part, this is because the GAM is considered to be an extremely strategic function. In addition, the GAM function encompasses complex communication, culture, and people management issues spanning multiple countries and business units. It has been said that the requirements specification for a global account manager is similar to that of a managing director of a substantial company!

Table 13.4 Evaluating cultural fit

Look at the statements given in the first column. For each statement, put a cross against the degree to which you agree or disagree for your own firm. When you have completed the evaluation for your own firm, go down the list of statements again, this time using a different symbol, such as a circle, to indicate what the customer would say about its own company. Each statement should now have two symbols against it, one for the supplier and one for the customer. The degree to which they match gives you an overview of the cultural fit. *Note*: There are no right or wrong answers – only different kinds of cultures.

Statement	Strongly agree	Tend to agree	Tend to disagree	Strongly disagree	Insufficient knowledge
Employees are made aware of the current financial position of the firm					
Management information is widely distributed					
There is a formal, robust planning system					
Day-to-day financial controls are tight					
Promotion is based on merit					
The firm is a good employer					
Reward is based on performance					
The firm has strong leadership					
Senior managers are approachable					
The strategy and direction of the business is clear					
The business is well managed					
People tend to stay because they like working there					
The organization treats its customers well					
People gripe when they meet at the coffee machine					
There is a rigid organization hierarchy and structure					
Sometimes one department will deliberately "sink" another department's projects					
You can tell from someone's office and car what their work grade is					
The firm encourages personal initiative					
Individuals have considerable flexibility about their working hours					
Business units tend to be autonomous					
Our two organizations share many strategic goals					

So far in this chapter, we have considered what the key account manager does (his/her roles) and the competencies needed; we have also considered the personal characteristics that high-performing key account managers display. The final part of the picture, which is often neglected, is matching the key account manager to the key account that will suit them best.

■ Matching the key account manager to the key account

An important but neglected aspect of delivering world-class KAM is to optimize the effectiveness of the key account manager by matching them to the key account with which they will produce the best results. Too many companies take great pains to recruit and train their key account managers to the highest standards, but then squander this investment by allocating a key account manager to an account on which they are wasted. Allocating key accounts to key account managers based on seniority or geography is nonsense. The objective should be to understand the particular strengths of each key account manager and then match them to a key account or key accounts where they can use these strengths to best advantage.

> Allocating key accounts to key account managers based on seniority or geography is nonsense. The objective should be to match the key account manager to a key account where they can use their strengths to best advantage.

An example would be a key account manager who has excellent negotiating abilities but is less strong in strategic vision. This key account manager should not be matched to a strategic partner: if he is, he will feel uncomfortable and will not perform to the best of his abilities. Still worse, he may irritate the client by focusing on hard price negotiation when the customer expects to have discussions about strategy. Conversely, if a key account manager is great at building personal relationships but less good at spotting opportunities or risk taking, she should not be matched with a key account which has great potential but needs a risk-taking entrepreneurial type to identify and exploit areas for development. If she is given this account to manage, she will feel she is underperforming and the customer may view her as slow to react.

The fact is that key account managers have different strengths and weaknesses, and prefer to operate differently. Matching the right key account manager to the right key account is a way of ensuring that the appropriate KAM strategy is adopted. If the key account is valuable but tough to handle, the supplier would be well advised to appoint a strong negotiator as the key account manager. Most key account managers could handle tough negotiations some of the time, but only a few could handle them all the time. Just the same is true of strategic discussions or entrepreneurial risk taking. Placing the key account manager with particular strengths into the relationships that most require these strengths is going to result in better overall performance.

> Placing the key account manager with particular strengths into the relationships that most require these strengths is going to result in better overall performance.

In this section, we will suggest how the key account manager could be matched to the key account. To do this, we need to briefly revisit the notion of the key account portfolio introduced earlier.

The key account portfolio and management strategies

The principle of the key account portfolio is that not all key accounts are the same. Some are more attractive than others (although all are relatively attractive compared to the whole of the customer base). Moreover, suppliers have greater business strengths with some key accounts than with others.

Plotting each key account on these two dimensions of the relationship (key account attractiveness and relative business strength) results in a key account portfolio matrix (Figure 13.1).

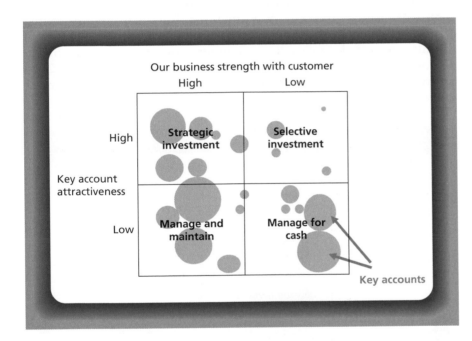

Figure 13.1
Key account portfolio matrix.

Very attractive key accounts with whom the supplier has a good relationship (High/High, or top left in the matrix) are suitable for strategic investment and close partnership conversations. Very attractive key accounts with whom the supplier does not yet have a good relationship (High/Low, top right) should be managed with a selective investment approach. These might be key account prospects where the relationship is in the early stages, or they might be key accounts where the supplier has a small share of spend but where this could be increased with the right relationship management approach.

Less attractive key accounts where there is a good relationship (Low/High, bottom left) need management and maintenance. These might be key accounts where the supplier has a large share of spend but there is little growth potential, or where the costs of servicing the client make it financially less rewarding. Finally, less attractive key accounts with a lesser relationship (Low/Low, bottom right) need careful management for cash. These might be very large customers who take a transactional view and are very price-driven, but are still key accounts because of the sheer volume they order.

As this discussion reveals, the position of the key account within the portfolio matrix indicates the appropriate strategy that the supplier should adopt to optimize its returns from the relationship, which in turn suggests what type of key account manager should be in charge of the relationship.

Strategic investment accounts need to be managed with a strong strategic vision. The supplier would benefit from treating these as partnerships. There may be shared meetings and joint projects such as product innovation and testing or process benchmarking. This may involve shared investment. The key account manager should have strong business and consultancy skills, be able to take a long-term view and operate comfortably at boardroom level. This is the *Business manager* type (Figure 13.2), so called because the skill set needed here is akin to that of the general manager of a business unit.

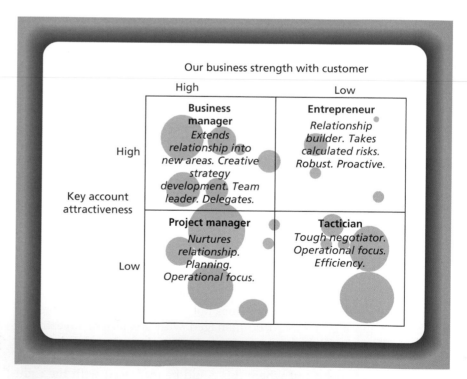

Figure 13.2
Key account
manager type.

Selective investment accounts are those where the optimal strategy is to identify opportunities for the supplier to gain market share. Some of the opportunities may involve some risk; for example, products or services might have to be tailored, or the supplier might have to buy in additional products or skills to deliver the offer the customer wants. For this reason, the best key account manager for these relationships is an *Entrepreneur*, who is motivated to identify opportunities and to go after them, even if that brings additional risks of failure and rejection. Not only entrepreneurs build relationships quickly, but they also have a sharp eye for the next opportunity and are not afraid to exploit their contacts to go after it.

Manage and maintain accounts are those where the focus should be on operational issues. Sometimes, these can be long-standing key accounts which are not attractive as they used to be; the problem for the supplier in this situation is to withdraw or renegotiate services that the key account received in its heyday. For this, a *project manager* type of key account manager is needed. This is not literally someone who has previously worked as a project manager (although it may be). The project manager is able to take an objective view of the relationship and manage it for operational efficiency. This will include skills in resource allocation and monitoring, so that these kinds of key account relationships do not use up too much valuable resource that would be better deployed elsewhere. Project manager types will also be able to examine requests and invitations to tender (ITTs) from the key account and reject those which the supplier cannot easily fulfil profitably.

Manage for cash accounts are, as the name suggests, key accounts which may be very aggressive in their bargaining. Their behaviour is multiple transactional rather than relationship-oriented. They will be quick to exploit any weakness. Manage for cash accounts are unlikely to be interested in a strategic relationship with this, or any supplier and it would be a waste of time and resources if the supplier were to pursue a strategic partnership. Instead, a *Tactician* should be appointed as key account manager. Tacticians are tough negotiators and very practical people with a good eye for detail that enables them to focus on efficiency.

Identifying your preferred KAM style

In practice, all key account managers are a mix of business managers, entrepreneurs, project managers, and tacticians, since all of these are essential facets of the KAM role. However, every key account manager will have a preference for one of the four styles. In some cases, the preference is so marked that you will have already been able to identify individuals who are clearly business managers or who are clearly tacticians. In other cases, the preferences are less marked.

To help you find out what your preferred KAM style is, complete Table 13.5 to find out what kind of key account manager you are.[2] Remember, there are no right or wrong answers to any of these questions. All four styles are valuable. The purpose of the diagnostic questionnaire is simply to give you some insight into where your KAM strengths may lie and to help you decide how you might get the best results out of the key account or key accounts you manage.

---

[2] Our thanks to Dr. Iain Davies, who developed the KAM style diagnostic based on the work of Dr. Sue Holt.

Table 13.5 KAM style diagnostic

	Yes	No
1 I tend to collect commercial information on clients from one principle client contact rather than multiple contact points.		
2 Targets and goals are important in gauging performance; I am governed by short-term financial goals rather than long-term financial goals.		
3 I make assessments of my customers' organizational culture on intuition and gauge by my principle contact rather than on high levels of structured analysis.		
4 I work in a flexible rather than highly organized manner.		
5 My proposals for my key accounts are normally based on a business case rather than an attempt to create strategic alignment.		
6 I make decisions based more on intuition as opposed to detailed research into the key account.		
7 I respond to current customer behaviour rather than an in-depth analysis of the long-term goals of the company.		
8 I am a risk taker.		
9 Meeting objectives and taking action are more important than detailed research and understanding.		
10 I don't follow strict implementation plans, but change them to meet new circumstances.		
11 I am sometimes relatively disorganized in my work patterns.		
12 I prefer to win new business as opposed to seeing through existing projects.		
13 I don't really use a defined process to identify key customers.		
14 I bid for all profitable business within designated customers, as opposed to only strategically aligned business.		
15 I don't work closely with operations.		
16 I build and utilize a trusted small group of personal relationships (as opposed to an extensive group) when formulating ideas, research, and decisions.		
17 I am not comfortable with other colleagues dealing directly with my client.		
18 I am flexible in my methods of communication, using whichever is best suited for that moment in time.		
19 I have a "culture blind" approach to management and treat people from different cultures just as I would people from home.		
20 I am more comfortable managing customers who are mainly interested in price than in a long-term relationship.		
Total Score		

If you have an internal mentor who is helping you develop your career as a key account manager, you might like to consider sharing the results of the KAM style diagnostic with them for additional feedback.

To determine your KAM style, add up the total number of ticks in the "Yes" box and read off your preferred KAM style from Table 13.6.

Table 13.6 Identifying your KAM style

Number of "Yes" ticks	KAM style	Notes
1–5	Business manager	You are good at strategic relationships. There are relatively few good business managers; you could also consider developing your career into a GAM role.
6–10	Project manager	You are an efficient, organized, able account manager. You may be more comfortable with long-established relationships that need nurturing, rather than the "hurly burly" of new account development.
11–15	Entrepreneur	You are a go-getting risk taker with an eye for an opportunity. You may like to focus on key account acquisition and development rather than longer-term relationship management.
16–20	Tactician	You are a strong manager and negotiator. A really good tactician is a rarity! You will tend to get given the tougher accounts, so make sure that your compensation package takes account of the more difficult task you face.

Finale

Key account management is one of the most demanding and exciting new roles to emerge for many years. The skills and competencies required from a world-class key account manager are so great that a top key account manager could run an entire business, not just a relationship. Indeed, some key account managers and global account managers find themselves managing relationships that are more valuable to their company or some entire business units, or national territories.

Our purpose in compiling this book has been to use our research into KAM planning and our experience of working with many key account managers and global account managers to set out a toolkit and processes that can help you develop into a world-class key account manager and your company into a world-class key supplier.

> A top key account manager could easily run an entire business, not just a relationship.

We wish you every success in your journey.

Happy planning!

CHAPTER 14

A step-by-step system for preparing a strategic plan for a key account

Summary

Part 1
- What is key account planning?
- A summary of the contents of a strategic key account plan.
- A step-by-step approach to preparing a strategic key account plan.
- A step-by-step approach to preparing a tactical key account plan.

■ The purpose of strategic plans for key accounts

The overall purpose of preparing a strategic plan for a key account is the identification and creation of competitive advantage for both the customer and the supplier.

■ What is key account planning?

Key account planning is just a logical sequence and a series of activities leading to the setting of objectives and the formulation of strategies and plans for achieving them.

■ Why is key account planning necessary?

Key account planning is necessary because of the following:

- Increasing turbulence, complexity, and competitiveness.
- The absolute necessity to understand in depth the real needs of powerful customers.
- The need to put together offers that will create competitive advantage for the customer and opposed to merely helping them avoid disadvantage.
- The need to avoid becoming a price-driven, commodity supplier.
- The speed of technological change.
- The need for you
  - to help identify sources of competitive advantage;
  - to force an organized approach;
  - to develop specificity;
  - to ensure consistent relationships.
- The need for *superiors*
  - to inform.

- The need for *non-marketing functions*
  - to get support.
- The need for *subordinates*
  - to get resources;
  - to gain commitment;
  - to set objectives and strategies.

■ A summary of the contents of a strategic key account plan

A summary of what appears in a strategic marketing plan and a list of the principal marketing tools/techniques/structures/frameworks which apply to each step is given in Figure 14.1. It is important to observe from Figure 14.1 that there are three main components to key account planning. The first is *the process* itself. This is a managerial process, which consists of several steps.

The second is the *output* of the process, which is the strategic plan for the key account. The third is the diagnostic tools that can be used to carry out the whole planning process.

It is crucial to understand the difference between the three components and it is a sad reflection on managers that they often get so involved in the process and in the use of the diagnostic tools, that they miss the whole point, which is the output (i.e. the strategic plan itself), which spells out what the supplier is planning to do to create sustainable competitive advantage for the customer and for itself.

Hence, this chapter gives firstly: the strategic plan itself; secondly the process and the tools and techniques that are relevant to carrying out the process; and thirdly, the contents of a 1-year tactical plan. Throughout, the reader is directed to appropriate parts of the book for more detailed explanations.

■ A key account planning system

This marketing planning system is in three sections.

Section A sets out a series of templates which, when completed, will constitute the strategic plan for a key account. It must be stressed that in an ideal world *all* the templates should be completed. This may, however, prove extremely difficult. Nonetheless, we recommend that as much as possible should be completed.

Section B takes you through a step-by-step approach to the preparation of a strategic key account plan with a series of worksheets which are referenced in the templates in Section A.

Section C takes you through the preparation of a 1-year tactical plan for your key account. What actually appears in a 1-year key account plan is given under the heading "The 1-year key account plan documentation".

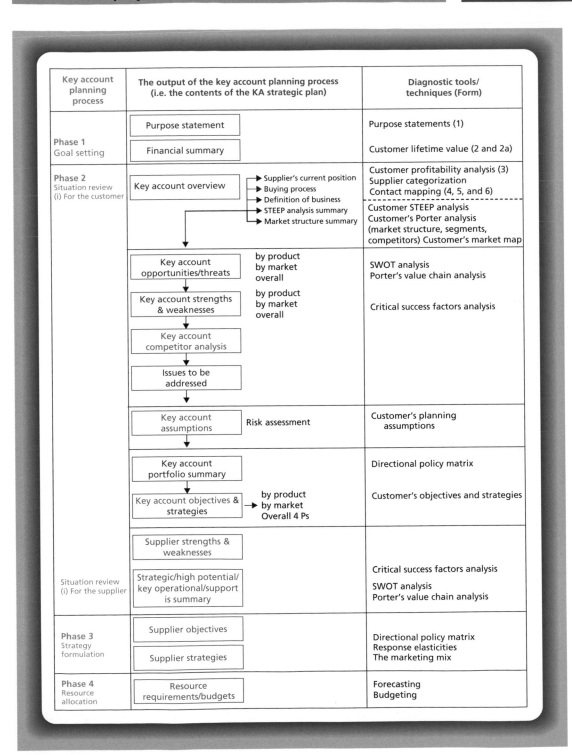

Figure 14.1
Key account planning process, output, and tools.

SECTION A

Templates for what should appear in a strategic key account plan

> ## Supplier strategic key account plan for
>
> Customer name ....
>
> Name of key account manager ....

Contents

Form 1 (see Worksheet 14.1)

Mission or purpose statement for the key account

● Role or contribution
● Distinctive competence
● Future indications
  – We *will*...
  – We *might*...
  – We will *never*...

Note: In order to determine the correct strategy for this key account, it is essential that the position of this particular customer in the supplier's overall portfolio of key accounts is pinpointed and understood (See matrix below. For a more detailed explanation of the crucial importance of this in determining the mission for a particular key account, see Chapter 4).

Form 2 (see Worksheet 14.2(a))

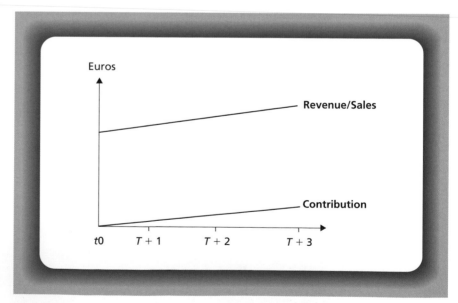

Figure 14.2
Financial summary.

This should be accompanied by a brief commentary.

Form 2a (see Worksheet 14.2(b))

Relationship lifetime	Year 1 (£/$/€)	Year 2 (£/$/€)	Year 3 (£/$/€)	Year 4 (£/$/€)
Revenues Product A Product B				
Total customer revenues Product costs Costs to serve Customer-specific overheads				
Total customer costs				
Year by year profit				
Total notional value				
Discount factor*				
Present value of future profits				
Customer lifetime value				

Background information on the supplier's position to date

Forms 3, 4, 5, and 6, which follow, set out some background information on the supplier's current position in the key account

Form 3 (see Worksheet 14.3)

Customer trading history with the supplier

Sales by product/ product group	t_0 (current year)						$t-1$						$t-2$					
	Supplier sales		Sales increase/ decrease	Supplier profit			Supplier sales		Sales increase/ decrease	Supplier profit			Supplier sales		Sales increase/ decrease	Supplier profit		
	£m		%	£m		%	£m		%	£m		%	£m		%	£m		%
Supplier total																		
Size of customer wallet	*																	
Share of customer wallet	Supplier ÷ total																	
Definition of wallet	**																	

*Customer's spend on the category of goods/services currently/potentially supplied by you.

**Scope of wallet: content and limits (what is included, what is excluded) if appropriate, make some comments on the customer's strategy for managing their supplier.

Notes on trading history

Notes on customer's supplier management strategy
(see supplier categorization matrix in Figure 14.3. For a more detailed explanation, see Chapter 10)

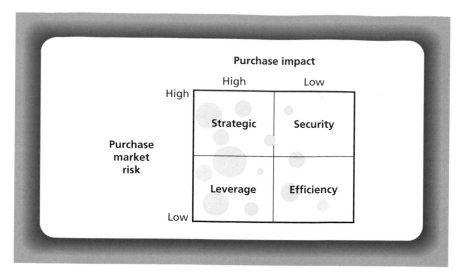

Figure 14.3
Supplier
categorization
matrix.

Comments on events influencing all of the above.

Form 4 (see Worksheet 14.4)

Supplier's account team

Name	Title/function	Role*

*Examples: Overall account manager; Customer operations; Market analysis; Quality issues.

Form 5 (see Worksheet 14.5(a))

Principal customer contacts/relationships

(Draw conclusions about how the customer goes about buying its products and services)

Name	Title/Function	Role in relationship with supplier *	Level of relationship with supplier	Level of importance to supplier
Stage of inter-company relationship overall				

*Examples: Principal contact; Buyer; Marketing.

Form 6 (see Worksheet 14.5(b))

Contact map showing the power structure and importance of contacts

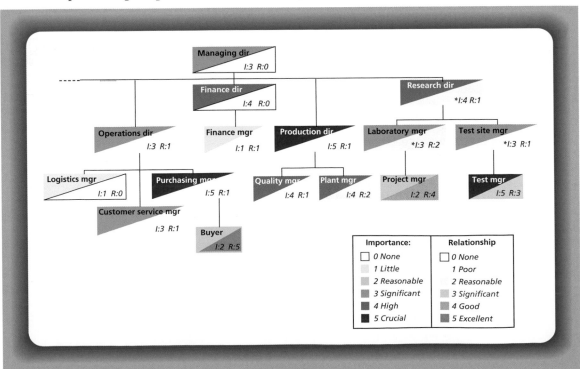

Key

Relationship levels:	Importance levels
The relationship reflected here is that between the supplier as a company and the individual in the customer. Individuals within the supplier may have good or bad personal relationships with each person, but that is not what this table captures. Record the customer's view, even if it includes legacy opinions which you may regard as no longer valid.	The level of importance recorded here should reflect the level of importance of this person in the development of the relationship with the supplier.

Level	You/others in your company have	Level	In developing supplier relationships this person
0	Never met this person, and they would know very little about us.	0	Is irrelevant
1	Just an acquaintance with this person *or* this person has a very poor opinion about us and/or vice versa.	1	Has no influence or control.
2	Some dealings with each other, but not consistently, and we do not have anything more than a basic relationship *or* this person has opinions about us which inhibit our relationship with them.	2	Has influence/control over their own personal relationship with providers.
3	A reasonable understanding and a satisfactory working relationship with this person, but it does not extend to the exchange of confidences or special assistance.	3	Has influence/control over a defined group within the organization
4	A good relationship and work very well together. We are well disposed towards each other and reflect that to our own companies.	4	Has a strong influence in the overall direction of the organization
5	An excellent working relationship; we trust each other and have a high opinion about each other. We are good friends and go out of our way to help each other.	5	The most/one of the most important/influential person(s) in the organization

Situation review: key account overview

The customer's position in its market

Forms 7–14, which follow, set out a situation review of the *customer's* position in its markets, the issues it faces, and their objectives and strategies.

Form 7 (see Worksheet 14.6)

The Customer's business: definition of the customer's business

1 Define the customer's business in terms of their customers' needs rather than what they sell.
2 What markets are they in?
3 Where are these markets?
4 What is the customer's scope in these markets? (for more information, see Chapter 2).

Forms 8 and 9

The Customer's market

Summarize the customer's market using a STEEP analysis of the customer's market and the Porter analysis see the forms below (for more information, see Chapter 3).

Form 8 (see Worksheet 14.7)

STEEP analysis of customer's environment

STEEP factor	Change/development	Which means that? (for the customer)
Social		
Technological		
Economic		
Ecological/Environmental		
Political/Legal/Regulatory		

Form 9 (see Worksheet 14.8)

Customer's Porter analysis

Market participants	Segments What are they?	Micro environment factors What's happening with these people/companies?	Importance H/M/L	Opportunity or threat O/T
Customer's customers				
Customer's competitors (current, new, potential)				
Suppliers to customer				

Form 10 (see Worksheet 14.9)

The customer's market map

Form 11 (see Worksheet 14.9)

The Customer's role/participation in their markets

From the customer's market map, draw clear conclusions/implications for the customer.

Form 12 (see Worksheet 14.10)

The opportunities and threats facing the customer

From the analysis sheets on Forms 8–11, list the opportunities and threats facing the customer and their relative importance, using the sheet below.

Customer's opportunities and threats statement	Likelihood H/M/L	Impact H/M/L
Opportunities		
Threats		

Form 13 (see Worksheet 14.11)

The customer's strengths and weaknesses relative to competitors

From the analysis sheets on Forms 8–11

List the customer's relative strengths and weaknesses in each of its main product/market areas.

Customer strengths	Importance H/M/L

Customer weaknesses	Importance H/M/L

Form 14 (see Worksheet 14.12)

Situation review: issues facing the customer

List in order of importance the issues facing the customer that have emerged from Forms 8–12. Some will be from opportunities and threats and some from strengths and weaknesses.

Issue	Importance to the customer

Form 15 (see Worksheet 14.13)

List the customer's principal assumptions

Form 16

Customer's portfolio summary

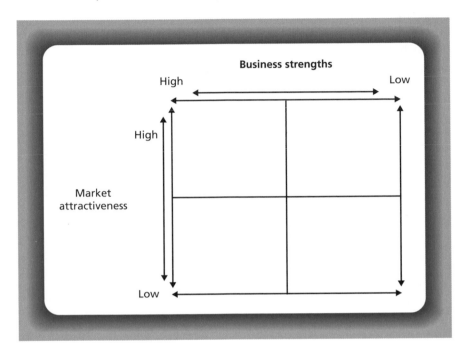

Example of a completed customer portfolio

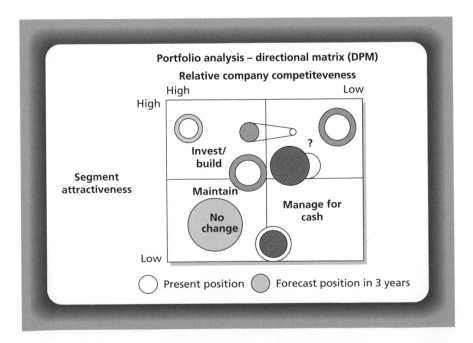

Form 17 (see Worksheet 14.15)

For each of the important markets in the customer's portfolio summary above, list their objectives and strategies for each for the next 3 years.

Customer's objectives and strategies for each important product/market

Product/Market	Objectives	Strategies

Situation review: the supplier's position in relation to the customer's business

Form 18 sets out the supplier's strengths and weaknesses in relation to the current and future needs of the customer based on the analysis in Forms 8–13

Form 18 (see Worksheet 14.16–14.18)

Supplier's relative strengths and weaknesses

	Importance H/M/L
Supplier's strengths (from the value chain analysis)	
Supplier's strengths (from analysis of the customers business)	
Supplier's weaknesses (from the value chain analysis)	
Supplier's weaknesses (from analysis of the customer's business)	

Phase 2 for the supplier: the process: situation review – summary of issues facing the customer and ways in which the supplier can help – Worksheet 14.19 (see Form 14).

Form 20 below shows a "Matrix" in which the issues faced by the customer (from Form 10) can be categorized by the supplier as a precursor to setting their own objectives and strategies.

Form 19

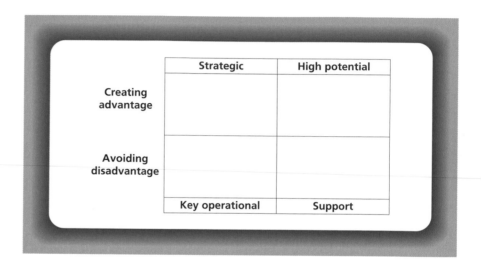

Key:

Strategic: Issues that will ensure the customer's long-term success.

High Potential: Issues that, whilst not crucial currently, could potentially lead to "differential advantage for the customer".

Key operational: Issues that, unless solved reasonably quickly, could lead to disadvantage for the customer.

Support: Issues that, whilst of a non-urgent nature such as information availability, nonetheless need to be solved to avoid disadvantage for the customer.

It can also be seen from Form 14 that solving some of the issues in the top half of the matrix, is likely to lead to the supplier creating advantage for the customer. Solving issues in the lower half of the matrix, whilst helpful, will only lead to the supplier helping the customer to avoid disadvantage.

The process (3)
supplier strategy formulation

Form 20 (see Worksheet 14.20)

Supplier strategy formulation – setting objectives

In completing Form 20, it is important to ensure that the revenue and volume objectives are realistic, based on the previous analysis.

Form 20

Supplier objectives

Business/financial

Purchases by product/ product group	LY		TY					TY + 1					TY + 2					TY + 3				
	Sales	Sales	Sales	Sales increase/ decrease	GM	GM	GM	Sales	Sales increase/ decrease	GM	GM	GM	Sales	Sales increase/ decrease	GM	GM	GM	Sales	Sales increase/ decrease	GM	GM	GM
	£m	£m	£m	%	£m	%		£m	%	£m	%		£m	%	£m	%		£m	%	£m	%	
Existing business																						
Total existing																						
New business	Business not received as on date of completing plan																					
Total new																						
Overall total																						
Customer wallet																						
Share of customer wallet																						

Other objectives (e.g. relationships, range of activity)

Objective	Measurement	LY	TY	TY + 1	TY + 2	TY + 3
Inter-company relationship	Target stage: basic cooperative, inter-dependent, integrated					
Range of activity	Target stage: for example introducing new lines of business; getting into new areas of the key account					

Form 21 (see Worksheet 14.21)

Supplier strategy formulation: setting strategies
to achieve the objectives (Part 1)

This is a crucial part of the planning process, for the supplier now has to detail the strategies to be employed to achieve their objectives, together with responsibilities and costs.

This is best done by taking each of the issues in turn from Form 20 and considering the precise actions that the supplier can take, given their own strengths and weaknesses, to help the customer to cope with it.

Thus, starting with the top left box from Form 19,

Customer strategic issues	Supplier strategies	Responsibility	Cost		
			Year 1	Year 2	Year 3
1	A				
2	B				
3	C				
	D				
	etc.				

Customer high-potential issues	Supplier strategies	Responsibility	Cost		
			Year 1	Year 2	Year 3

Customer key operational issues	Supplier strategies	Responsibility	Cost		
			Year 1	Year 2	Year 3

Customer support issues	Supplier strategies	Responsibility	Cost		
			Year 1	Year 2	Year 3

Form 22 (see Worksheet 14.22)

Supplier strategies – relationships

From Forms 5 and 6, set the relationship objectives, together with responsibilities, using the two forms (a) and (b) given below.
  Whatever costs are involved should be added to the costs of the other strategies from Form 22.

Form (a) Supplier relationship strategies
Additional to business strategies

Relationship development strategy	Target contact name(s) and role(s)

Form (b) Targeted relationship levels (by date) _ _ _ _ _ _ _ _ _ _)

KIE staff	Customer staff						
	Name 1	Name 2	Name 3	Name 4			
Name A	2 > 4			1 > 3			
Name B			1 > 2				
Name C							
Name D							

Form 23 (see Worksheet 14.23)

Summary of financials

On Form 16, the supplier calculated sales and gross margin for each of the three planning years.

Now, the supplier should take the gross margin for each year and deduct the total costs (taken from Form 16).

	Year *T* + 1	Year *T* + 2	Year *T* + 3
Total sales			
Total GM			
Less total costs (including relationship costs)			
Net profit/loss			

Comment on roles, responsibilities, alliancies, feasibility, etc.

SECTION B

The process: an introduction

As stated above, this is the equivalent of the strategic marketing planning process. It will generate substantial amounts of data and information, only some of which will appear in the actual key account strategic plan itself. Section A provides a series of templates that spell out precisely which parts of the information gathered during the process will appear in the plan itself.

■ The process phase 1: goal setting – the purpose statement

Worksheet 14.1 shows that a key account plan should begin with a purpose statement. This is perhaps the most difficult aspect of key account planning for managers to master, because it is largely philosophical and qualitative in nature. Many organizations find their different departments, and sometimes even different groups in the same department, pulling in different directions, often with disastrous results, simply because the organization hasn't defined the boundaries of the business and the way it wishes to do business.

The purpose statement (or lower-level mission statement) is appropriate at the strategic business unit, department product group, or key account level of the organization. The purpose statement in the key account plan should relate back to the organization's higher-level mission statement. Unfortunately, there are two types of mission or purpose statement, as shown in the following summary:

Type 1: "Motherhood" – usually found inside annual reports designed to "stroke" shareholders. Otherwise it is of no practical use.

Type 2: The real thing. A meaningful statement, unique to the organization concerned, which "impacts" on the behaviour of the executives at all levels.

The following is an example of a meaningless, vapid, motherhood-type mission statement, which most companies seem to have. They achieve nothing and it is difficult to understand why these pointless statements are so popular. Employees mock them and they rarely say anything likely to give direction to the organization. We have entitled this example "The Generic Mission Statement" and they are to be avoided at all costs.

> ## The Generic Mission Statement
>
> Our organization's primary mission is to protect and increase the value of its owner's investments while efficiently and fairly serving the needs of its customers. (.....insert organization name.......) seeks to accomplish this in a manner that contributes to the development and growth of its employees, and to the goals of countries and communities in which it operates.

See Form 1

The purpose statement for a key account strategic plan sets out your strategic intent or vision for that relationship (see Form 1). As a guideline, the following might be included:

Worksheet 14.1

1. *Role or contribution*:
   - Profit. Be specific. Refer to Chapter 5 here. This is crucially important, as the word "profit" has many different meanings.
   - Relationship building. It could be that you have to spend up to 5 years building a position of trust in the account, in which case it is impossible to maximize profits at the same time. See Chapters 5 and 6.
   - Other sources of value. It may well be that this is a customer who will give you credibility in your market, or who will create value for you in other ways. Again, you may have to do things for and with the customer that prevents you maximizing your profit (refer to Chapter 5).

2. *Distinctive competence*: Here, define your organization's essential skills/capabilities or benefits that you can bring to this customer compared to your competitors. If, in describing these, you could just as easily put a competitor's name to them, they are not distinctive competences. It may well be that the list includes benefits that you have yet to develop, which is acceptable.

3. *Future indications* List:
   What you *will* most definitely do for this customer;
   What you *might* do for this customer;
   What you will *never* do for this customer.

The key account purpose statement will need to be reviewed annually and it must be agreed across the organization, otherwise unrealistic objectives may be set for the account which are either just plain wrong, unachievable, or both.

■ The process phase 1: goal setting – financial summary

The purpose of this is to summarize for the people reading the plan the financial results over the full three planning period. It can be presented as a simple diagram along the lines shown in Worksheets 14.2(a) or as a table as shown in Worksheet 14.2(b). Information about how to calculate these numbers is given in Chapter 5 ("customer lifetime value").

See Forms 2 and 2a

Worksheet 14.2(a)

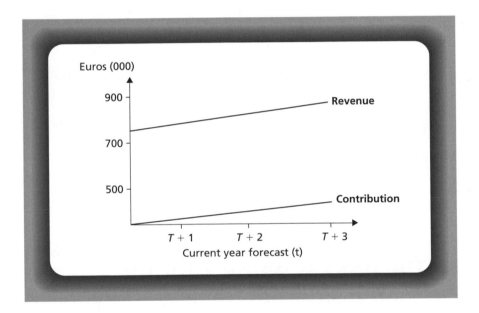

Worksheet 14.2(b):

Forecasting customer lifetime value

Relationship lifetime	Year 1 (£/$/€)	Year 2 (£/$/€)	Year 3 (£/$/€)	Year 4 (£/$/€)
Total customer revenues				
Total customer costs				
Year by year contribution/ profit				
Discount factor*				
Financial summary (Customer lifetime value)				

This should be accompanied by a brief commentary. For example:

"This 3-year business plan shows an increase in revenue from 7,000,000 euros to 9,000,000 euros and an increase in contribution/profit from 100,000 euros to 400,000 euros. The purpose of this strategic plan is to show how these increases will be achieved".

■ The process phase 2 for the customer: situation review – key account overview

Worksheet 14.3

See Form 3

(i) The customer's trading history with this supplier

The purpose of this is to inform readers/users of the plan about past sales, sales by product/group, size of the customer's wallet, share of customer's wallet, and the definition of the scope of the customer's wallet. It is helpful if there can be an explanation of factors which have influenced these results. Include this customer's strategy for managing their suppliers (if appropriate). For help on completing this analysis and for more detail on the calculation of customer profitability, see Chapter 5.

The next step is contact mapping. This involves mapping the supplier's key account team (Form 4), the principal customer contacts/relationships (Form 5), and the power structure and importance of contacts (Form 6).

Worksheet 14.4

(ii) Supplier's key account team

See Form 4

The purpose of this is to lay out the names, titles, and functions of the supplier's account team and to set out the principal current contacts and relationships.

Worksheet 14.5(a)

(iii) The key account's buying process

See Forms 5 and 6

Analyse how this customer goes about buying its products and services using the analysis sheet (see Chapter 3) shown in Worksheet 14.5(a). Then complete Forms 5 and 6.

Worksheet 14.5(a)

Customer Analysis Form	Customer							
Salesperson	Address							
Products					Telephone number			
	Buy class	New buy		Straight re-buy	Modified re-buy			
Date of analysis								
Date of reviews								
Member of Decision Making Unit (DMU)	Production	Sales & Marketing	Research & Development	Finance & Accounts	Purchasing	Data Processing	Other	
Buy Phase Name								
1 Recognizes need or problem and works out general solution								
2 Works out characteristics and quantity of what is needed								
3 Prepares detailed specification								
4 Searches for and locates potential sources of supply								
5 Analyses and evaluates tenders, plans, products								
6 Selects supplier								
7 Places order								
8 Checks and tests products								

Factors for consideration
1 price   4 back-up service   7 guarantees and warranties
2 performance   5 reliability of supplier   8 payment terms, credit, or discount
3 availability   6 other users' experience   9 other, e.g. past purchases, prestige, image, etc.

Adapted from Robinson, J., Farris, C.W. and Wind, Y. (1967). *Industrial Buying and Creative Marketing*, Allyn and Bacon).

Provide a map (see Figure 14.5(b)) and note the importance of contacts and the relationship level. The relationship level should be appropriate for the importance of the contact. Thus, you should have a closer relationship with the more important contacts. A less close relationship is acceptable for less important contacts.

Worksheet 14.5(b):

Contact mapping

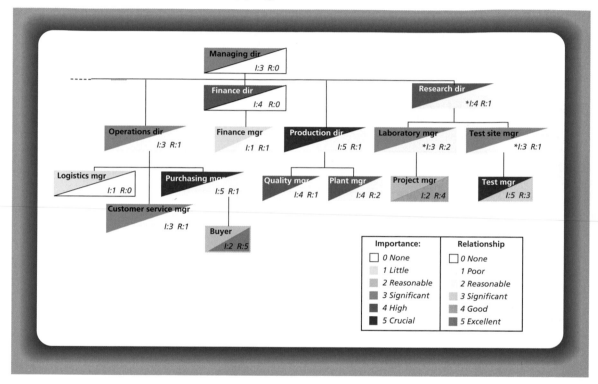

Worksheet 14.6

See Form 7

(iv) The customer's business

(a) Definition of the customer's business

The purpose of this is to spell out the definition and the scope of the customer's business (see Chapter 2)

1. Define the customer's business in terms of their customers needs rather than what they sell.
2. What markets are they in?
3. Where are these markets?
4. What is the customer's scope in these markets? (for more information, see Chapter 2).

Worksheet 14.7

(b) The customer's market

The purpose of this is to summarize the main thrust of the customer's market and their position in it, including social, technological, economic, ecological and political/legal issues that have affected and will affect the customer, with conclusions drawn (Worksheet 14.7). For more information on the STEEP analysis, see Chapter 4.

See Form 8

Worksheet 14.7

STEEP analysis of customer's business environment

STEEP factor	Change/Development	Which means that? (for the customer)
Social		
Technological		
Economic		
Ecological/ Environmental		
Political/Legal/ Regulatory		

Worksheet 14.8

(c) Customer's Porter analysis

The purpose of this is to examine the market structure influences that affect your customer.

As Worksheet 14.8 shows, this analysis includes the customer's market segments, the customer's competitors (including new and potential competitors), and other suppliers to the customer.

See Form 9

Customer's Porter analysis

Market participants	Segments What are they?	Micro environment factors What's happening with these people/companies?	Importance H/M/L	Opportunity or threat O/T
Customer's customers				
Customer's competitors (current, new, potential)				
Suppliers to customer				

Worksheet 14.9

(d) The customer's role/participation in its markets

The purpose of this is to show clearly how the customer's market works and their position in it, with conclusions for the customer clearly drawn.

See Forms 10 and 11

Draw a market map for the customer. Two examples of different formats for market maps are given below. Draw conclusions from the map(s) for the future of the customer (for further information, see Chapter 4).

Worksheet 14.9(a)

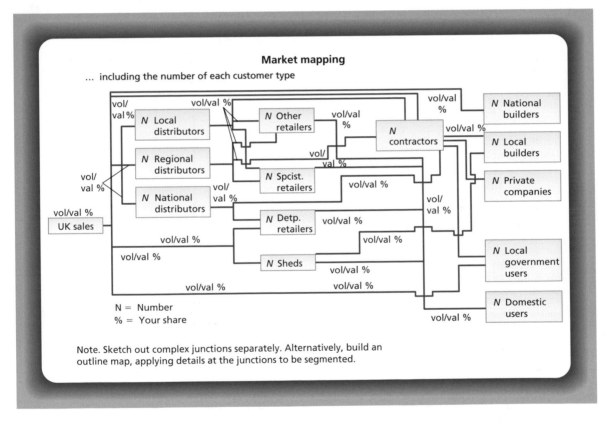

Market mapping

... including the number of each customer type

N = Number
% = Your share

Note. Sketch out complex junctions separately. Alternatively, build an outline map, applying details at the junctions to be segmented.

Worksheet 14.9(b)

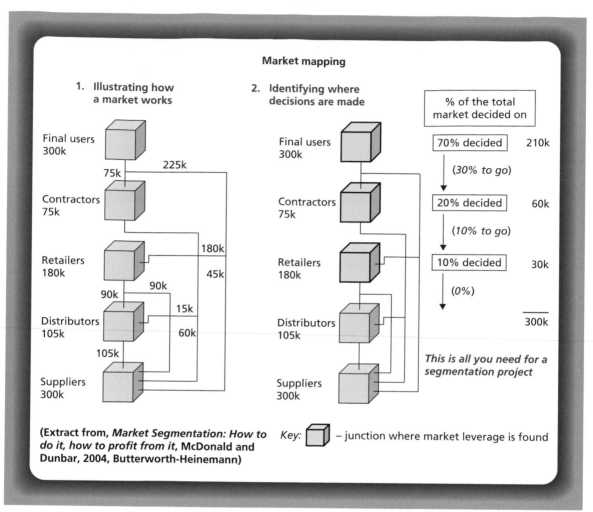

Market mapping

1. Illustrating how a market works

Final users 300k
75k / 225k
Contractors 75k
Retailers 180k — 180k / 45k
90k / 90k / 15k
Distributors 105k — 60k
105k
Suppliers 300k

2. Identifying where decisions are made

Final users 300k
Contractors 75k
Retailers 180k
Distributors 105k
Suppliers 300k

% of the total market decided on

70% decided	210k
(30% to go)	
20% decided	60k
(10% to go)	
10% decided	30k
(0%)	
	300k

This is all you need for a segmentation project

(Extract from, *Market Segmentation: How to do it, how to profit from it*, McDonald and Dunbar, 2004, Butterworth-Heinemann)

Key: ▢ – junction where market leverage is found

Key to Figure 14.9(b)

	300	105	180	300
	105 to distributors	Distributors	Retailers	Final users
Suppliers	90 to retailers	90 to retailers	180 to final users	180 from retailers
	60 to contractors	15 to contractors	180 to final users	45 from suppliers
	45 to final users			75 from contractors
	300	105	180	300

■ The process phase 2 for the customer: situation review – opportunities and threats – Worksheet 14.10

See Form 12

The purpose of this is to list the external opportunities and threats that face the customer in each of its main product/market areas relative to competitors and to highlight the implications for the customer (see Chapter 3). The customer's opportunities and threats are identified from the STEEP and Porter analysis and from the market map. Categorizing opportunities and threats by their likelihood and their impact on the customer's business will help the key account manager to identify the priority areas in which the supplier can help the customer, either by assisting the customer to exploit an opportunity or by helping it to avoid or minimize a threat. High likelihood, high impact opportunities, and threats are the priorities. Medium/medium opportunities and threats, whilst they may be of interest to the customer, are unlikely to be major priorities. Low/low opportunities and threats can probably be disregarded unless the situation changes.

■ The process phase 2 for the customer: situation review – the customer's strengths and weaknesses relative to competitors – Worksheet 14.11

See Form 13

List the customer's strengths and weaknesses relative to the opportunities and threats facing them. The examples of Porter's value chain are given below in Worksheets 14.11(a)–(c) and summary worksheets are provided in (d) and (e) below. Further analyses of strengths and weaknesses are given in Worksheets 14.11(f)–(h) below (see Chapter 3 for more information).

Worksheet 14.11(a)

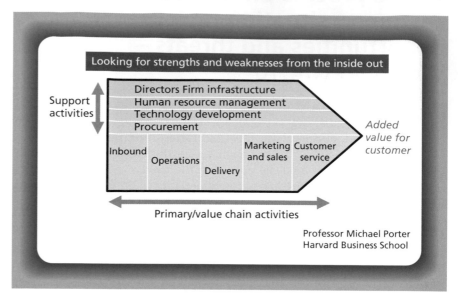

Looking for strengths and weaknesses from the inside out

Support activities

Directors Firm infrastructure
Human resource management
Technology development
Procurement

Inbound
Operations
Delivery
Marketing and sales
Customer service

Added value for customer

Primary/value chain activities

Professor Michael Porter
Harvard Business School

Worksheet 14.11(b)

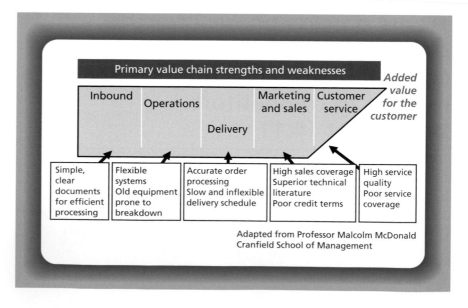

Primary value chain strengths and weaknesses

Added value for the customer

Inbound
Operations
Delivery
Marketing and sales
Customer service

Simple, clear documents for efficient processing	Flexible systems Old equipment prone to breakdown	Accurate order processing Slow and inflexible delivery schedule	High sales coverage Superior technical literature Poor credit terms	High service quality Poor service coverage

Adapted from Professor Malcolm McDonald
Cranfield School of Management

Worksheet 14.11(c)

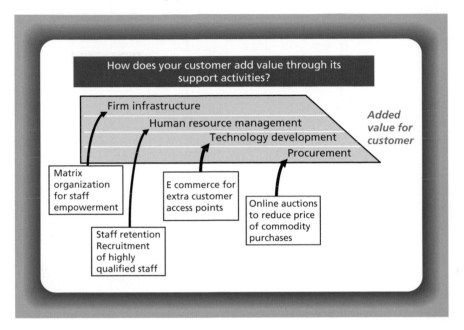

Worksheet 14.11(d)

Complete the two forms below.

Form 9(a): Customer's value chain based strengths

Value chain	Customer strengths	Which means that?	Different from competitors	Important to customers
Inbound				
Operations				
Outbound				
Marketing and sales				
Customer service				
Finance				
Procurement				
Technology development				
HR management				
Firm infrastructure				

Worksheet 14.11(e)

Customer's value chain based weaknesses

Value chain	Customer weaknesses	Which means that?	Different from competitors	Important to customers
Inbound				
Operations				
Outbound				
Marketing and sales				
Customer service				
Finance				
Procurement				
Technology development				
HR management				
Firm infrastructure				

Then complete the worksheet below (Worksheet 14.11(f)) if possible, with a view to specifying any financial strengths or weaknesses.

Then complete the worksheets below (Worksheets 14.11(g) and (h)) for as many parts of the customer's business as are important to it.

Worksheet 14.11(f)

Financial analysis

Financial ratio indicator	Formula	Source				Company standing	Industry standing	Does it appear as though improvement is needed?		Are there any initial thoughts about how our organization's products/services can help?
		Annual report						Yes	No	
Current ratio	Current assets / Current liabilities									
Net profit margin	Net profit / Net sales									
Return on assets	Net profit / Total assets									
Collection period	Debtors less bad debts / Average day's sales									
Stock turnover	Cost of goods sold / Stock									

Description of indicators		
	Current ratio	Measures the liquidity of a company – does it have enough money to pay the bills?
	Net profit margin	Measures the overall profitability of a company by showing the percentage of sales retained as profit after taxes have been paid. If this ratio is acceptable, there probably is no need to calculate the Gross profit or Operating profit margins.
	Return on assets	Evaluates how effectively a company is managed by comparing the profitability of a company and its investments.
	Collection period	Measures the activity of debtors. Prolonged collection period means that a company's funds are financing customers and not contributing to cash flow of the company.
	Stock turnover	Evaluates how fast funds are flowing through Cost of goods sold to produce profit. If stock turns over faster, it is not in the plant as long before it is saleable as a product.

Worksheet 14.11(g)

Strategic management planning exercise – SWOT analysis for how a key account selects suppliers

<table>
<tr>
<td colspan="2">

1. Segment description
It should be a *specific* part of the business and should *be very important* to the organization

</td>
<td colspan="2">

2. Critical success factors
In other words, how do customers choose their suppliers?

</td>
<td>

3. Weighting
(How important is each of these CSFs? Score out of 100)

</td>
<td>

4. Strengths/weaknesses analysis
How would their customers score them and their main competitors out of 10 on each of the CSFs? Multiply the score by the weight.

</td>
</tr>
</table>

	1		
	2		
	3		
	4		
	5		

Total 100

	You	Comp A	Comp B	Comp C	Comp D
1					
2					
3					
4					
5					
Total score					

5. Opportunities/threats
What are the few things outside their direct control that have had, and will have, an impact on this part of their business?

Threats

Opportunities
1	
2	
3	
4	
5	

6. Key issues that need to be addressed
What are the really key issues from the SWOT that need to be addressed?

Instructions for completing 2.16

Step 1: Select a key account and describe a specific part of this customer's business and the specific product(s) that your company do/could supply.

Step 2: Specify the customer's critical success factors (CSFs). In other words, what criteria does the customer use when selecting suppliers?

Step 3: Specify how relatively important each of these factors are to the customer (weighting).

Step 4: Score your company and at least 2 major competitors out of 10 on each of these CSFs. Multiply the score for each CSF by the weighting and arrive at a total score for your company and the two selected competitors.

Step 5: List the major opportunities and threats facing this customer.

Step 6: Specify in what ways your company can improve its competitive position or help the customer take advantage of the opportunities or overcome its threats.

Worksheet 14.11(h)

Strategic management planning exercise – SW analysis for a key account

1. Segment description
It should be a *specific* part of the business and should *be very important* to the organization

2. Critical success factors
In other words, how do customers choose?

1	
2	
3	
4	
5	

3. Weighting
(How important is each of these CSFs? Score out of 100)

Total 100

4. Strengths/weaknesses analysis
How would their customers score them and their main competitors out of 10 on each of the CSFs? Multiply the score by the weight.

	You	Comp A	Comp B	Comp C	Comp D
1					
2					
3					
4					
5					
Total score					

5. Key issues that need to be addressed
What are the really key issues that need to be addressed that arise from this SW analysis?

Step 1: Select a key account and describe a specific part of this customer's business.

Step 2: Specify the CSFs of the key account's customers. In other words, how do their customers choose a supplier?

Step 3: Specify how relatively important each of these factors are to the key account's customers (weighting).

Step 4: Score your key account and at least one of their major competitors out of 10 on each of these CSFs. Multiply the score for each CSF by the weighting and arrive at a total score for the key account and for at least one selected competitor.

Step 5: List the major opportunities and threats facing this customer.

Step 6: Specify in what ways your company can improve the key account's competitive position and help it to take advantage of its opportunities or overcome its threats.

Phase 2 for the customer: the process – situation review – issues to be addressed by the customer – Worksheet 14.12

See Form 14

The purpose of this section is to collect together all the issues facing the customer arising from the analysis used in Forms 8–12. Some will relate to opportunities and threats, some to strengths and weaknesses.

Phase 2 for the customer: the process – situation review – the customer's assumptions – Worksheet 14.13

See Form 15

Here, if you know them, list the planning assumptions made by the customer. Refer to the notes below.

There are certain key determinants of success in all companies about which assumptions have to be made before the planning process can proceed.

It is really a question of standardizing the planning environment. For example, it would be no good receiving plans from two product managers one of whom believed the market was going to increase by 10%, while the other believed the market was going to decline by 10%.

Examples of assumptions might include:

"With respect to the company's industrial climate, it is assumed that:

1 Industrial overcapacity will increase from 105% to 115% as new industrial plants come into operations.
2 Price competition will force price levels down by 10% across the board.
3 A new product in the field of "x" will be introduced by our major competitor before the end of the second quarter".

Assumptions should be few in number, and if a plan is possible irrespective of the assumptions made, then the assumptions are unnecessary.

Whilst this step is by no means essential, it is worthwhile remembering that no sensible planning can take place in any organization without making assumptions about key determinants of success, such as market growth, competitor activities, etc.

See Form 16

Phase 2 for the customer: the process – situation review – the customer's portfolio summary – Worksheet 14.14

This is an extremely difficult part of understanding the customer's business. Again, whilst not essential, it is without doubt the most effective way of understanding the objectives and strategies of your customer. Indeed, the customer themselves may not even think like this, but they will be very impressed if the supplier lets them see that they are really concerned about their objectives and strategies and ways in which they can help them.

A detailed methodology for completing this step is provided in Chapter 2.

Complete the matrix in Worksheet 14.14 below for the customers business. A completed example is provided below.

Customer's portfolio summary

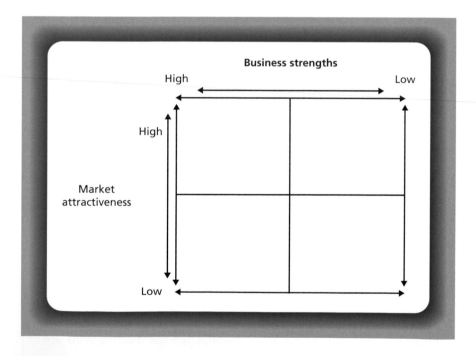

Worksheet 14.14

Example of a completed customer portfolio

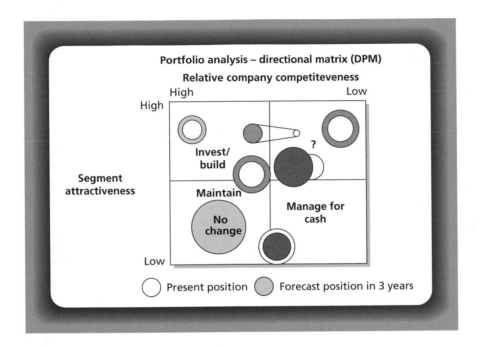

Portfolio analysis – directional matrix (DPM)

Relative company competiteveness

High / Low

Invest/build

Maintain

Segment attractiveness

?

Manage for cash

No change

○ Present position   ⬤ Forecast position in 3 years

Worksheet 14.15

For each of the markets in the customer's portfolio summary above, list their objectives and strategies for each for the next 3 years (see Form 17). A detailed explanation of objectives and strategies is given in Chapter 7.

Phase 2 for the supplier: the process – situation review – the supplier's strengths and weaknesses analysis in relation to the customer

See Form 18

This is in two parts

Part 1 relates to Porter's value chain in relation to the supplier. Worksheets 14.16 and 14.17 below relate to the supplier's operational strengths and weaknesses. It is important to remember that the supplier is only interested in strengths or weaknesses that are considered important by the customer. In this respect, consider the information gathered in Worksheets 14(a)–(h).

Worksheet 14.16

Worksheet: the supplier's value chain based strengths

Value chain	Strengths	Which means that?	Different from competitors	Important to customers
Inbound				
Operations				
Outbound				
Marketing and sales				
Customer service				
Finance				
Procurement				
Technology development				
HR management				
Firm infrastructure				

Worksheet 14.17

Worksheet: The Supplier's value chain based weaknesses

Value chain	Weaknesses	Which means that?	Different from competitors	Important to customers
Inbound				
Operations				
Outbound				
Marketing and sales				
Customer service				
Finance				
Procurement				
Technology development				
HR management				
Firm infrastructure				

Part 2 relates to strengths and weaknesses in relation to how the customer currently chooses suppliers (see Worksheet 14.18 below).

Key account management business strengths – SW analysis

1. Key account description It should be a *specific* part of the business and should *be very important* to your company	2. Critical success factors In other words, how does this customer select its suppliers?	3. Weighting (How important is each of these CSFs? Score out of 100)	4. Strengths/weaknesses analysis How would your customers score you and each of your main competitors out of 10 on each of the CSFs? Multiply the score by the weight.

	1				You	Comp A	Comp B	Comp C	Comp D
	2			1					
	3			2					
	4			3					
	5			4					
			Total 100	5					
				Total score					

5. In what specific ways must the supplier improve to meet the customer's requirements?

Instructions for completing Worksheet 14.18

For this key account describe a specific part of this customer's business and the specific product(s) that your company do/could supply.

Specify the customer's CSFs. In other words, what criteria does the customer use when selecting suppliers?

Specify how relatively important each of these factors are to the customer weightings.

Score your company and at least 2 major competitors out of 10 on each of these CSFs. Multiply the score for each CSF by the weighting and arrive at a total score for your company and the two selected competitors.

Phase 2 for the supplier: the process – situation review – summary of issues facing the customer and ways in which the supplier can help – Worksheet 14.19

See Form 19

Worksheet 14.19 below shows a "Matrix" in which the issues faced by the customer (from Form 10(c)) can be categorized by the supplier as a precursor to setting their own objectives and strategies.

	Strategic	High potential
Creating advantage		
Avoiding disadvantage		
	Key operational	Support

Key:

Strategic: Issues that will ensure the customer's long-term success.

High Potential: Issues that, whilst not crucial currently, could potentially lead to "differential advantage for the customer".

Key operational: Issues that, unless solved reasonably quickly, could lead to disadvantage for the customer.

Support: Issues that, whilst of a support nature, such as information availability, nonetheless need to be solved to avoid disadvantage for the customer.

It can also be seen from Form 20 that solving some of the issues in the top half of the matrix, is likely to lead to the supplier creating advantage for the customer. Solving issues in the lower half of the matrix, whilst helpful, will only lead to the supplier helping the customer to avoid disadvantage.

See Form 20

The Process: phase 3 – for the supplier – strategy formulation – supplier objectives – Worksheet 14.20

In completing the form given in Worksheet 14.20 below, it is important to ensure that the revenue and volume objectives are realistic, based on the previous analysis.

Worksheet 14.20

Form – supplier objectives

Business/financial

Purchases by product/product group	LY	TY				TY + 1				TY + 2				TY + 3			
	Sales	Sales	Sales increase/ decrease	GM	GM	Sales	Sales increase/ decrease	GM	GM	Sales	Sales increase/ decrease	GM	GM	Sales	Sales increase/ decrease	GM	GM
	£m	£m	%	£m	%	£m	%	£m	%	£m	%	£m	%	£m	%	£m	%
Existing business																	
Total existing																	
New business						Business not received as at date of completing plan											
Total new																	
Overall total																	
Customer wallet																	
Share of customer wallet																	

Other objectives (e.g. relationships, range of activity)

Objective	Measurement	LY	TY	TY + 1	TY + 2	TY + 3
Inter-company relationship	Target stage: basic cooperative, inter-dependent, integrated					
Range of activity	Target stage: for example introducing new lines of business; getting into new areas of the key account					

See Form 21

Phase 3 for the supplier: the process – strategy formulation – setting strategies – Worksheet 14.21 (Part 1)

This is a crucial part of the planning process, for the supplier now has to detail the strategies to be employed to achieve their objectives, together with responsibilities and cost. This is best done by taking each of the issues in turn from Form 19 and considering the precise actions that the supplier can take, given their own strengths and weaknesses, to help the customer to cope with them. Thus, starting with the top left box from Form 19, complete the worksheet given in Worksheet 14.21 below.

Worksheet 14.21

Customer strategic issues	Supplier strategies	Responsibility	Cost		
			Year 1	Year 2	Year 3
1 2 3	A B C D etc.				

Customer high-potential issues	Supplier strategies	Responsibility	Cost		
			Year 1	Year 2	Year 3

Customer key operational issues	Supplier strategies	Responsibility	Cost		
			Year 1	Year 2	Year 3

Customer support issues	Supplier strategies	Responsibility	Cost		
			Year 1	Year 2	Year 3

Relationships – Worksheet 14.22 (Part 2)

From Forms 5 and 6, set the relationship objectives, together with responsibilities, using the worksheets given in 14.22(a) and (b) below.
    Whatever costs are involved should be added to the costs of the other strategies from Worksheet 14.21.

Form (b) Supplier relationship strategies
Additional to business strategies

Worksheet 14.22(a)

Form (b) Supplier relationship strategies

Additional to business strategies

Relationship development strategy	Target contact name(s) and role(s)

Worksheet 14.22(b)

Targeted relationship levels (by date) _ _ _ _ _ _ _ _ _ _ _)

KIE staff	Customer staff						
	Name 1	Name 2	Name 3	Name 4			
Name A	2 > 4			1 > 3			
Name B			1 > 2				
Name C							
Name D							

Phase 4 for the supplier: the process – resource allocation and monitoring summary of financials – Worksheet 14.23

See Form 23

On Form 23, the supplier calculated sales and gross margin for each of the three planning years.

Now, the supplier should take the gross margin for each year and deduct the total costs (taken from Form 21) using Worksheet 14.23 below.

Worksheet 14.23

	Year *T* + 1	Year *T* + 2	Year *T* + 3
Total sales			
Total GM			
Less total costs (including relationship costs)			
Net profit/loss			

Comment on roles, responsibilities, alliancies, feasibility, etc.

■ Section B

The 1-year key account plan

This should be kept separate from the 3-year strategic marketing plan and should not be completed until the planning team has approved the strategic plan.

Specific sub-objectives for the strategies outlined in the key account strategic plan, supported by more detailed strategy and action statements, should now be developed. Here, include *budgets* and *forecasts* and a *consolidated budget*. These must reflect the objectives and strategies, and in turn the objectives, strategies, and programmes *must* reflect the agreed budgets and sales forecasts. Their main purpose is to delineate the major steps required in implementation, to assign accountability, to focus on the major decision points, and to specify the required allocation of resources and their timing.

If the procedures in this system are followed, a hierarchy of *objectives* will be built up in such a way that every item of budgeted expenditure can be related directly back to the initial financial objectives (this is known as task-related budgeting).

Thus when, say, sponsorship has been identified as a means of achieving an objective in a particular account (i.e. sponsorship is a strategy to be used), all sponsorship expenditure against items appearing in the budget can be related back specifically to a major objective. The essential feature of this is that budgets are set against both the overall objectives and the sub-objectives for each element of the plan.

The principal advantage is that this method allows operating units to build up and demonstrate an increasingly clear picture of what needs to be done for each customer. This method of budgeting also allows every item of expenditure to be fully accounted for as part of an objective approach. It also ensures that when changes have to be made during the period to which the plan relates, such changes can be made in a way that causes the least damage to the long-term objectives for the account.

■ Contingency plan

It is important to include a *contingency plan* in the 1-year key account. Notes on this are included below.

■ Guidelines for completion of a 1-year marketing plan

There is a minimum amount of information which should be provided to accompany the financial documentation. There is no need to supply market background information, as this should have been completed in the 3-year strategic key account plan.

■ Suggested format for a 1-year key account plan

1 (a) *Overall objectives (see Forms 1 and 2 in the 1-year key account plan documentation)*: These should cover the following:

Volume or value	Value last year	Current year estimate	Budget next year
Gross margin	Last year	Current year estimate	Budget next year

Against each there should be a few words of commentary/explanation.

   (b) *Overall strategies*: For example new products, advertizing, sales promotion, selling, customer service, pricing.

2 (a) *Sub-objectives (see Form 3 in the 1-year key account plan documentation)*: More detailed objectives should be provided, as appropriate.

 (b) *Strategies*: The means by which sub-objectives will be achieved should be stated.

 (c) *Action/tactics*: The details, timing, responsibility, and cost should also be stated.

3 *Summary of marketing activities and costs (see Form 4 in the 1-year key account plan documentation).*

4 *Contingency plan (see Form 5 in the 1-year key account plan documentation)*: It is important to include a contingency plan, which should address the following questions:

 (a) What are the critical assumptions on which the 1-year plan is based?

 (b) What would the financial consequences be (i.e. the effect on the operating income) if these assumptions did not come true? For example, if a forecast of revenue is based on the assumption that a decision will be made to buy a new plant by a major customer, what would the effect be if that customer did not go ahead?

 (c) How will these assumptions be measured?

 (d) What action will you take to ensure that the adverse financial effects of an unfulfilled assumption are mitigated, so that you end up with the same forecast profit at the end of the year?

To measure the risk, assess the negative or downside, asking what can go wrong with each assumption that would change the outcome. For example, if a customer growth rate of 5% is a key assumption, what lower growth rate would have to occur before a substantially different management decision would be taken? For a capital project, this would be the point at which the project would cease to be economical.

5 *Operating result and financial ratios (see Form 6 in the 1-year key account plan documentation).*

 Note: This form is provided only as an example, for, clearly, all organizations will have their own formats. This should include:

- net revenue
- gross margin
- adjustments
- marketing costs
- administration costs
- interest
- operating result
- return on sales (ROS)
- return on investement (ROI)

6 *Key activity planner (see Form 7 in the 1-year key account plan documentation)*: Finally, you should summarize the key activities and indicate the start and finish. This should help you considerably with monitoring the progress of your annual plan.

7 *Other*: There may be other information you wish to provide, such as sales call plans.

SECTION C

Templates for what should appear in a 1-year key account plan

Form 1

Short-term objectives

Volume	Value	Gross margin	Commentary
t + 1	t + 1	t + 1	

Form 2

Strategies

For each objective identified in Form 1 of the tactical plan, there should be at least one strategy. Strategies are about how the objectives will be delivered. They are about the 7 Ps (see Chapter 7).

Objective	Strategies									
O1										
O2										
O3										
O4										

Form 3

Tactics and resources

Objective	Strategies	Tactics	Who	When	Resource/Costs

Form 4

Suggested downside risk assessment format

Key assumption	Basic of assumption	What event would have to happen to make this strategy unattractive	Risk of such an event occurring (%)			Impact if events occurs	Trigger point for action	Actual contingency action proposed
			High P(7–10)	Medium P(4–6)	Low P(0–3)			

Form 5

Key activity planner

Date activity	Jan				Feb				March				April				May				June				July				Aug				Sept				Oct				Nov				Dec			
	1	2	3	4	1	2	3	4	1	2	3	4	1	2	3	4	1	2	3	4	1	2	3	4	1	2	3	4	1	2	3	4	1	2	3	4	1	2	3	4	1	2	3	4	1	2	3	4

Index